323.49 MCCOY
McCoy, Alfred W.
A question of torture :
R0022396150

APR   2006

Also by Alfred W. McCoy

*Closer Than Brothers: Manhood
at the Philippine Military Academy*

*Drug Traffic: Narcotics and Organized
Crime in Australia*

The Politics of Heroin in Southeast Asia

A QUESTION OF TORTURE

A QUESTION OF TORTURE

CIA Interrogation, from the Cold War
to the War on Terror

ALFRED W. McCOY

METROPOLITAN BOOKS

Henry Holt and Company   •   New York

Metropolitan Books
Henry Holt and Company, LLC
Publishers since 1866
175 Fifth Avenue
New York, New York 10010
www.henryholt.com

Metropolitan Books® and ⊞ ® are registered trademarks
of Henry Holt and Company, LLC.

Copyright © 2006 by Alfred W. McCoy
All rights reserved.
Distributed in Canada by H. B. Fenn and Company Ltd.

Grateful acknowledgment is made to *Scientific American* for
the illustration on page 36.

Library of Congress Cataloging-in-Publication Data

McCoy, Alfred W.
    A question of torture : CIA interrogation, from the Cold War
to the War on Terror / Alfred W. McCoy.—1st ed.
      p.   cm.
Includes bibliographical references and index.
ISBN-13: 978-0-8050-8041-4
ISBN-10: 0-8050-8041-4
1. Torture—United States—History.   2. United States. Central
Intelligence Agency.   3. Military interrogation—United States—History.
4. Intelligence service—United States—History.   I. Title.

HV8599.U6M33 2006
323.4'9—dc22   2005051124

Henry Holt books are available for special promotions
and premiums. For details contact: Director, Special Markets.

First Edition 2006

Printed in the United States of America

10   9   8   7   6   5   4   3   2   1

For my mother,
Margarita Piel McCoy,
and all that she tried to teach us

R0022396150

CONTENTS

A QUESTION OF TORTURE

INTRODUCTION

MY WORK ON this book began in another country, in another time, in another lifetime. In the summer of 1933, a grand Pierce-Arrow touring car sped past Switzerland's historic Schaffhausen castle and crossed into Germany. The powerful steel-cast, straight-eight engine pumped out an unmatched 125 horsepower, as the sedan swept north to the medieval market city of Nuremberg. With its chromed grill, massive front bumper, crouching-archer ornament, and trumpet-shaped headlamps, this automobile seemed a glistening herald of triumphal American engineering, plowing across the Bavarian countryside.

At the wheel, pushing the car to its limit of eighty-five miles an hour, was a German-American brewer, Rudolf Piel, touring his father's homeland in search of the latest technology for the family's famed Brooklyn brewery. In the passenger seat, his wife, Margarita, watched the usual daredevil driving with a practiced forbearance. In the back, their ten-year-old daughter, Peggy, was as always reading, glancing up from time to time at the passing farms, fields, and once, at a team of oxen that blocked the road. Sitting sentinel at her side was the family's German shepherd, Teufel.

Reaching Nuremberg, the oversize American sedan entered the town's medieval walls and twisted its way through the narrow cobbled streets. The passengers' meandering led to the Rathaus, where they strolled through the grand assembly hall, its high-timbered ceiling soaring and light streaming through leaded windows. With his meticulous way of looking for the serious, the important, Peggy's father insisted they tour the dungeons below, the "Lochgefangnisse."

This small family, their little girl in tow, followed a guide as he descended a narrow staircase into the stone foundations of the Rathaus and next through the dungeons, even then famed as exemplars of medieval justice. First they squeezed their way through a series of tiny cells, small wooden rooms built into the stonework, each with a narrow plank bed and low ceiling that made even a minute's visit seem oppressive.

Inside this dark world, Peggy discovered a new, disturbing feeling akin to despair. The stonework seemed covered with the black grime of centuries, unscrubbed. Without any windows, the air was still and heavy. The utter darkness, broken only by a few faint electric bulbs, was frightening.

Moving on, they entered a high-ceilinged interrogation chamber with a roped contraption to suspend bound prisoners painfully for questioning beneath a slit window where medieval magistrates had once observed. Near the winch were heavy, hewn stones that could be attached to the feet for increased pain. With her child's imagination, Peggy knew what must have happened.

The next room held an infinite variety of iron implements for physical torture—countless thumbscrews, calipers, chains, and spiked pressure devices. In their heavy, burnished iron, so perfectly preserved, these all seemed terribly cruel. Then, as the family walked through the tunnels and twisting lanes to a nearby tower, she came face-to-face with the famed Iron Maiden of Nuremberg—an iron-girded wooden box shaped like a bloated giant that crushed its victim between two beds of sharp, elongated iron spikes. Watching from her protected world, the girl thought this was all unimaginably monstrous. Then, the tour done, she emerged into the sunlight stunned and shaken by this visit to what she would later call "the torture museum."

The Pierce-Arrow swept north, by stages, to relatives in Düsseldorf, to the old family farm near Dortmund, and then east to the capital, where the family settled for a year. Berlin of 1933–1934 was in the throes of a vivid, traumatic time, making Peggy Piel witness to events so monumental, so powerful that they would remain in her memory for a lifetime.

Yet nothing she would see in Berlin's troubled present could rival her taste of Nuremberg's past: Not seeing the rapture on the faces of street-side crowds as Hitler passed in an open car. Not watching an entire city freeze in rigid attention while Hitler spoke over the radio— waiters, diners, and trams immobilized by his voice. Not observing the concierge's son, a Hitler Youth leader, terrorize their apartment building with random raids at all hours in search of subversion. Not even being chased through the streets by a mob of teenage toughs who pelted her with mud and stones, screaming over and over, "American Jew! American Jew!"

When the year was over, Peggy Piel came home to America, grew up, married a soldier during World War II, and raised two children, telling them of the things she had seen as a girl in Germany. Later, when she became a university professor and gained the habit of speaking with nuance, choosing her words with care, she would still say, "Torture is evil, pure and simple."

That little girl was, and is, my mother. If I have learned but a fraction of what she tried to teach us, every page that follows bears, in some way, the imprint of her experience. But I cannot, of course, start from her assumption of evil. I must, as an analyst of U.S. policy, begin with an open question, asking whether there might not be, in desperate times, some circumstances in which torture is effective, even justified. In short, this is a book about policy, not a study of morality, and it is written largely from a pragmatic perspective, probing the hidden history of torture inside the U.S. intelligence community over the past half century.

1

TWO THOUSAND YEARS OF TORTURE

IN APRIL 2004, the American public was stunned when CBS Television broadcast photographs from Abu Ghraib prison, showing Iraqis naked, hooded, and contorted in humiliating positions while U.S. soldiers stood over them, smiling.[1] As the scandal grabbed headlines around the globe, Secretary of Defense Donald Rumsfeld assured Congress that the abuse was "perpetrated by a small number of U.S. military," whom columnist William Safire branded as "creeps."[2] Other commentators—citing the famous Stanford prison experiment in which ordinary students role-playing the "guards" soon became brutal—attributed the abuse to a collapse of discipline by overstretched American soldiers in overcrowded prisons.[3]

But these photos are not, in fact, snapshots of simple sadism or a breakdown in military discipline. Rather, they show CIA torture methods that have metastasized like an undetected cancer inside the U.S. intelligence community over the past half century. If we look closely at these grainy images, we can see the genealogy of CIA torture techniques, from their origins in 1950 to their present-day perfection. Indeed, the photographs from Iraq illustrate standard interrogation practice inside the global gulag of secret CIA prisons that have operated, on executive authority, since the start of the war on terror. These photos, and the later investigations they prompted, offer telltale signs that the CIA was both the lead agency at Abu Ghraib and the source of systematic tortures practiced in Guantánamo, Afghanistan, and Iraq. In this light, the nine soldiers court-martialed for the abuse at Abu Ghraib were simply following orders. Responsibility for their actions lies higher, much higher, up the chain of command.

In this heated controversy, all of us, proponents and opponents of torture alike, have been acting out a script written over fifty years ago during the depths of the Cold War. Indeed, a search for the roots of Abu Ghraib in the development and propagation of a distinctive American form of torture will, in some way, implicate almost all of our society—the brilliant scholars who did the psychological research, the distinguished professors who advocated its use, the great universities that hosted them, the august legislators who voted funds, and the good Americans who acquiesced, by their silence, whenever media or congressional critics risked their careers for exposés that found little citizen support, allowing the process to continue.

What began as an isolated incident of abuse by a few "bad apples," "sadistic" soldiers on the "night shift," or some "recycled hillbillies from Cumberland, Maryland" would grow, in just six months, into a great political scandal that diminished the majesty of the American state, the world's preeminent power. As the U.S. press probed and Washington's bureaucracy hemorrhaged documents, revelations of abuse spread from Abu Ghraib to American military prisons worldwide. Despite eleven military investigations, twelve congressional hearings, and forty White House briefings all designed to bury the scandal, responsibility climbed, by degrees, from the handful of prison guards to the Pentagon and, ultimately, the president.[4] What started as an examination of the night shift in one cell block ramified into an inquiry, first into the Bush administration's interrogation policy, and then into the inner workings of the national-security state, the constitutional restraints on executive powers, and the limits of civil liberties—making other recent American political scandals appear, if not petty or parochial, at least somewhat more limited in their implications. Compared to weighty matters of state raised by Abu Ghraib, Watergate, narrowly construed, seems little more than the failure of one man's character; Iran-Contra an isolated albeit intriguing incident at the sunset of the Cold War; and, above all, l'affaire Monica Lewinsky sad, sordid, and forgettably partisan. At last, at the dawn of the twenty-first century, America's century, the United States had a crisis worthy of its grandeur as a global power, one revealing of the most profound ambiguities of our age—the tensions between security and freedom, morality and expediency, sovereignty and international- ism, the rule of law and the imperatives of covert operations, democ- racy at home and dominion abroad. Yet, ironically, the gravity of the scandal has discouraged television coverage, defied close analysis, and may ultimately drive Abu Ghraib from America's collective memory.

More deeply, this controversy is the product of a contradictory U.S. policy toward torture evident since the start of the Cold War. At the UN and other international forums, Washington opposed torture and advocated a universal standard for human rights. But, in contravention of these diplomatic conventions, the CIA propagated torture during those same decades. Several scholarly essays have noted this conflict in U.S. human rights policy without understanding the reason: no- tably, the persistence of torture techniques and the prerogative of their use within the intelligence community.[5]

At the deepest level, the abuse at Abu Ghraib, Guantánamo, and Kabul are manifestations of a long history of a distinctive U.S. covert- warfare doctrine developed since World War II, in which psychological torture has emerged as a central if clandestine facet of American for- eign policy. Thus, this book does not focus primarily on particular in- cidents, even important ones such as the events at Abu Ghraib, but instead examines these events as expressions of how American power has been brought to bear upon the world—so strong, so forceful, and so misapplied.

From 1950 to 1962, the CIA became involved in torture through a mas- sive mind-control effort, with psychological warfare and secret research into human consciousness that reached a cost of a billion dollars annu- ally—a veritable Manhattan Project of the mind.[6] After experiments with hallucinogenic drugs, electric shock, and sensory deprivation, this work then produced a new approach to torture that was psycho- logical, not physical, perhaps best described as "no-touch torture." The agency's discovery was a counterintuitive breakthrough— indeed, the first real revolution in the cruel science of pain in more than three centuries. To test and then propagate its distinctive form of torture, the CIA operated covertly within its own society, penetrating and compromising key American institutions—universities, hospitals, U.S. Agency for International Development, and the armed forces. As the lead agency within the larger intelligence community, the CIA has long been able to draw upon both military and civil resources to amplify its reach and reduce its responsibility. Moreover, the agency's attempts to conceal these programs from executive and legislative review have required manipulation of its own government through clandestine techniques, notably disinformation and destruction of incriminating documents.

Still, if genius is the discovery of the obvious, then the CIA's perfection of psychological torture was a major scientific turning point, albeit unnoticed and unheralded in the world beyond its secret safe houses. For more than two thousand years, interrogators had found that mere physical pain, no matter how extreme, often produced heightened resistance. By contrast, the CIA's psychological paradigm fused two new methods, "sensory disorientation" and "self-inflicted pain," whose combination causes victims to feel responsible for their suffering and thus capitulate more readily to their torturers. Although seemingly benign, the term "sensory disorientation" means, in this CIA usage, something far more invasive. Through relentless probing into the essential nature of the human organism to identify its physiological and psychological vulnerabilities, the CIA's "sensory deprivation" has evolved into a total assault on all senses and sensibilities—auditory, visual, tactile, temporal, temperature, survival, sexual, and cultural. Refined through years of practice, the method relies on simple, even banal procedures— isolation, standing, heat and cold, light and dark, noise and silence—for a systematic attack on all human senses. The fusion of these two techniques, sensory disorientation and self-inflicted pain, creates a synergy of physical and psychological trauma whose sum is a hammer-blow to the fundamentals of personal identity.

That notorious photo of a hooded Iraqi on a box, arms extended and wires to his hands, exposes this covert method. The hood is for sensory deprivation, and the arms are extended for self-inflicted pain. A week after the scandal broke, the U.S. prison chief in Iraq summarized this two-phase torture. "We will no longer, in any circumstances, hood any of the detainees," the general said. "We will no longer use stress positions in any of our interrogations."[7]

Although seemingly less brutal than physical methods, no-touch torture leaves deep psychological scars on both victims and interrogators. One British journalist who observed this method's use in Northern Ireland called sensory deprivation "the worst form of torture" because it "provokes more anxiety among the interrogatees than more traditional tortures, leaves no visible scars and, therefore, is harder to prove, and produces longer lasting effects."[8] Victims often need extensive treatment to recover from injury far more crippling than mere physical pain.[9] Perpetrators can suffer a dangerous expansion of ego, leading to escalating cruelty and lasting emotional disorders. Though any ordinary man or woman can be trained to torture, every gulag has a few masters who take to the task with sadistic flair—abhorred by their victims and valued by their superiors. Applied under the pressure of actual field operations after 1963, psychological methods soon gave way to unimaginable cruelties, physical and sexual, by individual perpetrators whose improvisations, plumbing the human capacity for brutality, are often horrifying.

Why, one might ask, is psychological torture so devastating, inflicting harm that is often more lasting than even the most brutal form of physical abuse? Insights from the treatment of Chilean victims tortured under General Augusto Pinochet's regime offer a point of entry into this complex question. Psychotherapist Otto Doerr-Zegers found that victims suffer "a mistrust bordering on paranoia, and a loss of interest that greatly surpasses anything observed in anxiety disorders." The subject "does not only react to torture with a tiredness of days, weeks, or months, but *remains a tired human being,* relatively uninterested and unable to concentrate."[10] These findings led him to a revealing question: "What in torture makes possible a change of such nature that it appears similar to psychotic processes and to disorders of organic origin?"

The answer, Doerr-Zegers argues, lies in the psychological, not physical, "phenomenology of the torture situation": (1) an asymmetry of power; (2) the anonymity of the torturer to the victim; (3) the "double bind" of either enduring or betraying others; (4) the systematic "falsehood" of trumped-up charges, artificial lighting, cunning deceptions, and "mock executions"; (5) confinement in distinctive spaces signifying "displacement, trapping, narrowness and destruction"; and (6) a temporality "characterized by some unpredictability and much circularity, having no end." Thus, much of the pain from all forms of torture is psychological, not physical, based upon denying victims any power over their lives. In sum, the torturer strives "through insult and disqualification, by means of threats . . . to break all the victim's possible existential platforms." Through this asymmetry, the torturer eventually achieves "complete power" and reduces the victim to "a condition of total or near total defenselessness."[11]

As Doerr-Zegers describes it, the psychological component of torture becomes a kind of total theater, a constructed unreality of lies and inversion, in a plot that ends inexorably with the victim's self-betrayal and destruction. To make their artifice of false charges, fabricated news, and mock executions convincing, interrogators often become inspired thespians. The torture chamber itself thus has the theatricality of a set with special lighting, sound effects, props, and backdrop, all designed with a perverse stagecraft to evoke an aura of fear. Both stage and cell construct their own kind of temporality. While the play both expands and collapses time to carry the audience forward toward denouement, the prison distorts time to disorientate and then entrap the victim. As the torturer manipulates circumstances to "maximize confusion," the victim feels "prior schemas of the self and the world . . . shattered" and becomes receptive to the "torturer's construction of reality." Under the peculiar conditions of psychological torture, victims, isolated from others, form "emotional ties to their tormentors" that make them responsive to a perverse play in which they are both audience and actor, subject and object—in a script that often leaves them not just disoriented but emotionally and psychologically damaged, in some cases for the rest of their lives.[12]

Once the CIA completed its research into no-touch torture, application of the method was codified in the curiously named *Kubark Counterintelligence Interrogation* manual in 1963. The agency then set about disseminating the new practices worldwide, first through U.S. AID's Office of Public Safety to police departments in Asia and Latin America and later, after 1975, through U.S. Army Mobile Training Teams active in Central America during the 1980s. In battling communism, the United States thus adopted some of its most objectionable practices—subversion abroad, repression at home, and torture.

Though torture seems so simple, so banally obvious in its brutality, it does have a lineage that allows us to track distinctive methods across time and continents, through agencies and bureaucracies. Much of the abuse synonymous with the era of authoritarian rule in Asia and Latin America seems to have originated in the United States. While dictatorships in those regions would no doubt have tortured on their own, U.S. training programs provided sophisticated techniques, up-to-date equipment, and moral legitimacy for the practice, producing a clear correspondence between U.S. Cold War policy and the extreme state violence of the authoritarian age. Significantly, torture spread around the Third World with the proliferation of these training programs and then receded when America turned resolutely against the practice at the end of the Cold War. In its pursuit of torturers across the globe for the past forty years, Amnesty International has thus been, in a certain sense, following the trail of CIA programs.

In these same troubled decades, U.S. leadership in the global fight against torture and inhumanity has waxed and waned. After World War II, American diplomats played a central role in drafting the UN's Universal Declaration of Human Rights and the Geneva Conventions on treatment of prisoners—documents that ban torture in both principle and practice. During the Cold War, however, Washington withdrew from active support of international human rights, ignoring or rejecting several major conventions. Then, at the Cold War's close, Washington resumed its advocacy of universal principles, participating in the World Conference on Human Rights in Vienna in 1993 and, a year later, ratifying the UN Convention Against Torture.[13] At the same time, CIA counterinsurgency efforts declined, and the agency carried out its comparatively limited interrogations by sending occasional targets overseas to allied agencies still notorious for torture. On the surface, therefore, the United States had, at the end of the Cold War, resolved the tension between its principles and its practices. But by failing to repudiate the CIA's propagation of torture, while adopting a UN convention that condemned its practice, the United States left this contradiction buried like a political land mine to detonate with phenomenal force, less than ten years later, in the Abu Ghraib prison scandal. Since the start of the war on terror, the intelligence community, led by the CIA, has revived the use of torture, making it Washington's weapon of choice. In effect, the development of the agency's techniques at the height of the Cold War, through a confused, even chaotic process, created a covert interrogation capacity that the White House could deploy at times of extraordinary crisis, whether in South Vietnam in 1968 or Iraq in 2003.

Indeed, the pervasive influence of the agency's torture paradigm can be seen in the recurrence of the same techniques used by American and allied security agencies in Vietnam during the 1960s, Central America in the 1980s, and Afghanistan and Iraq since 2001. Across the span of three continents and four decades, there is a striking similarity in U.S. torture techniques—from the CIA's original *Kubark* interrogation manual, to the agency's 1983 Honduras training handbook, all the way to General Ricardo Sanchez's 2003 orders for interrogation in Iraq. As we will see, these three key documents are almost identical in both conceptual design and specific techniques.

Yet, the American public has only a vague understanding of the scale of the CIA's massive mind-control project. Almost every adult American carries fragments of this past—LSD drug experiments, the Vietnam Phoenix program, and, of course, the Abu Ghraib photographs. But few are willing to fit these fragments together. There is a wilful blindness, a studied avoidance of this deeply troubling topic, similar to the silence that shrouds this sensitive subject in postauthoritarian societies. With the controversy over Abu Ghraib, however, incidents that once seemed isolated gain renewed significance. They form a clear mosaic of a clandestine agency manipulating its government and deceiving its citizens to propagate a new form of torture throughout the Third World.

Among the practices of the modern state, torture is the least understood, one that lures its practitioners, high and low, with fantasies of power and dominion. As we use the historian's tools to trace the hidden history of torture in America over the past half century, five intertwined aspects of its perverse psychology will emerge.

First, torture plumbs the recesses of human consciousness, unleashing an unfathomable capacity for cruelty as well as seductive illusions of omnipotence. Once torture begins, its perpetrators—reaching into that remote terrain where pain and pleasure, procreation and destruction all converge—are often swept away by dark reveries, by frenzies of potency, mastery, and control. Just as interrogators are often drawn in by an empowering sense of dominance, so their superiors, even at the highest level, can succumb to fantasies of torture as an all-powerful weapon. The contemporary view of torture as aberrant and its practitioners as abhorrent ignores its pervasiveness as a Western practice and its appeal, both to perpetrators and the powerful—particularly in times of crisis. As a CIA analysis of the Soviet Kremlin, perhaps applicable to the post-9/11 White House, explains: "When feelings of insecurity develop within those holding power, they become increasingly suspicious and put great pressures upon the secret police to obtain arrests and confessions. At such times police officials are inclined to condone anything which produces a speedy 'confession,' and brutality may become widespread."[14]

Second, states that sanction torture often allow it to spread beyond a few selected targets to countless suspected enemies. When U.S. leaders have used torture to fight faceless adversaries, Communist or terrorist, the practice has proliferated almost uncontrollably. Just four years after the CIA compiled its 1963 manual for use against a handful of counterintelligence targets, its agents were operating forty interrogation centers in South Vietnam that killed more than twenty thousand suspects and tortured thousands more. A few months after the CIA used its techniques on a small number of "high-target-value" Al Qaeda suspects, the practice spread to the interrogation of hundreds of Afghans and thousands of Iraqis. Modern states using torture, even in a very limited way, run the risk of becoming increasingly indiscriminate in its application.

Third, torture offers such a persuasive appearance of efficient information extraction that its perpetrators remain wedded to its use, refusing to acknowledge evidence of its limited utility and high political cost. In any society, medieval or modern, rulers, emboldened by the knowledge that their breath can draw blood from unseen victims, suffer an inflation of ego that clouds an appreciation of torture's drawbacks. At least twice during the Cold War, the CIA's torture training contributed to destabilization and delegitimation of key American allies, President Ferdinand Marcos in the Philippines and the shah of shahs in Iran. Yet the agency could not see that its doctrine was destroying the very regimes it was designed to defend. As its most troubling legacy, the CIA's psychological method, with its scientific patina and avoidance of obvious physical brutality, has created a pretext for the preservation of torture as an acceptable practice within the intelligence community.

Fourth, even when exposed to public scrutiny, torturers arouse such fear and fascination, attraction and revulsion, that they are rarely prosecuted for their crimes. While they walk free among us empowered, threatening, and even, dare we say, erotically enticing, we are simultaneously fearful and fascinated. Yet when they are brought down, ousted if not jailed, we turn on them, scornful, even mocking. Amid such public ambiguity, torturers elude justice in ways numerous and, to outsiders, mysterious—negotiating democratic transitions in weak states and manipulating government structures in strong ones, through a process political scientists call *impunity*.

Finally, as we learned from France's battle for Algiers in the 1950s and Britain's Northern Ireland conflict in the 1970s, a nation that sanctions torture in defiance of its democratic principles pays a terrible price. For nearly two millennia, the practice has been identified with tyrants and empires. For the past two centuries, its repudiation has been synonymous with the humanist ideals of the Enlightenment and democracy. When any modern state tortures even a few victims, the stigma compromises its majesty and corrupts its integrity. Its officials must spin an ever more complex web of lies that, in the end, weakens the bonds of trust and the rule of law that are the sine qua non of a democracy. And, beyond its borders, allies and enemies turn away in collective revulsion.

Under the pressures of the Cold War, Washington ignored many of the humanitarian precepts whose validity had been demonstrated so undeniably during its fight against fascism in World War II. Yet even as it prepared to compromise these principles, the United States became a forceful if fleeting advocate for international human rights. Indeed, meeting in New York in 1948, delegates to the United Nations, led by former first lady Eleanor Roosevelt, adopted the Universal Declaration of Human Rights—the foundation for all later UN humanitarian conventions.[15] Among its many idealistic provisions, this covenant specified, in Article 5, that "no one shall be subjected to torture or to cruel, inhuman or degrading treatment." But the declaration provided few specifics and no mechanism for enforcement.[16]

Just a year later, the United States also ratified Geneva Convention III Relative to the Treatment of Prisoners of War, with its strong prohibitions against torture. Article 13 states that "prisoners of war must at all times be humanely treated," while Article 87 bars "corporal punishment, imprisonment in premises without daylight and, in general, any form of torture or cruelty." Article 89 offers an unambiguous ban on harsh treatment: "In no case shall disciplinary punishments be inhuman, brutal or dangerous to the health of prisoners of war."[17] Similarly, under Geneva Convention IV Relative to the Protection of Civilian Persons in Time of War, the United States accepted the broad language of Article 31: "No physical or moral coercion shall be exercised . . . to obtain information from them or from third parties."[18] The United States had thus committed itself to a new, strict standard for human rights, whether in war or peace.

But by the mid-1950s, a confluence of pressures, legislative and clandestine, led Washington to suspend its support for these humanitarian principles. For American conservatives, the founding of the United Nations had raised the threatening specter of "world government," inspiring a movement in Congress for the Bricker Amendment that would limit executive authority over foreign affairs—a threat the Eisenhower administration defeated by reducing its backing for human rights at the UN.[19] Less visibly, the CIA's massive mind-control project may have created an internal momentum that influenced Washington's changed position and led its allies to adopt torture as an instrument of state—reviving a practice with a long, problematic history in Europe and the West.

* * *

Through its use in judicial interrogation, torture had played a central role in European law for more than two thousand years. While ancient Athens had limited torture to extraction of evidence from slaves, imperial Rome extended the practice to freemen, for both proof and punishment. "By *quaestio* [torture] we are to understand the torment and suffering of the body in order to elicit the truth," wrote the imperial jurist Ulpian in the third century A.D. But he also recognized that torture was a "delicate, dangerous, and deceptive thing," often yielding problematic evidence. "For many persons have such strength of body and soul that they heed pain very little, so that there is no means of obtaining the truth from them," he explained, "while others are so susceptible to pain that they will tell any lie rather than suffer it."[20]

With the rise of Christian Europe, the use of torture in courts of law faded for several centuries. Torture was antithetical to Christ's teachings and so, in 866, Pope Nicholas I banned the practice.[21] But after a Church council abolished trial by ordeal in 1215, European civil courts revived Roman law with its reliance on torture to obtain confessions—an approach that persisted for the next five centuries.[22] With the parallel rise of the Inquisition, Church interrogators also used torture for both confession and punishment, a procedure that was formalized under Pope Innocent IV in 1252. By the fourteenth century, the Italian Inquisition used the *strappado* to suspend the victim by ropes in five degrees of escalating duration and severity—a scale preserved in modern memory in the phrase "the third degree" to mean harsh police questioning.[23]

The impact of judicial torture on European culture went far beyond the dungeon, coinciding with a subtle shift in theological emphasis from the life of Jesus to the death of the Christ—a change reflected in artistic representations, both painting and sculpture, of his body being scourged, tortured, and crucified. From limited details of Christ's agonies in the Gospels, medieval artists, in the words of one scholar, "approximated these grisly violations with the unerring eye of a forensic pathologist," creating an image of the pain inflicted on his battered body that mimed, and may have legitimated, the increasingly gruesome legal spectacle of torture and public execution.[24] Later, in the sixteenth and seventeenth centuries, the absolutist regimes elaborated on this embrace of torture. "Military torture was prodigious," wrote Alec Mellor of these sixteenth-century states, "religious torture was regularized; and judicial torture was enriched daily by new varieties."[25]

But in the eighteenth century, evaluation of evidence on its merits replaced forced confessions. For several centuries, there had been a growing disquiet among continental jurists about the accuracy of evidence extracted by torture. As one sixteenth-century criminal handbook observed, those tortured often succumb to "the pain and torment and confess things that they never did." Indeed, the burgomaster of Bamberg, Germany, Johannes Julius, wrote his daughter from a dungeon where he awaited execution for witchcraft: "It is all falsehood and invention, so help me God . . . They never cease to torture until one says something." A slow shift away from these medieval blood sanctions in the seventeenth century to a lesser penal servitude, akin to modern imprisonment, laid the foundation for torture's abolition. After his coronation in 1740, Frederick II of Prussia banned ordinary torture and wrote a dissertation calling the practice "as cruel as it is useless." His friend Voltaire famously condemned the practice in polemics denouncing judicial torture, both the *question ordinaire* and *question extraordinaire,* sparking a movement that led to its abolition across Enlightenment Europe by the early 1800s. With its jury system and common law precedents, England had no judicial foundation for torture. Its sole experience came from eighty-one torture warrants for treason under Tudor-Stuart rule—which derived from the doctrine of sovereign immunity and soon faded, leaving no legal basis for torture in British common law.[26]

During the nineteenth century, European states gradually replaced the symbols of torture—the Tower of London, the Bastille, and public execution—with the apparatus of a scientific criminology that included police, courts, and prisons. By 1874, Victor Hugo could claim "torture has ceased to exist." But the respite proved short-lived for, in the years following World War I, rival authoritarian states—Hitler's Third Reich and Stalin's Soviet Union—revived the practice, applying modern methods to expand the diversity and intensity of physical pain.[27]

In the 1920s, torture thus reappeared in Europe, in the words of a famed English jurist, as "an engine of the state, not of law." After taking power in 1922, Benito Mussolini declared "man is nothing" and used his OVRA secret police to torture the enemies of his all-powerful state. Similarly, Hitler's Gestapo engaged in limited, largely concealed torture during the regime's first years, relying on protracted isolation, crude beatings, and humiliation to break political opponents, whether Communist or Gypsy, Catholic or Jew. Then, in June 1942, SS chief Heinrich Himmler ordered interrogators to use the third degree of beatings, close confinement, and sleep deprivation. At the Dachau concentration camp in the late 1930s, SS doctors under Kurt Plotner tested mescaline on Jews and Gypsies, finding that it caused some to reveal their "most intimate secrets." But the Gestapo was "not ready to accept mescaline as a substitute for their more physical methods of interrogation."[28] At war's end, the United States prosecuted the "Nazi doctors" at Nuremberg, producing principles known as the Nuremberg Code prescribing, under Article Four, that medical experiments "should be so conducted as to avoid all unnecessary physical and mental suffering."[29]

Despite the Third Reich's defeat in 1945, its legacy persisted in the former occupied territories, particularly among French officers in colonial Algeria. As partisans who fought the German occupation during World War II, some of these officers had suffered Nazi torture and now, ironically, used the experience to inflict this cruelty on others. In a vain attempt to crush a national revolution with repression, France launched a massive pacification that, from 1954 to 1962, resulted in the forcible relocation of two million Algerians, the deaths of 300,000 more, and the brutal torture of several hundred thousand suspected rebels and their sympathizers. By branding the guerrillas "outlaws" and denying them the Geneva protections due lawful combatants, the French kept such brutality within the bounds of formal legality through the seven years of war. To contain the political damage from these excesses, the government's Wuillaume Report excused the army's systematic torture of the rebels: "The water and electricity methods, provided they are carefully used, are said to produce a shock which is more psychological than physical and therefore *do not consti-*

tute excessive cruelty." Forcing water down a victim's throat to simulate drowning, a technique then favored by the French army and later used by the CIA, was, the report insisted, perfectly acceptable. "According to certain medical opinion, the water-pipe method," Wuillaume wrote, "involves no risk to the health of the victim."[30]

When the Front de Libération National launched an urban uprising in Algiers in 1956–57, the Tenth Paratroop Division under Colonel Jacques Massu employed such tortures to break the resistance infrastructure in the old Casbah. Knowing well the inevitability of interrogation, the FLN command asked only that its fighters stay silent for the first twenty-four hours after capture. But the French mix of water pipe, electric shock, beating, and burning extracted sufficient intelligence to track down guerrillas in the Casbah's narrow confines. And all the rebel suspects taken to the army's Villa des Tourelles safe house for torture under cover of dark were dead by dawn, dumped in shallow graves outside the city. These secret "summary executions," which one senior officer called "an inseparable part of the task associated with keeping law and order," were so relentless that 3,024 of those arrested in Algiers went "missing"—a crippling blow to the FLN.[31]

Although the French army won the battle for Algiers, its campaign proved counterproductive as the revolt spread, transforming the FLN from small cells into a mass party, and France itself recoiled against the costs of counterinsurgency, moral and material. The editor of an Algiers newspaper, Henri Alleg, who was tortured by the Tenth Paratroop during the battle, wrote a moving memoir titled, with a bow to Voltaire, *The Question*, describing the effect of the army's water-pipe method. "I tried, by contracting my throat, to take in as little water as possible and to resist suffocation by keeping air in my lungs for as long as I could," Alleg recalled. "But I couldn't hold on for more than a few moments. I had the impression of drowning, and a terrible agony, that of death itself, took possession of me." With an angry introduction by Jean-Paul Sartre, the book, published in 1958, became a cause célèbre when the French government banned it, making it an underground bestseller in Paris and prompting well-publicized translations in both English and German.[32]

"The French army won an uncontested military victory," argues the distinguished French historian of the Algerian war, Benjamin Stora. "But in fact the political victory was far from being won because the use of torture heightened awareness among the French public. The society went through a serious moral crisis." As the fighting ground on without end, the Paris press focused on the army's torture; and public support for the war effort, once nearly unanimous, slowly eroded to the point that France finally quit Algeria in 1962, after 130 years. In the war's painful aftermath, as Pierre Vidal-Naquet argued in *Torture: Cancer of Democracy,* public indifference to torture abroad had the long-term effect of eroding civil liberties at home—even in a democratic society.[33]

America inherited much of this ambiguous European experience of torture. Through the influence of the Enlightenment, the United States had gained a revulsion, enshrined in the Constitution's ban on cruel and unusual punishment. And Europe's recent history of torture in Germany and Algeria also provided vivid lessons in the political costs of lost legitimacy. As the former CIA director William Colby recalled in his memoirs, he came to South Vietnam in the 1960s mindful of Algeria: "France's near-victory there was fatally undermined by a French journalist's accusation that torture was an accepted practice in the French Army's prosecution of that antiguerrilla war."[34] Yet the frequent recourse to torture by European regimes, absolutist and authoritarian, also created seductive precedents and specific practices that Washington would adopt, secretly, for its Cold War against the last of the European dictatorships, the Soviet Union.

2

MIND CONTROL

AS THE IRON Curtain came down across Europe in 1948, the human mind became a Cold War battleground. Just as the War Department had mobilized physicists to develop radar and atomic weapons during World War II, so the CIA now recruited psychologists to discover new means of mind control. Nuclear physics had been relatively advanced in 1941, but at the start of the Cold War scientific understanding of human psychology was, as one military researcher observed, still "quite primitive."[1] Yet Soviet scientists had already launched an intense effort to crack the code of human consciousness, so the CIA now felt forced to mount a massive program that soon made it a powerful patron in the infant field of behavioral science.

Ironically, America's initial contact with torture came in conflicts with its proponents, against two regimes now synonymous with systematic brutality. During World War II, Washington created the Office of Strategic Services, and then used this espionage agency at war's end to attract German scientists—including those who had directed Nazi experiments into human physiology and psychology—as resources in its struggle against the Soviet Union. Under Operation Paperclip, American agent Boris Pash recruited Nazi scientists, including Dr. Kurt Plotner, who had tested mescaline on Jewish prisoners during the war. After the OSS was reborn as the CIA in 1947, the agency revived these Nazi-inspired drug experiments, now testing LSD (lysergic acid diethylamide) and THC (marijuana) for interrogation of suspected spies and double agents.[2]

From its founding in 1947, the CIA was disturbed by the Soviet ability to extract public confessions in ways that hinted at secret mind-control methods. The prominent Yale psychologist Irving L. Janis was one of the first to warn the intelligence community of this war being waged on the frontiers of cognitive science. Since 1923, he reported in his 1949 study for the Air Force, Moscow's State Institute of Experimental Psychology had been doing research into ways that "hypnosis could be used to elicit false confessions in a public trial." At recent show trials for "many different personalities," ranging from old Bolsheviks in Moscow to a Catholic cardinal in Budapest and Protestant pastors in Sofia, Bulgaria, Communist police had shown "consistent success" in extracting "false confessions," making it probable, Janis argued, that "some special psychological technique is being used." In particular, the sudden change in Hungary's Jozsef Cardinal Mindszenty, known for his "intransigent moral stamina," from a brilliant "ecclesiastical orator" to a man who spoke to the court "in a kind of monotonous mechanical chant," made Janis suspect that "a series of electroshock convulsions is being administered . . . to reduce resistance to hypnotic suggestion." With a mix of drugs and electroshock, the Soviets, Janis warned, may have discovered techniques "to induce a somnambulistic trance . . . in perhaps 90 percent or more of all defendants from whom they might wish to elicit a public confession."[3]

Calling Communist mastery of hypnosis "a serious threat to democratic values in times of peace and war," Janis advised the intelligence community to conduct a "systematic investigation by means of carefully controlled experiments," including:

(a) specialized technological studies on methods of placing an uncooperative person into a somnambulistic trance in which guilt, etc., can be implanted (e.g., the effectiveness of various drugs, electric convulsive treatments, etc., in weakening resistance);

(b) an overall attempt to duplicate the public confessions obtained in Soviet-dominated trials (e.g., can we take a group
of confirmed atheists and, by means of specially devised
hypnotic techniques, get all of them to accuse themselves
of past iniquities in the sight of the Lord, and to confess a
number of sins they had never actually committed?)[4]

With words weighted by his prestige as a Yale professor, Janis had
validated the Soviet mind-control threat. Most important, he recommended a program of extreme cognitive experimentation, with drugs
and electroshock, that the CIA would follow for the next fifteen years.

The agency's in-house research seemed to confirm Janis's concerns
about a Soviet mind-control challenge. In 1950, a CIA analysis of
Stalin's 1937 show trials for fellow Communists found that "the style,
context and manner of delivery of the 'confessions' were such as to be
inexplicable unless there had been a reorganization and reorientation
of the minds of the confessees." Such sudden, radical personality
change, the analysis concluded, "cannot be brought about by the traditional methods of physical torture," raising the disturbing possibility
that the Soviets had discovered "newer or more subtle techniques," including psychosurgery, electroshock, and "psychoanalytic methods."
In a 1951 memorandum, "Defense Against Soviet Mental Interrogation and Espionage Techniques," the CIA justified the use of extreme
measures, beyond the law, to counter this Soviet threat: "International
treaties . . . have never controlled the . . . use of unconventional methods of warfare, such as . . . fiendish acts of espionage, torture and
murder of prisoners of war, and physical duress and other unethical
persuasive actions in the interrogation of prisoners." Within months, a
series of disturbing public confessions by American soldiers captured
in Korea seemed to confirm these concerns. "There is ample evidence," reported the chief of the CIA medical staff in 1952, "that the
Communists were utilizing drugs, physical duress, electric shock and
possibly hypnosis against their enemies. With such evidence, it is difficult not to keep from becoming rabid about our apparent laxity. We
are forced by this mounting evidence to assume a more aggressive role
in the development of these techniques."[5]

Announcing the CIA's battle against Communist "brain warfare," the agency's director, Allen Dulles, made a rare public statement before a Princeton alumni reunion in 1953, warning that the Soviet Union was engaged in secret work with drugs and electroshock aimed at "the perversion of the minds of selected individuals who are subjected to such treatment [so] that they are deprived of the ability to state their own thoughts. Parrot-like, the individuals so conditioned can merely repeat thoughts which have been implanted in their minds."[6]

During these early years of the Cold War, several popular writers stoked public fears about Communist mind control. "I can hypnotize a man—*without his knowledge or consent*—into committing treason against the United States. If I can do it, so could psychologists of other nations in the event of another war," warned Dr. George Estabrooks, a Colgate University psychologist and America's leading expert on hypnosis, in a 1950 article for the popular men's magazine *Argosy.* "Two hundred trained foreign operators, working in the United States, could develop a uniquely dangerous army of hypnotically controlled Sixth Columnists," he continued, ratcheting up the rhetoric of fear. "A small corps of carefully trained hypnotists attached to an armed force could wreak more far-reaching havoc than an atom bomb." Then, with some prescience, Estabrooks pointed out that modern hypnotism was now a "full-fledged science" that could be intensified by "subjecting the 'patient' to bright lights, loud noises, and sleepless nights." The effect would be to break the victim more thoroughly—just as the Nazis had addled the hapless Van der Lubbe in court appearances for the Reichstag fire and the Communists had confused Cardinal Mindszenty at his Budapest show trial.[7]

In similarly sensational articles, Edward Hunter, a career CIA propagandist who posed as a freelance journalist for the *Miami Daily News* and other papers, alerted the public to the threat of Chinese Communist "brainwashing"—his literal translation of the Chinese colloquialism *hsi nao,* to "wash brain." In his wildly popular book, *Brain-Washing in Red China,* published in 1951, Hunter called this practice "the principal activity on the Chinese mainland when the Communists took over," soon becoming a method for systematically filling the minds of 450 million people with "hate and warmongering." He called this form of indoctrination "psychological warfare on a scale incalculably more immense than any militarist of the past," arguing that it must be "stopped and counteracted . . . if we ourselves are to be safe . . . from 'brain-washing' and 'brain-changing'—and 'liquidation' and 'evaporation.'"[8]

Although the CIA may well have manipulated the climate of fear through propagandists like Hunter, there was, by the mid-1950s, something akin to genuine hysteria over Communist mind control. Recalling the temper of those times, the psychologist Robert J. Lifton said that popular culture portrayed Communist brainwashing as an "all-powerful, irresistible, unfathomable, and magical method of achieving total control over the human mind."[9]

In response to the Communist challenge, the CIA would spend several billion dollars over the next decade to probe two key aspects of human consciousness—the mechanisms of mass persuasion and the effects of coercion on individual consciousness. This complex, at times chaotic, mind-control project had two goals: improved psychological warfare to influence whole societies and better interrogation techniques for targeted individuals.[10] Gradually, these two strands diverged, one emerging in the public domain and the other disappearing into a covert netherworld. Research into psychological warfare methods explored mass persuasion through the U.S. Information Agency and the academic field of mass communications—surfacing, in time, as the legitimate arenas of diplomacy and scholarly study. By contrast, as it probed the impact of drugs, electric shock, and sensory deprivation on individual consciousness, interrogation research moved ever deeper inside a clandestine complex of military, intelligence, and medical laboratories.

In the Cold War's early dangerous, desperate years, Washington's national security agencies were determined to match their Moscow adversaries weapon for weapon. "It is now clear that we are facing an implacable enemy whose avowed objective is world domination by whatever means," read the influential report by ex-president Herbert Hoover on government operations in 1954. "We must . . . learn to subvert, sabotage, and destroy our enemies by more clear, more sophisticated, and more effective methods than those used against us."

Offering a prediction that proved sadly accurate, the report added: "It may become necessary that the American people will be made acquainted with, understand and support this fundamentally repugnant philosophy."[11]

If Moscow had the KGB, Washington would create the CIA; if Russian scientists manipulated human behavior, then their American counterparts must follow. When Washington adopted the National Security Act in July 1947, creating both the National Security Council as a top-level executive agency and the CIA as its instrument, it effectively removed foreign intelligence from meaningful congressional oversight.[12] The act contained a brief clause allowing the new agency to perform "other functions and duties relating to intelligence affecting the national security" that the president, through the NSC, might direct—investing these executive agencies with extraordinary authority to operate outside the law, whether for covert operations, assassinations, or torture.[13] Five months after the agency's founding, the council promulgated NSC 4–A, a "top secret" authorization for the CIA to conduct overt propaganda programs that "must be supplemented by covert psychological operations."[14]

The CIA's "defensive" behavioral research soon culminated in the creation of its largest and most notorious mind-control program, MKUltra. In retrospect, this secret research moved through two distinct phases: first, esoteric, often bizarre experiments with hypnosis and hallucinogenic drugs, from 1950 to 1956; then, more conventional research into human psychology until 1963 when the agency compiled the fruits of this costly investigation in a definitive interrogation manual. This first phase of esoteric drug experimentation has been the subject of congressional inquiries, a half-dozen major books, and endless public fascination.[15] But, ultimately, this was a failed research effort whose only significance lies in its role in a scientific process of trial and error that would ultimately take the CIA in a very different direction.

In April 1950, then-CIA director Roscoe Hillenkoetter launched Operation Bluebird to discover more effective methods for interrogation by using teams with a psychiatrist, a polygraph expert, and a hypnotist. Under this project, Boris Pash, formerly employed in Operation

Paperclip, reviewed Nazi interrogation techniques, including "drugs, electro-shock, hypnosis and psycho-surgery." Operation Bluebird also conducted the first CIA experiments with the newly discovered hallucinogenic drug LSD, testing doses on twelve subjects before expanding the program to thousands of unwitting U.S. soldiers at Maryland's Edgewood Chemical Arsenal.[16] Even at this early stage, Bluebird's aim was to explore "the possibility of control of an individual by application of special interrogation techniques." Reflecting the agency's initial fascination with exotic methods, Bluebird was also directed to examine "offensive uses of unconventional interrogation techniques, including hypnosis and drugs."[17]

Two years later, the CIA's Office of Scientific Intelligence started Project Artichoke to look at interrogation through "the application of tested psychiatric and psychological techniques including the use of hypnosis in conjunction with drugs." For the most part, Artichoke used American subjects, notably seven patients at the drug-treatment facility in Lexington, Kentucky, who were kept on dangerous doses of LSD for seventy-seven days straight.[18] In July 1952, Artichoke notified the CIA director about testing of its techniques on two suspected Soviet double agents, with "light dosages of drugs coupled with hypnosis . . . to induce a complete hypnotic trance. This trance was held for approximately one hour and forty minutes of interrogation with a subsequent total amnesia produced by post-hypnotic suggestion." Commenting on this successful application of sodium pentathol, a supposed truth serum, the report waxed euphoric: "For a matter of record, the [CIA] case officers involved in both cases expressed themselves to the effect that the ARTICHOKE operations were entirely successful and team members felt that the tests demonstrated conclusively the effectiveness of the combined chemical-hypnotic technique in such cases."[19] Inside the agency's headquarters, Artichoke conducted several hundred hypnotic experiments "apparently utilizing the staff employee volunteers as subjects."[20]

Although Project Artichoke used both willing and unwitting subjects, the agency imposed nominal "medical and security controls which would ensure that no damage would be done to individuals volunteering."[21] Moreover, to discourage any duplication of effort, the

CIA director also instructed Artichoke's principals to collaborate closely with Army and Navy researchers and exchange information with British and Canadian scientists. From surviving documents, it seems this coordination developed a loose division of labor, with the Army doing much of the drug testing through its Chemical Warfare Laboratories and the Navy directing behavioral experiments through its Office of Naval Research (ONR).[22]

Finally in April 1953, the CIA gathered its sprawling array of mind-control research under the umbrella of a unified project, MKUltra—placing it under a single scientist, Dr. Sidney Gottlieb of its Technical Services Division, and making him, in turn, responsible to a single superior, spymaster Richard Helms. As the assistant deputy director of plans, a euphemism for covert operations, Helms would play a key role in the mind-control effort for the next twenty years, protecting behavior-modification research from both internal review and external attack. Until its funding, totaling some $25 million, was curtailed in 1963, MKUltra supervised 149 projects and 33 more subprojects all focused, in diverse ways, on the control of human consciousness. The work continued at a reduced level until 1973, when Helms, now director of the CIA and fearful of a damaging exposé, terminated the project and destroyed its files.[23]

The MKUltra researchers were given extraordinary powers. At the program's outset, Helms proposed, and Director Dulles agreed, that 6 percent of the budget for the agency's TSD could be spent "without the establishment of formal contractual relations." Helms noted that talented academic and medical researchers "are most reluctant to enter into signed agreements of any sort which connect them with this activity since such a connection would jeopardize their professional reputations."[24] In effect, Helms ran the program covertly within the agency, avoiding oversight even by the CIA's director, because he "felt it necessary to keep details of the project restricted to an absolute minimum number of people."[25]

Under MKUltra, the agency's investigations reached out into American civil society—its universities and hospitals—to involve "physicians, toxicologists, and other specialists" during both "the basic research phase" and later "intensive tests on human subjects."[26] In an internal investigation in 1963, the CIA's inspector general found that the initial "research and development" phase was structured to conceal "the interests of the CIA" from all but "key individuals."[27] By the late 1950s, for example, respected medical researchers used secret CIA funding for LSD experiments at Boston Psychopathic, Mt. Sinai, and Columbia University hospitals, simultaneously reporting medical results in academic journals and secret findings to the agency.[28] Through this combination of university-based experiments and its own field tests of these results, the CIA launched a major national effort to develop a new psychological paradigm for torture.

From 1953 to 1963, MKUltra and allied projects dispensed $25 million for human experiments by 185 nongovernmental researchers at eighty institutions, including forty-four universities and twelve hospitals.[29] At first, Director Dulles complained that "we have no human guinea pigs to try these extraordinary techniques."[30] To overcome this critical shortage, the agency adopted testing methods marked by cruelty, illegality, and, with surprising frequency, failure. Seeking unwitting subjects, the CIA injected not only North Korean prisoners, but also spiked drinks at a New York City party house, paid prostitutes to slip LSD to their customers for agency cameras at a San Francisco safe house, pumped hallucinogens into children at summer camp, attempted behavior modification on inmates at California's Vacaville Prison, and collected powerful toxins from Amazon tribes. For "terminal experiments"—those that were pushed to possibly fatal limits— agents trolled Europe for dubious defectors or double agents deemed "expendable."[31]

To a surprising degree, experiments with LSD dominated the CIA's early mind-control research. In later testimony before the Senate, one CIA officer recalled that "we were literally terrified" by reports of Soviet use of LSD "because this was the one material that we had ever been able to locate that really had potential fantastic possibilities if used wrongly."[32] MKUltra's chief scientist, Sidney Gottlieb, said "the impetus for going into the LSD project specifically rested in a report, never verified, . . . that the Russians had bought the world supply."[33] The drug had first been synthesized in 1943 at Sandoz Pharmaceuticals in Switzerland by Dr. Albert Hofmann, a staff chemist who took a

small dose and soon thought "I was dying or going crazy"—a "terrifying" effect that attracted immediate interest from espionage agencies
when his research was published four years later. At the start of the
CIA's drug program, the Army, Hofmann recalled, "sent a representative . . . to speak to me about the procedure for producing large quan-
tities of LSD" to test its military use as an "incapacitating agent" or,
more colloquially, a "weapon without death." Though these plans
proved impractical, Sandoz sent LSD to the Food and Drug Administration, which, Hofmann believed, "distributed" it to the CIA. Simultaneously, the Soviets, probably supplied by Czech chemists, studied
LSD, Hofmann said, "in military and parapsychological investigations, . . . searching for an antidote."[34]

Gottlieb also devised his own LSD tests on unsuspecting subjects,
once spiking the drinks of colleagues during a meeting at a Maryland
lodge, in November 1953. One of the other CIA scientists, Dr. Frank
R. Olson, suffered an immediate mental breakdown and, several days
after taking the drug, jumped or was pushed from the tenth floor of
New York's Statler Hotel, where the agency had confined him for
observation—a crime that the CIA covered up for the next twenty
years by reporting the death to his family as suicide. After telling an internal agency inquiry that the fatality was "just one of the risks running
with scientific experimentation," Gottlieb received a mild reprimand
for "poor judgment" and continued to play a prominent role in drug experiments. In 1975, an investigation of the CIA headed by Vice President Nelson Rockefeller finally revealed that Olson's death was drug
induced, though the report exculpated the agency by alleging that "this
individual may have had a history of emotional instability." His family
called a press conference to announce it would sue the government, to
inscribe the truth into "American memory." Within weeks, President
Gerald Ford apologized formally to the Olson family in the Oval Office
and authorized a parsimonious hush payment of $750,000.[35]

By this time, all the early enthusiasm for exotic techniques had
long faded in the cold light of more sober, independent analysis. In
1958, for example, a staff psychologist at the National Institute of
Mental Health had dismissed the hyperbole over hypnosis, saying:

"Unless knowledge of the art is more elaborate in the secret publications or lore of intelligence agencies than it is in the open sources of science, it is unlikely that present techniques of hypnosis can figure in any significant way in interrogation." Though there was no similarly succinct rejection of drugs, funding for this research tapered off during the 1960s.[36]

Gradually, as drugs failed to deliver useful results, the agency's mind-control project shifted to more mundane behavioral research, which has generally been ignored by scholars and journalists entranced by the red-herring, or "public bogey," of esoteric LSD testing. Yet it was this process of academic trial and error through countless psychological experiments, all dutifully and dully reported in scholarly journals, that produced the real breakthroughs in the CIA's search for effective interrogation techniques.[37]

As early as 1950, after just a few months of investigation, the CIA decided to "transfer the psychological part of the [research] program to an outside agency, where more adequate facilities . . . and volunteers could be utilized as subjects." One of the first of these contracts was for $300,000, through the Navy, to a "Department of Psychology" at an unnamed university, launching a close collaboration of the CIA, the Office of Naval Research, and experimental psychology. Within two years, the ONR would become an influential patron in this still infant scientific field, with 117 contracts at fifty-eight universities under its Psychological Sciences research program.[38]

In retrospect, the agency's alliance with behavioral science seems marvelously synergistic, placing mind-control research at the apex of the academic agenda and providing patronage that elevated cooperative scientists, particularly psychologists, to the first rank of their profession. Indeed, of the billions expended on mind-control research in the 1950s, the intelligence community allocated $7 million to $13 million annually for behavioral studies at major universities by channeling funds through private foundations, some legitimate and others fronts—including the Ford and Rockefeller foundations. One of the main conduits was the Bureau of Social Science Research, which was established at the American University in 1950 and employed, during the next decade, eminent social scientists such as Robert Bower, Albert Biderman, and Louis Gottschalk.[39]

Emerging from World War II as the most militarized among the social or biological sciences, psychology already had a professional mind-set that made it a natural CIA ally in the search for new interrogation techniques. Not only did hundreds of psychologists serve in the wartime army and navy as professionals, but after the war university psychologists, affiliated with the American Psychological Association's Division of Military Psychology, did contract Pentagon research, presenting academic papers on topics such as "the group structures of combat rifle squads" or "evaluations of B-29 crews in training and in combat." More broadly, psychologists studied the human mind, gaining knowledge and power without being restrained, like psychiatrists, by the Hippocratic oath, making them more flexible in their service to the state, its military, and clandestine agencies.[40] At the Cold War's peak in the 1950s, the agency cultivated an intimate relationship with this academic discipline, providing critical funding, flying planeloads of psychologists to international conferences, and monitoring the annual meetings of the American Psychological Association for useful papers.[41] By mobilizing some of the finest minds working in the field of cognitive science, indeed some of the most creative intellects of their generation, the CIA would create, within just a decade, a new form of interrogation grounded in a deeper understanding of human consciousness.

Through covert trial and error, the CIA, in collaboration with university researchers, slowly identified three key behavioral components integral to its emerging techniques for psychological torture. At Montreal's McGill University, the discovery, by gifted Canadian psychologist Dr. Donald O. Hebb, of the devastating impact of sensory deprivation became the conceptual core of the agency's paradigm. Working under direct and indirect CIA contracts, distinguished American behavioral scientists—Albert Biderman, Irving L. Janis, Harold Wolff, and Lawrence Hinkle—advised the agency about the role of self-inflicted pain in Communist interrogation. Finally, a young Yale psychologist, Stanley Milgram, did controversial research under a government grant showing that almost any individual is capable of torture—a critical finding for the agency as it prepared to disseminate its method worldwide. By the project's end in the late 1960s, this torture research had involved three of the "100 most eminent psychologists of the 20th century"—Hebb, Milgram, and Janis—as well as several presidents of the American Psychiatric Association and the American Psychological Association.[42] In silent, sadly eloquent testimony to the corrupting influence of this research, it is ironic that Hebb, an ethical and erudite scholar, should be best remembered today for work that made him, in effect, the progenitor of psychological torture.

Clearly, the topic of much of this scholarly research was indeed torture. Some studies conducted by the BSSR at American universities with Air Force funding explored "the relative usefulness of drugs, electroshock, violence, and other coercive techniques during interrogation of prisoners." Early findings were classified, such as Biderman's analysis of Communist interrogation of POWs under an Air Force contract in 1959, *A Study for Development of Improved Interrogation Techniques.* But some of the BSSR's later work was also published in leading academic journals, notably Biderman's article for a 1960 issue of *Sociometry,* "Social-Psychological Needs and 'Involuntary' Behavior as Illustrated by Compliance in Interrogation." A year later, showing how these secret contracts skewed legitimate scientific research, this same group published a compilation of essays by various contributors, *The Manipulation of Human Behavior,* with a reputable publisher, John Wiley. Inadvertently revealing the ultimate aim of the research, Biderman reported that psychological torture seemed "the ideal way of 'breaking down' a prisoner" because "the effect of isolation on the brain function of the prisoner is much like that which occurs if he is beaten, starved, or deprived of sleep."[43]

As it turned away from unsuccessful drug experiments, CIA-funded studies of sensory deprivation at McGill University proved fruitful. The agency's shift to a behavioral approach was given real impetus by a joint American-British-Canadian effort launched at a secret

Montreal meeting on June 1, 1951. Two days earlier, the venerable senior scientist from the British Ministry of Defence, Sir Henry T. Tizard, had landed from London and checked into a single room, with bath, at Montreal's Ritz-Carlton Hotel for a visit whose public face was an address to the Canadian Association of Physicists. Between morning and dinner sessions with the physicists on June 1, Tizard slipped away for a meeting marked in his private diary only as "discussion with Solandt, etc." As we know from other sources, "Solandt" was Dr. Ormond Solandt, chairman of the Canadian Defense Research Board; "etc." meant senior CIA researcher Cyril Haskins and several Canadian scientists; and their "discussion" set a behavioral research agenda that led to the discovery of psychological torture.[44]

Many years before in August 1940, during a historic scientific mission to North America, Sir Henry had transformed the face of applied physics, making radar a powerful allied weapon in the fight against fascism and, more broadly, the physical sciences a servant of the state. Now, a decade later, Tizard was instrumental in fostering allied behavioral research that made psychological torture NATO's secret weapon against communism and cognitive science the handmaiden of state security. Apart from the considerable prestige he brought to this meeting, Tizard also wielded enormous formal power as the grand boffin of Britain's nexus of military-scientific committees—the Defence Research Policy Committee, the Advisory Council on Scientific Policy, the Joint Intelligence Bureau, and the Commonwealth Committee on Defence Science.[45]

With his magisterial authority and the mannerisms of an "intelligent frog," Sir Henry opened the Montreal session by saying "there had been nothing new in the interrogation business since the days of the Inquisition." Although, according to the CIA's minutes, he urged emphasis on "propaganda and political warfare," the discussion gradually convinced him of the promise of behavioral research. Significantly, the principals agreed there was "no conclusive evidence" that the Soviets had made anything akin to "revolutionary progress," and dismissed their interrogation techniques as "remarkably similar . . . to the age-old methods." Behind closed doors, therefore, the defensive pretence for this cruel science evaporated. Instead, these cold warriors decided to pursue control over human consciousness for its own sake, agreeing on a joint research program to further their "cold war operations."[46] Within just a few years, this effort would include a British "intelligence research unit" at Maresfield, Sussex; an Anglo-American facility near Frankfurt for lethal experiments on captured Soviet-bloc "expendables"; CIA-funded psychology research at leading U.S. universities; periodic conferences to exchange results; and, above all, classified Canadian studies of sensory deprivation at McGill.[47]

Among the Canadians present at the June 1951 meeting was Hebb, then chair of the Human Relations and Research Committee of the Canadian Defence Research Board, who received, from 1951 to 1954, a modest defense grant of $10,000 under "Contract X-38" to study sensory deprivation. One year later, Hebb reported on his research into the "effects of radical isolation upon intellectual function" at a secret symposium convened by Canada's Defence Research Board. Using student volunteers at McGill, where he was also head of the Psychology Department, Hebb had discovered that even short-term deprivation produced a devastating impact on the human psyche. After just two to three days in his isolating "black box," Hebb found that "the subject's very identity had begun to disintegrate." What had the doctor done? Drugs? Electroshock? Threats? No, something far simpler, far more fundamental.[48]

Masking the project as an attempt to prevent "railroad and highway accidents," several of Hebb's graduate students published the experiment's first summary in a 1954 issue of the *Canadian Journal of Psychology,* explaining the simple means used to achieve this dramatic impact on human consciousness. Their subjects, twenty-two male college students, were paid twice the average daily wage just "to lie . . . in a lighted cubicle 24 hours a day" with all sensory stimuli muted—light "diffused" by translucent goggles, "auditory stimulation" limited by soundproofing and constant low noise, and "tactual perception" blocked by thick gloves and a U–shaped foam pillow about the head. According to a later report in the *Guardian,* "early photographs show volunteers, goggled and muffled, looking eerily similar to prisoners arriving at Guantánamo." Most students quit after two or three days. Many refused to finish the experiment. All

suffered eerie hallucinations akin to mescaline use as well as "deteri-
oration in the capacity to think systematically." Claiming a major scientific discovery, Hebb's team concluded that the extreme effects
from such brief loss of stimuli provide "direct evidence of a kind of
dependence on the environment that has not been previously recognized." In his own publications, Hebb expressed surprise that mere
"perceptual isolation" under otherwise "cheerful and happy" conditions should produce such a rapid "breakdown" in thought processes
"with problem-solving and intelligence-test performance significantly impaired." After just four hours of isolation, he found that
subjects "could not follow a connected train of thought," and even
twenty-four hours after their release "motivation for study or the like
was seriously disturbed."[49]

Writing in *Scientific American* a few years later, one of Hebb's students offered a fuller explanation of the extraordinary impact of something so simple as sensory deprivation. After just forty-eight hours of
isolation, most subjects experienced hallucinations similar to the effect
of the powerful drug mescaline. Some subjects saw "rows of little yellow
men with black caps on and their mouths open." One saw "a procession
of squirrels with sacks over their shoulders marching 'purposefully.'"

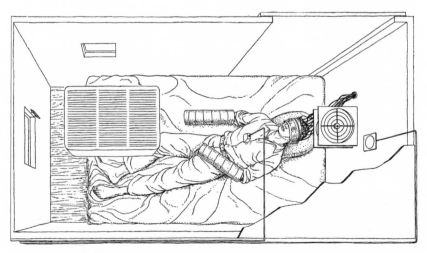

Dr. Donald O. Hebb's experimental cubicle, constructed at McGill University
in Montreal, to study the effect of protracted isolation. (*Scientific American*)

Another heard a choir singing "in full stereophonic sound." A third felt "pellets fired from a miniature rocket ship." By monitoring brain waves of subjects throughout the isolations, Hebb's researchers concluded that "a changing sensory environment seems essential for human beings." Through the monotony of isolation, "the activity of the cortex may be impaired so that the brain behaves abnormally."[50]

Though these results might seem, at first glance, benign if not banal, their implications, when developed by Hebb's less ethical successors in this larger CIA interrogation project, would allow a devastating assault on the human psyche. Once refined by further testing, the research discovered a human mental equilibrium so delicate that just a few simple tools—goggles, gloves, and a foam pillow—could induce a state akin to acute psychosis in many subjects within just forty-eight hours.

The CIA's Technical Services Division (TDS) was remarkably quick to recognize the implications of Hebb's experiments among the hundreds of projects backed by millions of dollars in secret funding from three governments. As more than 6,000 psychologists filled New York City's Statler Hotel in September 1954 for the annual convention of the American Psychological Association, a lone, anonymous CIA scientist moved among them, trolling the corridors for relevant research. There was surprisingly little of interest, the agent reported to his TSD chief, in the 445 research papers and 86 symposia. Even the papers at the symposium on drugs and behavior were generally humdrum if not ho-hum—Dr. G. R. Wendt's discussion of mescaline experiments was "evasive," Conan Kornetsky on drug tests at Lexington Hospital had "nothing of interest to our program," and Daniel Wilner on juvenile addiction had "no pertinent information for our purposes." But among the "good many papers in clinical psychology," there was, in fact, one of considerable interest—a presidential address by D. O. Hebb of McGill on "Drives and the C.N.S (Conceptual Nervous System)," describing a promising "project carried out by the Canadian army." In a private meeting, one "Dr. Webster of McGill University" told this CIA representative that the experiment was an attempt "to eliminate as much as possible all sensations." In his report, the agent meticulously noted all the important details—student volunteers "were blindfolded and their ears covered with foam rubber and their feet and hands were covered with large mitts and they were placed in soundproof rooms," where they were read "childish rhymes." Significantly, the subjects "tended to lose their sense of time" and became "very irritable and requested time after time to hear the simple childish rhymes." None held out "longer than a week." Highlighting the importance of these findings for the agency, the report concluded that "this experiment gets at some of the psychological factors found in prisoner-of-war treatment where the individual is completely isolated in solitary confinement."[51]

The implications of this small experiment, for both cognitive science and CIA interrogation, were, in fact, profound. Seven years after the McGill team's first publications, over 230 articles on sensory deprivation appeared in the world's leading scientific journals. For Hebb himself, the experiments allowed timely testing of his neurological theories, winning him a Nobel Prize nomination by McGill, the presidency of the American Psychological Association, and, in the words of a professional encyclopedia, a "distinctive place in the history of twentieth-century psychology." But back home in Canada, Parliament began grumbling about this wasteful research in 1954, and the country's Defence Research Board, fearing a security breach, suddenly canceled the project's funding. Hebb soon found his data was, as he put it, "snatched immediately to some organization in the States."[52]

The CIA, following Hebb's lead, moved quickly to explore the implications of sensory deprivation for interrogation. As early as March 1955, for example, the agency's Office of Security had already done a research paper describing "total isolation" techniques as "an operational tool of potential."[53] That same year, Morse Allen, a militant anti-Communist who headed the CIA's Artichoke project, met with a brain surgeon at the National Institute of Mental Health, Dr. Maitland Baldwin, about his recent, rather promising experiment. After forty hours inside a specially constructed sensory deprivation box, an army volunteer began "an hour of crying loudly and sobbing in a most heartrending fashion" before kicking his way out. This dramatic denouement persuaded Baldwin that "the isolation technique could break any man, no matter how intelligent or strong-willed." By now, Morse Allen felt further work with volunteers proved little, and wanted real-world testing of subjects "for whom much is at stake (perhaps life and death)," pressing even for "terminal experiments" to see how deeply coerced sensory deprivation could disturb the mind. Though feeling that anything more than six days of sensory deprivation would "almost certainly cause irreparable damage," Baldwin agreed to do these "terminal type" tests if the agency would provide both subjects and cover. In the end, however, a CIA medical officer blocked the project as "immoral and inhuman," suggesting that those who favored the experiment might "volunteer their heads for use in Dr. Baldwin's 'noble' project."[54]

But the stakes were too high for moral concerns to stop this critical pursuit. In another non-coercive experiment at the National Institute of Mental Health in 1955–56, Dr. John C. Lilly, later famed for his work with dolphins, immersed two volunteers "in a tank containing slowly flowing water," eyes covered with "blacked-out mask (enclosing the whole head)," and an extremely "low" sound level. After just three hours with sensory stimuli limited to "some faint sounds of water from the piping," both subjects went from normally "directed type of thinking about problems," to consciousness of "residual stimuli . . . to an almost unbearable degree," and finally to "reveries and fantasies of a highly personal and emotionally charged nature" with powerful visual hallucinations. Learning of his work, intelligence officials, as author John Marks put it, "swooped down on Lilly . . . interested in the use of his tank as an interrogation tool," pressing him to immerse "involuntary subjects" until they were "broken down to the point where their belief systems . . . could be altered." Lilly evidently did some of this work, but, under his own strict ethical guidelines, made himself and a colleague the sole subjects until 1958 when, realizing that intelligence agencies had no interest in sensory deprivation for its "positive benefits," he resigned from the NIMH.[55]

A team of four Harvard University psychiatrists conducted a similar but larger experiment in 1957 that the CIA found promising, though still limited. Although these researchers cited concern for polio patients as the project's justification, their experiment, like many, was funded by the ONR's covert behavioral program (Nonr 1866 [29]).

And even they admitted the findings were relevant to "brainwashing." Instead of immersion in water, this test's seventeen paid volunteers were "placed in a tank-type respirator with a specially built mattress" arranged "to inhibit movement and tactile contact." To create an atmosphere of sensory monotony, the respirator's motor ran constantly for "a dull, repetitive auditory stimulus" and low "artificial light was minimal and constant." After seventeen hours, one subject, a twenty-five-year-old dental student, "began to punch and shake the respirator," his "eyes full of tears, and his voice shaking," as he struggled in vain to break out of the iron lung until an attendant released him. At least four volunteers terminated from "anxiety and panic," and only five subjects remained for the experiment's full thirty-six hours. Among the seventeen subjects, half had hallucinations and all suffered "degrees of anxiety." Apparently addressing their covert patrons, the Harvard psychiatrists concluded that "sensory deprivation can produce major mental and behavioral changes in man," and recommended its capacity to induce psychosis as "more 'natural' than the pharmacological and physical methods currently used"—not, of course, in polio treatment but, if we can finish their sentence, in CIA torture. In the words of the agency's later interrogation manual, this Harvard study "confirmed earlier findings" that:

1. the deprivation of sensory stimuli induces stress;
2. the stress becomes unbearable for most subjects;
3. the subject has a growing need for physical and social stimuli; and
4. some subjects progressively lose touch with reality, focus inwardly, and produce delusions, hallucinations, and other pathological effects.[56]

As testimony to the significance of sensory deprivation, in June 1958 the intelligence community funded, under a covert ONR behavioral contract also numbered Nonr 1866 [29], a special symposium at Harvard Medical School. This remarkable gathering attracted leading cognitive scientists such as Jerome S. Bruner, a pioneer in the application of behavioral science to education, and Norbert Wiener, the father of cybernetics; several CIA contract researchers; and Hebb himself. Although the Harvard convener hailed Hebb for "courageously" acting on his "ingenious idea" of studying sensory deprivation, the honoree limited his participation to a public confession that the work had not been done for prevention of railway accidents but dealt, "actually, with the problem of brainwashing," although he was "not permitted to say so in the first publishing." A colleague of Hebb's gave the first full report of the experiments, admitting that one of their main aims was "to measure the subject's susceptibility to propaganda," which had increased markedly in isolation. Most significantly, their experiment had established that "variation in the sensory environment . . . would contribute to the breakdown of the organized activity of complex central processes" in the brain. In short, anyone could produce "surprisingly drastic effects" on consciousness by simple, nonviolent changes in the environment—heat, sound, sight, and touch.[57]

Another symposium paper, by Dr. George E. Ruff, a University of Pennsylvania psychiatrist doing sensory-deprivation research for the Air Force, indicated the potential of this work for prisoner interrogation, noting that all experiments to date had allowed the subject to leave "the chamber if he 'wants out.'" Ruff predicted, in words that the agency should have found enticing, that involuntary isolation "would produce behavior unlike that observed where an escape route is available."[58]

With ample funding from the Army and the National Science Foundation, another seminar participant, Princeton psychologist Jack A. Vernon, soon replicated Hebb's stunning results on one hundred students, showing, first, that "physical violence" in interrogation "appears unwise" or counterproductive and, by contrast, that nonviolent sensory deprivation could be used to "build a very effective brainwashing technique."[59]

Then, in 1960, one of the agency's most active contractors, Lawrence Hinkle of Cornell, confirmed the significance of Hebb's research for the CIA's mind-control effort. Through a comprehensive review of "interrogation . . . for the purposes of intelligence," Hinkle found Hebb's work, in light of the neurological literature, the most promising of all known techniques. "It has long been the custom,"

Hinkle noted, "of captors, police, and inquisitors, to isolate their prisoners in places that are cold, damp, hot, unventilated, unsanitary, uncomfortable, and so on; to deprive them of food, fluids, sleep, and rest and medical care; and to beat, torture, harry, overwork and threaten them, as well as question them interminably with leading questions." But which of these methods, Hinkle asked, is most effective? All the standard interrogation techniques have varying, unpredictable, impacts on the brain's functioning, and even the most venerable police procedures "incur a risk" by generating "compliant behavior without necessarily eliciting accurate information." For example, the enforced standing used by Soviet interrogators can induce fainting or "circulatory impairment," leading to delirium that renders the subject's information dubious. Similarly, since sleep deprivation induces the brain's "special vulnerabilities," the subject's performance quickly deteriorates. Of all the possible techniques, isolation seems "from the interrogator's point of view . . . the ideal way of 'breaking down' a prisoner, because, to the unsophisticated, it seems to create precisely the state that the interrogator desires: malleability and the desire to talk, with the added advantage that one can delude himself that he is using no force or coercion." Even the prisoner may be deceived, saying the "interrogator never laid a hand on me." Yet, as Hebb's work had found, "the effect of isolation on the brain function of the prisoner is much like that which occurs if he is beaten, starved, or deprived of sleep."[60]

All this research, though intriguing, did not answer the question of paramount importance to Morse Allen and others at the CIA: What would happen if the subjects were prisoners, not volunteers, and there were no "escape route"? One of Hebb's colleagues in psychiatry at McGill, Dr. D. Ewen Cameron, was working on parallel studies that soon captured the CIA's interest. A respected researcher and past president of the American Psychiatric Association, Cameron claimed, in scientific papers, that he had duplicated "the extraordinary political conversions . . . in the iron curtain countries," in one case "using sleeplessness, disinhibiting agents [drugs], and hypnosis."[61]

One of the CIA's staff psychologists, John Gittinger, noticed Cameron's 1956 article in which he had described an extreme form of sensory deprivation called "psychic driving" and notified his agency superiors. As Cameron explained in the *American Journal of Psychiatry,* he had used "an adaptation of Hebb's psychological isolation" by bombarding patients with endless repetitions of taped messages about parental rejection or incestuous longings while they were in a drug-induced "clinical coma," or in "hypnosis under stimulus drugs" such as LSD. The combined effect produced a state "analogous to . . . the breakdown of the individual under continuous interrogation." Consequently, the CIA sent its close collaborator from the National Institute of Mental Health, Maitland Baldwin, to Montreal for an informal chat with Cameron, powerfully entrenched after fifteen years as head of McGill's psychiatric treatment facility, the Allan Memorial Institute. Three months after Baldwin's "informal chat," Allan Memorial, at Cameron's behest, applied to the Society for the Investigation of Human Ecology, one of the agency's main fronts for mind-control research, for support to study "The Effects upon Human Behavior of the Repetition of Verbal Signals." Cameron proposed to use his "patients" at Allan Memorial as unwitting subjects in a brutal research regimen that would intensify Hebb's sensory isolation by electroshocks and incessant repetition of audiotapes. Specifically, Cameron would study:

1. The breaking down of ongoing patterns of the patient's behavior by means of particularly intensive electroshocks (depatterning).
2. The intensive repetition (16 hours a day for 6–7 days) of the prearranged verbal signal.
3. During the period of intensive repetition the patient is kept in partial sensory isolation.
4. Repression of the [psychic] driving period is carried out by putting the patient, after the conclusion of the period, into continuous sleep for 7–10 days.[62]

At last, the CIA had a scientist eager to conduct "terminal experiments in sensory deprivation," and one with his own ready supply of human subjects. As soon as Cameron's grant application arrived at Human Ecology's New York office on January 23, 1957, the CIA's local mole forwarded it to agency headquarters where Dulles, who knew the doctor well from their wartime work on Nazi psychology, personally approved the project on February 25. Within days, the CIA designated Cameron's promising research as MKUltra Subproject 68, placed it under Gottlieb's direct supervision, and laundered generous annual payments of $20,000 through Human Ecology. Between 1957 and 1963, approximately one hundred patients admitted to the Allan Institute with moderate emotional problems became unwitting or unwilling subjects in an extreme form of behavioral experimentation conducted under the cover of treating schizophrenia. To cite one of the tragic examples: a recently qualified psychiatrist, Dr. Mary Morrow, agreed to routine psychological testing when she applied for a staff position but soon found herself drugged and subjected to weeks of involuntary electroshocks and sensory deprivation. In another case, a young housewife, Jeanine Huard, who had sought help for ordinary postpartum depression, was given a similarly dangerous cocktail of drugs, electrical shock, and protracted sleep. In these CIA-funded experiments, Cameron was using his patients to test a three-stage method for what he called depatterning—first, drug-induced coma for up to eighty-six days; next, electroshock treatment three times daily for thirty days; and, finally, a football helmet clamped to the head for up to twenty-one days with a looped tape repeating, up to half a million times, messages like "my mother hates me." In contrast to Hebb's six-day maximum for voluntary isolation, Cameron confined one patient, known only as Mary C., in his "box" for an unimaginable thirty-five days of total sensory deprivation. Cameron claimed his methods were producing a real breakthrough. In May 1960, for example, he told an Air Force conference that his experiments using "strict sensory isolation," making his patients de facto prisoners, had proven "much more disturbing" to the human psyche than Hebb's voluntary, or "self-imposed," deprivation by student volunteers.[63]

But by late 1963, after seven years of support, the CIA, with Dulles now retired, grew tired of the limited practical results and terminated Cameron's project. Canadians had come to regard him as a crackpot, with Hebb branding his colleague as "criminally stupid" and Solandt saying his work "was something the Defence Research Board would have no part in." Six months later, Cameron, stripped of all funding, suddenly resigned as director of Allan Memorial, packed all the papers from MKUltra Subproject 68 into his car, and drove across the border into New York State.[64]

In 1967, three years after Cameron's sudden resignation, the Allan Institute conducted a follow-up study and found that 60 percent of the seventy-nine subjects who had reached stage 3 of his depatterning were still suffering persistent amnesia. In addition, a full 23 percent of his former subjects had serious physical complications. After the press exposed Cameron's CIA funding in 1980, nine of his former patients filed a civil suit against the agency in Washington. Two litigants, Mary Morrow and Jeanine Huard, were still suffering from prosopagnosia, a brain disorder that blocks recognition of faces or even common objects. After a federal judge rejected a CIA motion to dismiss in October 1988, the agency settled out of court for the legislated maximum of $750,000. About the same time, the Canadian government made an even more miserly payment of $180,000 to nine victims. The following May, the president of the American Psychiatric Association, Dr. Paul Fink, issued a formal statement "expressing our deep regret that psychiatric patients became unwitting participants in those experiments." By contrast, the Canadian Psychiatric Association closed ranks and refused to apologize, instead issuing a statement that praised Allan Memorial's contributions to their profession.[65]

In these years of covert experimentation, other contract researchers identified a second key element in the agency's emerging paradigm— self-inflicted pain. This discovery emerged from a series of studies by two respected neurologists at Cornell Medical Center, Lawrence Hinkle and Harold Wolff, who founded the Human Ecology Society in 1953–54, soon making it the most important CIA conduit for legitimate scientific research. In his proposal offering to bend behavioral science to the agency's needs, Wolff asked the CIA to provide all its information on interrogation and intimidation to facilitate his comprehensive review of human control, the precursor, he said, to "experimental investigations designed to develop new techniques of offensive/defensive intelligence use." In a revealing passage, Wolff's grant proposal promised that "potentially useful secret drugs (and various brain damaging procedures) will be similarly tested." To conduct this risky research, Wolff made clear that "we expect the agency to make available suitable subjects and a proper place for the performance of necessary experiments." With generous CIA funding of $5 million for just three years of operations, the Human Ecology Society backed innovative research by its two principals and allowed the agency access to the country's leading behavioral scientists. From 1955 to 1958, for example, the CIA channeled funds through Human Ecology to test LSD on twenty-six sexual psychopaths at Ionia State Hospital in Michigan. In a synergy of the covert and the overt, the agency also laundered nearly $200,000 through the society to support research into cultural differences, producing more effective propaganda techniques for the CIA and assisting the ascent of the researcher, Dr. Charles Osgood, to the presidency of the American Psychological Association.[66]

With backing secured, Hinkle and Wolff conducted a seminal study of Communist interrogation for the CIA's TSD in 1956. In a sanitized version of their findings published by the *Archives of Neurology and Psychiatry,* the authors reported that successful Communist interrogation relied not on esoteric "brainwashing" with drugs or electroshock but on standard "police practices" that the KGB had inherited from its czarist predecessor. After four weeks of "isolation, anxiety, lack of sleep, uncomfortable temperatures, and chronic hunger," most Russian prisoners suffered "profound disturbances of mood" that made them willing to cooperate with their KGB interrogators. Instead of exotic methods, the KGB simply made victims stand still for eighteen to twenty-four hours—producing "excruciating pain" as ankles double in size, skin becomes "tense and intensely painful," blisters erupt oozing "watery serum," heart rates soar, kidneys shut down, and delusions deepen. After seizing power in 1949, Chinese Communists adopted many of the Soviet procedures, although they also employed manacles and leg chains, no longer used by the KGB. Significantly, the authors found no reason to differentiate the "nonviolent" KGB methods "from any other form of torture."[67]

This Cornell report may have contributed to the agency's shift from the search for a miracle mind-control drug to the more mundane exploration of human psychology. Indeed, when the agency's two-phase method was finalized seven years later, it would follow many of the KGB's distinctive techniques. By their sophisticated analysis of Soviet torture, Hinkle and Wolff had, in effect, identified another critical facet of the CIA's emerging model for interrogation—self-inflicted pain.

In searching for other university research that contributed to the CIA's evolving torture paradigm, the famed Yale obedience experiments by a young psychologist, Stanley Milgram, seem a likely candidate. Since the agency regularly laundered MKUltra funds through other federal agencies to some 185 nongovernment researchers and has refused to release their names, we have no way of knowing the full scope of academic investigation that might have advanced the CIA's study of torture.[68] But the timing, at the peak of the agency's academic involvement, and the topic, torture, raise the possibility that Milgram's work may well have been a part of its larger mind-control project. And, of equal import, his close ties to the ONR lend substance to this speculation. Moreover, Yale's senior psychologist, Irving L. Janis, had written the seminal Air Force study of the Soviet mind-control threat, recommending the sort of experiment Milgram now proposed.[69]

After the American Council for Learned Societies rejected Milgram's application for $2,000 to test the effect of mescaline on art appreciation in late 1960, he wrote Luigi Petrullo, head of the ONR's Group Psychology Branch, proposing to study whether ordinary people would torture innocent victims with electric shock. After follow-up correspondence with the ONR, Milgram expanded his slender research design and, in January 1961—a period when the CIA's mind-control studies were focused fully on human psychology—applied to the National Science Foundation for a grant to study the "Dynamics of Obedience." After sending a three-man review team to New Haven and receiving assurances from its own legal counsel that liability for any damage to the subjects would be Yale's, the NSF gave Milgram a substantial $24,700 grant—an exceptional mix of caution and largesse that hints at NSF reluctance and possible ONR or CIA pressure. Indeed, in later years when Milgram proposed other projects without ONR's backing, the NSF rejected all his applications, even though they featured a similar method using a mechanical device to test aspects of human behavior.[70]

With this generous federal grant, Milgram tested forty "ordinary" residents of New Haven, Connecticut, to see if they would, on command, torture a helpless "victim" with escalating electric shocks. Skillful staging lent authority to these commands. At Yale's "elegant" Interaction Laboratory, a uniformed experimenter seated the subjects before an "impressive" machine labeled "Shock Generator Type ZLB" and ordered them to activate thirty switches, ranging from 15 to 450 volts. At 75 volts, the victim, who was actually a railroad auditor acting out this role, gave a "little grunt." At 315 volts, he produced a "violent scream." And after 330 volts, he "was not heard from." When the volunteers heard but could not see the victim, 65 percent of them flicked switches on command all the way to the supposedly fatal maximum level, 450 volts. If the volunteers were asked just to assist, but not to act, compliance was almost 100 percent. If, by contrast, a nonauthority figure without the white coat gave the commands, obedience was zero. In some subjects, the test induced what Milgram called "extreme levels of nervous tension" marked by "sweating, trembling, and stuttering." One poised businessman was, Milgram said, reduced in just twenty minutes to "a twitching, stuttering wreck, who was rapidly approaching a point of nervous collapse." Rejecting the idea that those who delivered maximum voltage were "monsters, the sadistic fringe of society," Milgram concluded that social convention led normal individuals to accept authority and ignore the victim's pain. Whether his analysis was valid or not, one result of this research was clear: At the end of each simulated-torture session, ordinary New Haven citizens walked out of the Yale laboratory with a check for $4.50 and the disturbing knowledge that they, like Gestapo interrogators, could inflict pain and even death on an innocent victim. Indeed, one subject, a military veteran named William Menold, recalled feeling like "an emotional wreck," a "basket case," from the realization "that somebody could get me to do that stuff."[71]

When first published, Milgram's results were controversial and his many professional critics concentrated their fire on his lack of ethics in the handling of human subjects. Milgram himself secretly shared this view, telling his diary it was "ethically questionable . . . to lure people

into the laboratory and ensnare them into a situation that is stressful."
A critic writing in *American Psychologist* charged that this "traumatic"
experiment was "potentially harmful" to its subjects. One Yale colleague complained about this aspect to the American Psychological
Association, which then denied Milgram membership for a year. After
finishing his contract at Yale, he moved on to Harvard, where he was
later denied tenure, largely for the same reason. However, Milgram's
intelligence connections apparently saved his career. He was soon
hired, with a promotion to full professor, by the new graduate dean at
the City University of New York, Mina Rees, who had recently retired
as deputy director of the Office of Naval Research.[72]

Nobody has asked, even decades later, why the ONR would have
been so solicitous of Milgram's career and why the NSF would have
funded an experiment of so little scientific value. Although Milgram
himself said he was testing theories about Nazi torturers, World War II
was long over and his ONR patrons, like their intelligence confreres at
the CIA, were now obsessed with winning the Cold War.[73] In retrospect, the timing, topic, military ties, conflicted NSF funding, and
NSF rejection of all his later projects, if taken together, provide indications, albeit circumstantial, that Milgram's experiment was a by-
product of the larger CIA mind-control project.

Whatever his ultimate funding source, Milgram's published results
answered the key question the agency faced as it began global dissemination of its interrogation method: if trained in the new torture techniques, would ordinary police officers in Asia and Latin America be
willing to practice what they had been taught? In time, the CIA's field
experience confirmed Milgram's laboratory results: any ordinary soldier or police officer could be taught to torture.

By the early 1960s, the CIA was ready to move beyond research to
application. Most important, the years of secret experimentation had
convinced agency scientists that "esoteric" methods simply did not
work and more basic psychological techniques were, by contrast, dev-
astatingly effective. As the CIA psychologist John Gittinger later told
the U.S. Senate, "the general idea we were able to come up with is that
brain-washing was largely a process of isolating a human being, keeping

him out of contact, putting him under long stress in relationship to interviewing and interrogation, . . . without having to resort to any kind of esoteric means."[74]

At the same time, in 1963, the CIA's inspector general discovered the super-secret MKUltra project during a routine audit and compiled a twenty-four-page report for the director condemning these experiments for putting "the rights and interests of all Americans in jeopardy." The report noted that "research in the manipulation of human behavior is considered by many authorities in medicine . . . to be professionally unethical." Significantly, the inspector added, "some aspects of MKUltra raise questions of legality" under the CIA's charter.[75] The inspector was particularly critical of the program's drug testing on unwitting subjects, since the agents were "not qualified scientific observers" and had no way of treating subjects who became seriously ill.[76]

In response to this report, the CIA suspended MKUltra. But powerful backers such as Richard Helms objected, saying that "for over a decade Clandestine Services has had the mission of maintaining a capability for influencing human behavior." Though Helms warned the suspension threatened the agency's "positive operational capability to use drugs," and thus won permission for experiments to continue at a lower level for another decade, the important research work had, by this point, been completed and investigations gradually drew to a close.[77]

In 1963, the CIA distilled its findings in its seminal *Kubark Counterintelligence Interrogation* handbook. For the next forty years, the *Kubark* manual would define the agency's interrogation methods and training programs throughout the Third World. Synthesizing the behavioral research done by contract academics, the manual spelled out a revolutionary two-phase form of torture that relied on sensory deprivation and self-inflicted pain for an effect that, for the first time in the two millennia of this cruel science, was more psychological than physical.

Reflecting its underlying behavioral approach, the *Kubark* manual proclaims, on page 1, that "sound interrogation . . . rests upon . . . certain broad principles, chiefly psychological." The report's "fundamental hypothesis" is that effective questioning, both coercive and non-coercive, involves "methods of inducing regression of the personality to whatever earlier and weaker level is required for the dissolution of resistance and the inculcation of dependence." Thus, all interrogation techniques "are essentially ways of speeding up the process of regression." As the subject clings "to a world that makes some sense" and struggles to "reinforce his identity and powers of resistance," the interrogator counters with a "confusion technique . . . designed not only to obliterate the familiar but to replace it with the weird" until this systematic assault on personal identity becomes "mentally intolerable."[78]

Such confusion can best be effected by attacking the victim's sense of time, by scrambling the biorhythms fundamental to every human's daily life. Creation of existential chaos starts from the moment of arrest, which "achieves, if possible, surprise and the maximum amount of mental discomfort in order to catch the suspect off balance and to deprive him of the initiative." Then, in words repeated almost verbatim twenty years later in the CIA's Honduran training handbook, *Kubark* suggests interrogators engage in the "persistent manipulation of time, by retarding and advancing clocks and serving meals at odd times—ten minutes or ten hours after the last food was given. Day and night are jumbled." By "thwarting" the detainee's effort "to keep track of time, to live in the familiar past," interrogators are "likely to drive him deeper and deeper into himself, until he is no longer able to control his responses in an adult fashion."[79]

The manual then goes on to spell out the essential features of the CIA's psychological paradigm. "The more completely the place of confinement eliminates sensory stimuli," the report reads, drawing on the McGill research by Hebb and Cameron, "the more rapidly and deeply will the interrogatee be affected. Results produced only after weeks or months of imprisonment in an ordinary cell can be duplicated in hours or days in a cell which has no light . . . which is sound proofed, in which odors are eliminated, etc." In this first stage, interrogators are instructed to employ simple, nonviolent techniques, such as hooding or sleep denial, to disorient the subject. To intensify this confusion, they might also attack personal identity, often with personal or sexual humiliation. Explaining the destructive force of self-inflicted pain, *Kubark* states: "It has been plausibly suggested that, whereas pain inflicted on a person from outside himself may actually focus or intensify his will to resist, his resistance is likelier to be sapped by pain which he seems to inflict upon himself."[80]

Citing Albert Biderman's BSSR study on coercion approvingly, the *Kubark* manual argues that "the threat to inflict pain . . . can trigger fears more damaging than the immediate sensation of pain"—in effect, restating the paradigm's key principle that psychological pain is more devastating than its physical variant. But to render their threats credible under actual field conditions, interrogators might sometimes accelerate the prisoner's disorientation by inflicting physical pain through beatings, electric shock, or more malign methods. Once the subject is disoriented, interrogators can then move on to the stage of self-inflicted pain through techniques such as enforced standing with arms extended. In this latter phase, victims are made to feel responsible for their own suffering, thus inducing them to alleviate their agony by capitulating to the power of their interrogators. In assessing Biderman's major research, *The Manipulation of Human Behavior*, the *Kubark* manual comments critically that its "contributions consistently demonstrate too theoretical an understanding of interrogation" and it has "practically no valid experimentation." Similarly, *Kubark* noted that experiments at "McGill University, the National Institute of Mental Health, and other sites have attempted to come as close as possible to the elimination of sensory stimuli." Some of these "findings point toward hypotheses that seem relevant to interrogation, but conditions like those of detention for purposes of counterintelligence interrogation have not been duplicated for experimentation."[81] This deficiency—the lack of verifiable results from human subjects— would soon be resolved as the CIA began to apply its paradigm, particularly in South Vietnam.

The *Kubark* manual was by no means a dead document, filed away for future reference, but instead became the basis of a major agency training program that ran for about a decade. Calling it the CIA's "premier course," one former agent, Bill Wagner, attended the three-week interrogation program at The Farm, the agency's celebrated training center near Williamsburg, Virginia, in 1970. Competition for admission was so strong among ambitious young agents that many secured slots by first volunteering for the role of "captives." For weeks, these volunteers, following the *Kubark* method, "were deprived of sleep, kept doused with water in cold rooms, forced to sit or stand in uncomfortable positions for long periods, isolated from sunlight and social contacts, given food deliberately made unappetizing (oversalted, for instance . . .), and subjected to mock executions." Even for hardened agents participating in a controlled training exercise inside their own agency, *Kubark*'s prescriptions were so devastating that at least ten percent of the volunteers "dropped out" and many later refused to take the course when their turn came. "They lost their stomach for it," Wagner explains. By the time this controversial program was shut down during Congress's investigations of the agency in the mid-1970s, an entire generation of CIA agents and interrogators had been trained in psychological torture.[82]

Beyond the obvious effectiveness of the CIA's new methods, psychological torture afforded intelligence agencies everywhere an additional advantage: leaving none of the usual signs, the practice easily eluded even the strictest of human-rights protections. This feature was made clear by Britain's experience where the interrogation was used, with limited gains and high political costs, in a global campaign against terrorists. By 1957, as Cameron was launching his CIA research at McGill University, Britain had established the intelligence research unit at Maresfield and, within two years, completed tests verifying the Canadian findings. As reported in a 1959 issue of the British medical journal *Lancet,* an experiment with twenty volunteers at Lancaster Moor Hospital, a government mental institution, replicated every detail of Hebb's experiment, including the goggles, gloves, and, in a slight variation, a soundproofed cubicle—the latter specially constructed at great cost with unidentified funds. All subjects passed through stages of "agitation, . . . thinking difficulties, and finally . . . panic." Despite strong incentives to continue, fourteen quit within forty-eight hours. Five suffered "nightmares of which drowning, suffocating, and killing people &c. were features." Despite the surface legitimacy of its publication in *Lancet,* the timing and cost of the experiment make it likely that this was military, not medical, research. Leaving aside the question of funding, this test of sensory deprivation had produced even greater emotional disturbance than its Canadian original, providing ample evidence of its efficacy for British intelligence. In the early 1960s, Britain's military began training its elite forces in these psychological methods, offensively to conduct counterinsurgency, and defensively to survive the stress of capture.[83]

In the violent eclipse of the British Empire, these interrogation techniques, as a later official inquiry reported, "played an important part in counter insurgency operations . . . in the British Cameroons (1960–61), Brunei (1963), British Guiana (1964), Aden (1964–67), [and] Borneo/Malaysia (1965–66)." After allegations of brutality by its forces, Britain adopted, in February 1965, a "joint directive on military interrogation" that cited the Geneva Conventions to bar any "violence to life and person" or "outrages upon personal dignity." Explaining the logic of these prohibitions, the directive stated that "torture and physical cruelty of all kinds are professionally unrewarding since a suspect so treated may be persuaded to talk but not to tell the truth." The directive stated forcefully that "successful interrogation . . . calls for a psychological attack."[84] After further allegations of "cruelty and torture" at the British Army's Interrogation Centre in Aden during an Arab terror campaign in 1966, an official inquiry by Roderic Bowen, Q.C., added requirements for external supervision.[85] But despite these restrictions, British intelligence evidently preserved its knowledge of the psychological practices that were now, under these tighter guidelines, at the cusp of illegality.

When a record 304 bombs erupted across Northern Ireland between January and June 1971, London deployed this extreme interrogation against the underground Irish Republican Army. In effect, like France in Algeria and America in Iraq, Britain felt compelled to fight terror with torture. In April, the English Intelligence Centre gave Belfast's police, the Royal Ulster Constabulary, a top-secret training course in what were called the "five techniques" for "interrogation in depth." Although all instruction was done "orally" and no orders were "committed to writing or authorized in any official document," the British government later admitted that these methods had been approved at a "high level." After investing security forces with special powers of summary arrest and limitless internment, Belfast unleashed Operation Demetrius on August 9, quickly "sweeping-up" some eight hundred suspected IRA terrorists.[86]

Among the hundreds arrested, fourteen suspects were selected for a secret program to test the interrogation doctrine under field conditions. In the words of a later finding by the European Court of Human Rights, these fourteen subjects were taken to "unidentified centres" where they were subjected to "five particular techniques" that were "sometimes termed 'disorientation' or 'sensory deprivation' techniques." Their perverse simplicity and "combined application" revealed the influence of both Hebb's experiments and the CIA's two-phase method, with its trademark mix of sensory disorientation and self-inflicted pain. In the court's words, these techniques involved:

(a.) wall-standing: forcing the detainees to remain for periods of some hours in a "stress position," described by those who underwent it as being "spreadeagled against the wall, with their fingers put high above the head against the wall, the legs spread apart and the feet back, causing them to stand on their toes with the weight of the body mainly on the fingers";

(b.) hooding: putting a black or navy coloured bag over the detainees' heads and . . . keeping it there all the time except during interrogation;

(c.) subjection to noise: pending their interrogations, holding the detainees in a room where there was a continuous loud and hissing noise;

(d.) deprivation of sleep: pending their interrogations, depriving the detainees of sleep;

(e.) deprivation of food and drink: subjecting the detainees to a reduced diet during their stay at the centre and pending interrogations.[87]

Within weeks, press reports detailing these harsh measures forced Britain's Conservative government to appoint a committee of inquiry,

chaired by Sir Edmund Compton, into allegations of "physical brutality." In October 1971, while the committee was still investigating, the
Times of London sparked a bitter debate in Parliament with an exposé
of torture in Northern Ireland. Home Secretary Reginald Maudling
defended the security forces, arguing that tough tactics were imperative because "intelligence is of enormous importance in defeating gun-
men." But a member from Northern Ireland, Frank McManus, shot
back that the case was going before Europe's Court of Human Rights
and the government was "in serious danger of coming into serious international disrepute."[88]

Published only four weeks later, the Compton committee's report
stoked these partisan fires with its contorted justifications for each of
the "five techniques." Wall standing for up to forty-three hours "provides
security for detainees and guards." The hood serves a similar "security"
function. The continuous noise bombarding detainees "prevents their
overhearing . . . and is thus a security measure." All these tough tactics were, Compton said, necessary against terrorists because "information must be sought while it is still fresh . . . and thereby save the
lives of members of the security forces and of the civil population." Although the wall standing did constitute "physical ill-treatment," the report insisted that there was "no evidence at all of a major trauma." But
how could Compton miss psychological torture so traumatic that, according to expert diagnosis, "overt psychiatric illness" was still evident
over two years later? Hewing narrowly to his brief, Compton had focused on physical abuse. Treating each of the "five techniques" sepa-
rately, he ignored their cumulative effect, a central feature of the CIA
psychological paradigm. This extraordinary "whitewash" prompted a
special parliamentary session, with the government justifying interrogation that "yielded information of great value . . . about individuals
concerned in the IRA campaign, . . . about the location of arms
dumps and weapons."[89]

In rapid-fire ripostes to Compton and his defenders, Amnesty International explained that "the purpose and effects of these techniques
is to disorientate and break down the mind by sensory deprivation."
These features won them, Amnesty said, "special place in our cata-
logue of moral crimes" and made them "as grave an assault on . . . the

human person as more traditional techniques of physical torture."[90] Amnesty's medical assessment and moral outrage were well-founded, astutely recognizing how psychological torture could more easily evade scrutiny than the physical variety. Indeed, a later committee into interrogation headed by Hubert Lister Parker, Baron of Waddington, that was formed midst the firestorm over Compton's report, soon discovered the difficulties in restraining psychological torture when state security was determined to use it. Parker's committee reviewed Hebb's original experiments, staged demonstrations of the techniques, and heard expert medical testimony that sensory isolation can induce "an artificial psychosis or episode of insanity." Despite all this detailed evidence, committee members agreed unanimously that they could not measure "scientifically" either the degree or the duration of these psychological effects—the determining factors that would distinguish aggressive interrogation from either cruelty or torture. "Where," Lord Parker asked in his final report, "does hardship and discomfort end and for instance humiliating treatment begin, and where does the latter end and torture begin?" The answer, he said, turns on "words of definition" and thus "opinions will inevitably differ" over where a particular action might lie. On the slippery slope of psychological techniques, there were no easy definitional footholds.[91]

Reports and committees notwithstanding, the Irish Republic complained formally to the European Human Rights Commission, which, in 1976, submitted an 8,400-page report finding that "the combined use of the five techniques . . . shows a clear resemblance to those methods of systematic torture which have been known over the ages." Setting aside the physical to focus on the psychological, the commission ruled unanimously that these five techniques were, in fact, "a modern system of torture." Consequently, in February 1977, the case advanced to the European Court of Human Rights where Britain's attorney general appeared, chastened, to give "this unqualified undertaking that the 'five techniques' will not in any circumstances be reintroduced as an aid to interrogation." Again showing the definitional elusiveness of psychological torture, the court later found Britain guilty of "inhuman and degrading treatment" but not torture—a distinction, the judges said, that derived "principally from a difference in the intensity of the suffering inflicted." In sum, the complexities of psychological torture had eluded even this human rights court.[92]

It is worth noting that, alone among the seventeen justices ruling on this case, Judge Dimitrios Evrigenis of Greece grasped the character of psychological torture. In his dissenting opinion, he argued that this court's conception of torture has "already been overtaken by the ingenuity of modern techniques." Through "subtle techniques developed in multidisciplinary laboratories which claim to be scientific," there are now "new forms of suffering that have little in common with the physical pain caused by conventional torture." In effect, "torture no longer presupposes violence." These modern methods can, without any physical violence, bring about "the disintegration of an individual's personality, the shattering of his mental and psychological equilibrium and the crushing of his will." In assessing Britain's "combined use of the five techniques from the factual point of view," the judge was "sure that the use of these carefully chosen and measured techniques must have caused . . . extremely intense physical, mental and psychological suffering, inevitably covered by the strictest definition of torture."[93]

Indeed, independent medical examination of these victims found that the British Army had developed a particularly lethal mix of physical and psychological methods. A British psychologist, Tim Shallice, reported that twelve of the Irish prisoners had been subjected to a "hybrid technique" with sensory deprivation by hooding, sleep deprivation, self-inflicted pain by protracted wall standing, and crude physical beatings for any who moved from the wall. So devastating was the combination that three of the men, in the opinion of a university psychiatrist, had become "psychotic" after just twenty-four hours of this interrogation with symptoms marked by "loss of the sense of time, . . . hallucinations, profound apprehension and depression, and delusional beliefs."[94]

Under actual field conditions, the CIA's psychological paradigm—of which this British interrogation is a textbook example—was often supplemented by conventional physical tactics, whether from simple cruelty or a need to accelerate psychological breakdown. With the physical thus compounding the psychological, medieval and modern methods sometimes seemed indistinguishable. Inside the CIA's interrogation center at Bagram Air Base near Kabul in 2002, for example, American guards would force prisoners "to stand with their hands chained to the ceiling and their feet shackled," creating an effect similar to the Italian Inquisition's *strappado*. At Iraq's Abu Ghraib prison in 2003, U.S. military police would parade Iraqi prisoners naked with plastic sandbags over their heads, combining psychological humiliation with the pain of restricted breathing—just as medieval victims were once displayed in town squares with iron masks clamped on their heads, suffering both "imagined ridiculousness" and "physical torture through obstruction of the mouth or the nose."[95]

Yet there are also subtle, significant differences in the CIA's techniques, which dispensed with crude physical implements to make the pain seem self-inflicted. In place of the Inquisition's "crippling stork" that twisted the victim's body to fit into an iron frame, CIA interrogators made their victims assume "stress positions" without any external mechanism. Similarly, both the Paris Inquisition's "water question" and the CIA's "water boarding" forced fluids down the victim's throat to simulate a sense of drowning. The Church, of course, sought to purge evil with physical punishment, while the agency aims to induce the survival reflex of a near-death experience and thus break the victim psychologically.[96]

These modern innovations, while absent from the research first codified in the CIA's *Kubark* manual, would evolve, over time, as the agency set about propagating its new torture techniques worldwide. Like many important discoveries, the CIA's psychological paradigm, once a complex problem that had challenged brilliant behavioral scientists, soon became, through this global journey, a simple technique easily mastered by any police sergeant with a secondary education. It would prove, moreover, a surprisingly supple procedure, readily refined by any officer or operative with taste for torture.

3

PROPAGATING TORTURE

IN THE GLOBAL dissemination of its new interrogation doctrine during the Cold War, the CIA moved through two distinct phases, first operating undercover through police-training programs in Asia and Latin America and later collaborating with Army teams that advised local counterinsurgency forces, largely in Central America. Throughout this thirty-year effort, the CIA's torture training grew increasingly brutal, moving by degrees beyond the original psychological techniques to harsh physical methods through its experience in the Vietnam War.

From 1962 to 1974, the CIA worked through the Office of Public Safety, a division of U.S. AID that posted police advisers to developing nations.[1] Established by President John F. Kennedy in 1962, OPS grew, in just six years, into a global anti-Communist operation with an annual budget of $35 million and over four hundred U.S. advisers assigned worldwide. By 1971, the program had trained over one million police officers in forty-seven nations, including 85,000 in South Vietnam and 100,000 in Brazil.[2] Concealed amid the larger effort, CIA interrogation training soon proved controversial, as police agencies across the Third World became synonymous with human rights abuses—particularly in South Vietnam, Uruguay, Iran, and the Philippines.

To launch this Cold War effort in the early 1960s, the Kennedy administration formed the interagency Special Group–Counter Insurgency, whose influential members—General Maxwell Taylor, national security adviser McGeorge Bundy, CIA director John McCone, and Under-secretary of State U. Alexis Johnson—could cut across bureaucratic boundaries to get the job done.[3] As a National Security Action Memorandum indicated in 1962, "the President desires that careful consideration be given to intensifying civil police programs in lieu of military assistance where such action will yield more fruitful results in terms of our internal security objective."[4] Although "the police program is even more important than Special Forces in our global C-I [counterinsurgency] effort," said staff member Robert Komer in an April 1962 memo, finding a "congenial home" for this multi-agency initiative was to prove difficult.[5] In effect, the problem was how to expand U.S. AID's existing police program into an instrument for a more aggressive CIA internal-security effort among Third World allies. The solution, apparently, was to increase the public safety program within U.S. AID and simultaneously place it under the control of CIA personnel—notably the program's head, Byron Engle.[6] During his decade as OPS chief, Engle recruited CIA personnel for the program and provided close coordination with the agency's intelligence mission.[7]

The hybrid nature of OPS allowed CIA field operatives an ideal cover for dissemination of the agency's interrogation techniques. In South Vietnam, for example, OPS trained Vietnamese police in what the U.S. chief adviser called "stringent wartime measures designed to assist in defeating the enemy." At the provincial level, Vietnamese National Police Field Forces, trained by OPS, worked with CIA mercenaries in apprehending suspected Communists for interrogation.[8] In Latin America, the CIA used OPS to recruit local police for training at a clandestine center in Washington, International Police Services, that operated behind a blind provided by U.S. AID's International Police Academy. In its audit of OPS in 1976, the General Accounting Office reported that "there were allegations that the academy . . . taught or encouraged use of torture," but its investigation did not support a formal finding of that nature.[9]

By contrast, Amnesty International documented widespread torture, usually by police, in twenty-four of the forty-nine nations that had hosted OPS police-training teams.[10] Staffers for Senator James Abourezk (Democrat, South Dakota) also found evidence of torture training at the IPA by examining student graduation theses. In his 1968 essay, for example, trainee Nickolas V. Fotinfpfulos of Greece described "the psychological tactics and techniques of an effective interrogation of reluctant witnesses by means of instrumental aids or drugs."[11] After devoting four pages of his fourteen-page thesis to a history of European torture, Luu Van Huu of the South Vietnam police summarized lessons learned: "We have 4 sorts of torture: use of force as such; threats; physical suffering, imposed indirectly; and mental or psychological torture."[12] In his 1971 paper, Le Van An, also of the South Vietnam police, defended torture: "Despite the fact that brutal interrogation is strongly criticized by moralists, its importance must not be denied if we want to have order and security in daily life."[13]

Elsewhere in its worldwide campaign, the CIA worked through public safety advisers in Brazil and Uruguay to provide local police with training and interrogation equipment. Through its field offices in Panama and Buenos Aires, the agency's Technical Services Division, the unit responsible for psychological research, shipped polygraph and electroshock machines in diplomatic pouches to public safety offices across the continent.[14] For all its global reach, however, OPS's operations were, as the Vietnam War heated up during the 1960s, increasingly concentrated in South Vietnam.

Although early OPS advisers tried to transform the Vietnamese police into an effective counterinsurgency force, the clear failure of this effort by 1963 created pressure for a new approach. Arriving at the South Vietnamese capital, Saigon, in December of that year, CIA station chief Peer DeSilva soon learned that "the Vietcong were monstrous in their application of torture and murder." Inspired by a doctrine of counterterror, DeSilva began a campaign "to bring danger and death to the Vietcong functionaries themselves, especially in the areas where they felt secure."[15]

The CIA thus set about simultaneously expanding and centralizing South Vietnam's scattered intelligence operations, which all fell, at least nominally, under Saigon's Central Intelligence Organization housed at the National Interrogation Center. There, four agency advisers were assigned to train the Vietnamese hands-on by interrogating the hundreds of prisoners locked up within its concrete walls. After a year of DeSilva's leadership, each of the forty-plus provinces in South Vietnam had an Intelligence Coordination Committee and its own concrete prison compound called the Provincial Interrogation Center. In these same years, the CIA sent many more experts, "most of whom had worked on Russian defectors," from its Technical Services Division to train the Vietnamese interrogators. Instead of the "old French methods" of crude physical torture, most evident among the Saigon police, the Vietnamese, in the words of one CIA trainer, "had to be re-taught with more sophisticated techniques." At the provincial centers, however, physical methods continued to prevail, including electric shock, beatings, and rape.[16]

Taking this covert war to the countryside in 1965, CIA careerist William Colby launched the agency's Counter Terror program. "CIA representatives," wrote agency analyst Victor Marchetti, "recruited, organized, supplied, and directly paid CT teams, whose function was to use . . . techniques of terror—assassination, abuses, kidnappings and intimidation—against the Viet Cong leadership." A year later, the CIA "became wary of adverse publicity surrounding the use of the word 'terror' and changed the name of the CT teams to the Provincial Reconnaissance Units." Colby also supervised construction of the Provincial Interrogation Centers, each headed by a CIA employee who, Marchetti tells us, "directed each center's operations, much of which consisted of torture tactics against suspected Vietcong, such torture usually carried out by Vietnamese nationals."[17] By 1965–66, the CIA had thus developed a nationwide intelligence collection system that reached from the National Interrogation Center in Saigon down to the society's rice roots via the Provincial Interrogation Centers and the PRU counterterror operations.

The program expanded in 1967 when the CIA, working with other agencies, established a centralized pacification bureaucracy, Civil Operations and Rural Development Support. Under this umbrella, the CIA drew all the scattered counterinsurgency operations—OPS police training, military intelligence, the CIO, and its own interrogation units—into CORDS and then used this labyrinthine bureaucracy as cover for a murderous covert operation called the Phoenix program. With limitless funding and unrestrained powers, Phoenix represented an application of the most advanced interrogation techniques to the task of destroying the Vietcong's revolutionary underground. From its overall strategy to its specific interrogation techniques, Phoenix was the culmination of the CIA's mind-control project.

As conventional counterinsurgency failed to defeat the enemy, the U.S. mission created Phoenix to correct a major contradiction in its complex, collaborative relationship with South Vietnam's weak government. The Vietnamese National Police, despite a doubling of its strength to 120,000 between 1966 and 1972, suffered poor leadership and "pervasive corruption" that blunted its effectiveness against the Vietcong's underground government. And the South Vietnamese army, as one of its officers explained, felt that "this unarmed enemy was not their proper adversary." With the police unable and the army unwilling to engage in effective counterinsurgency, the Vietcong's control of the countryside grew unchecked—creating a pressing need, the CIA felt, for a new kind of clandestine operation to attack this invisible Communist infrastructure.[18]

In Saigon, Phoenix used sophisticated computer information banks to centralize data on the Vietcong infrastructure, identifying key Communist cadres for interrogation or elimination. In the countryside, the program made use of this intelligence through specially trained counterguerrilla teams, the PRUs, attached to the CIA's forty Provincial Interrogation Centers. Miming the clandestine cell structure of the Vietcong units, each PRU began as a six-man team that elaborated, through a pyramid structure, into a provincial unit of 146.[19]

Notwithstanding later CIA rhetoric designed to give Phoenix a sanitized, professional patina, it soon devolved into a brutality that produced many casualties but few verifiable results. For all its technological gloss, the program's strategy remained grounded in DeSilva's vision of physical and psychological counterterror. After a PRU had brought in suspected Communists, interrogators from the Provincial Interrogation Center, often under CIA supervision, tortured the prisoners and summarily executed many without trial or due process. Some PRUs degenerated into petty protection rackets, extracting bribes from accused Communists and eliminating suspects on the basis of unsubstantiated gossip. Although early recruits were often well motivated, as the PRUs spread the units began to attract social outcasts, including convicted criminals, who embraced their basic task, murder, by tattooing themselves "Sat Cong" (Kill Communists). According to a 1970 report in the *New York Times,* each PRU "consists of a dozen or more South Vietnamese mercenaries, originally recruited and paid handsomely by the CIA," who were usually "local hoodlums, soldiers of fortune, draft-dodgers, defectors."[20]

At the same time, Phoenix and allied programs allowed the CIA to continue its research into the effects of coercion on human consciousness. No longer restricted to isolated drug trials or simulated psychology experiments, the agency was now operating a nationwide network of interrogation centers that used torture to generate intelligence, providing a limitless supply of human subjects. In mid-1966, the agency sent a Page-Russell electroshock machine and three psychiatrists—two from its staff and the third a California practitioner, Dr. Lloyd H. Cotter—to conduct experiments at Bien Hoa Mental Hospital, just north of Saigon. In effect, they were testing, under field conditions, whether Ewen Cameron's McGill depatterning techniques could actually alter human behavior. As he explained in an article for the *American Journal of Psychiatry,* Cotter applied electroconvulsive treatment three times weekly and withheld food to force patients to work, finding himself "impressed" with the results. Simultaneously, inside a walled compound on the grounds of the same hospital, the two CIA doctors subjected several Vietcong prisoners to a dozen electroshocks the first day and sixty during the next seven days until one died. When the last prisoner expired a few weeks later, the CIA operatives packed up their machine and flew home without breaking any of the Vietcong.[21]

In similar experiments at Bien Hoa Hospital in July 1968, another CIA crew arrived with a skilled neurosurgeon who, in one journalist's account, "implanted tiny electrodes in each brain" of three Vietcong prisoners. In the first rudimentary tests, the CIA behaviorists used "radio frequencies . . . to cause their subjects suddenly to defecate or vomit." Then, after placing the captives in a room and giving them knives, the CIA men, "pressing the control buttons on their handsets . . . tried to arouse their subjects to violence." After a week of repeated failure, the scientists headed home while "the prisoners were shot by Green Beret troopers and their bodies burned."[22]

The character of CIA operations in Vietnam first emerged, albeit obliquely, in 1969, during the investigation of Colonel Robert B. Rheault, a West Point graduate and Special Forces commander, for the summary execution of a suspected Vietcong spy named Thai Khac Chuyen. After the Green Berets captured a roll of film revealing that their Vietnamese operative was a double agent working for the enemy, they used sodium pentathol ("truth serum") and lie-detector tests, probably with CIA assistance, for an interrogation that supposedly confirmed his treason. Thinking the agency had ordered his "elimination," the Special Forces unit at Nha Trang drugged Chuyen with morphine, shot him with a .22 caliber pistol, and dumped his body at sea. Furious, the U.S. commander in Vietnam, General Creighton Abrams, ordered a "no-holds-barred" investigation that culminated in murder charges against Colonel Rheault, his alleged triggerman Captain Robert F. Marasco, and six other Green Berets. At the behest of the Nixon White House, the CIA refused to allow its agents to testify, ultimately forcing the Army to back down and dismiss charges against Colonel Rheault and his co-accused. In its analysis of the case, the New York Times argued that the killing was a product of confused intelligence operations that had been the impetus, two years earlier, for the formation of the Phoenix program to train Vietnamese assets "in the fine art of silent killing." Indeed, Captain Marasco later admitted that he had shot the double agent on "very very clear orders from the CIA," and claimed that there had been "hundreds" of similar summary executions in South Vietnam. Despite the dismissal of charges, the investigation had alerted Congress and the public to the covert war against the Vietcong, one that apparently included summary killings of suspected VC agents.[23]

After nearly four years of these murky operations, Congress and the press finally exposed the Phoenix program in 1970. William Colby, chief of pacification in Vietnam, testified before the Senate Foreign Relations Committee that, in 1969 alone, Phoenix had killed 6,187 members of the 75,000-strong Vietcong infrastructure. Although he admitted to some "illegal killings," Colby rejected a suggestion by Senator J. William Fulbright (Democrat, Arkansas) that it was "a program for the assassination of civilian leaders."[24]

Despite mounting congressional opposition, the U.S. command, according to the *New York Times,* launched a renewed pacification effort in 1971, aimed at the "neutralization" of 14,400 Communist agents by killing or capture.[25] In the wake of this press exposé, the House Operations Subcommittee conducted the first wide-ranging congressional probe of CIA counterinsurgency operations, finding that Phoenix had killed 9,820 Vietcong suspects in the past fourteen months. "I am shocked and dismayed," said Representative Ogden R. Reid (Republican, New York). "Assassination and terror by the Viet Cong or Hanoi should not, and must not, call forth the same methods by Saigon, let alone the United States, directly or indirectly."[26]

Several days later, Colby told the subcommittee that Phoenix had killed 20,587 Vietcong suspects since 1968. The Saigon government provided figures attributing 40,994 Vietcong deaths to the Phoenix program.[27] When Reid charged that Phoenix was responsible for "indiscriminate killings," Colby defended his program as "an essential part of the war effort" that was "designed to protect the Vietnamese people from terrorism." Although the CIA had started the program, the agency, Colby explained, had already transferred the apparatus to the Vietnamese National Police so that it was now, in his words, "entirely a South Vietnamese program."[28]

In these same hearings, K. Barton Osborn, a military intelligence veteran who had worked with the Phoenix program in 1967–68, described "the insertion of the six-inch dowel into the ear canal of one of my detainee's ears and the tapping through the brain until he died; and the starving to death of a Vietnamese woman who was suspected of being part of the local [Vietcong] political education cadre." He also recalled "the use of electronic gear such as sealed telephones attached to the . . . women's vagina and the men's testicles . . . [to] shock them into submission." In his eighteen months with the Phoenix program, not a single VC suspect had survived interrogation. All these "extrale-gal, illegal, and covert" procedures were, Osborn testified, found in the *Defense Collection Intelligence Manual,* issued to him during training at Fort Holabird. Adding to the lethal aura, by 1972 the Phoenix total for enemy "neutralization" had risen to 81,740 Vietcong eliminated and 26,369 prisoners killed.[29]

To discredit such damaging testimony, the U.S. Army Intelligence Command conducted a thorough investigation of Osborn's charges which Colby released, in a declassified summary, during his 1973 con-firmation hearings as CIA director. Though the Army's classified report nitpicked many of Osborn's secondary details, it did not challenge his overall sense of Phoenix's systematic brutality—a negative assessment confirmed by both eyewitness accounts and official studies.[30]

In early 1968, for example, two CORDS evaluators, John G. Ly-brand and L. Craig Johnstone, conducted an official review of the pro-gram in II Corps (Central Vietnam), finding that: "The truncheon and electric shock method of interrogation were in widespread use, with al-most all [U.S.] advisers admitting to have witnessed instances of the use of these methods." The study found that "Most advisers claimed they did not personally take part in [tortures] but 'turned their backs on them.'" Similarly, an American who advised PRU irregulars in Binh Thuan Province during 1968–69, Richard Welcome, indicated that Americans allowed their Phoenix allies wide latitude: "Prisoners were abused. Were they tortured? It depends on what you call torture. Electricity was used by the Vietnamese, water was used, occasionally some of the prisoners got beat up. Were any of them put on the rack, eyes gouged out, bones broken? No, I never saw any evidence of that at all." Even Colby him-self, the program's founder, admitted "various of the things that Mr. Os-born alleges might have happened." In the wink-nudge, turn-a-blind-eye approach that Phoenix participants adopted to abuses by their Saigon al-lies, Colby added that "Phoenix . . . was not to be a program of assassi-nation and we issued instructions . . . that not only were Americans not to participate . . . but they were to make their objections known . . . I did receive some reports of this nature . . . and took them up with the gov-ernment of South Vietnam . . . I knew there were people killed, there is no question about it, . . . but I certainly reject the idea that it was a systematic program of assassination." Reviewing this evidence, one recent rather conservative history of Phoenix concluded that "the large majority of South Vietnamese interrogators tortured some or all of the Communist prisoners in their care" and "a smaller number tortured villagers suspected of collaborating with the Communists."[31]

As the Vietnam War wound down, public opinion, disturbed by impending defeat and reports of the harsh CIA tactics, created a climate for reform. In December 1974, *New York Times* reporter Seymour Hersh published a front-page story that the CIA's Operation Chaos had conducted illegal mail interception and phone tapping against antiwar activists. In response to these revelations, President Gerald Ford appointed Vice President Nelson Rockefeller to investigate, and both houses of Congress formed special inquiries. Instead of stonewalling, as then-CIA director Helms had done with the MKUltra files, Colby, by now director, skillfully restrained the inquiries by feeding investigators just enough information to convince them that they were uncovering the truth.[32] Not surprisingly, the Rockefeller commission found that the CIA, in monitoring U.S. citizens, had done things that "should be criticized" but concluded that the agency had already reformed itself. Alone among these inquiries, the special Senate Committee, led by Frank Church (Democrat, Idaho), held hearings that probed aggressively for abuses. But a critical history of the CIA found that the Senate's inquiries into MKUltra and subsequent torture training programs did not go beyond the anecdotal.[33]

Although the Senate hearings inspired four well-documented books on the CIA's drug and behavioral experiments, there was no internal investigation or criminal prosecution of culpable officials. "I thought in 1978 when our books were appearing, when we were doing media work all over the world," recalled Alan Scheflin, author of *The Mind Manipulators*, "that we would finally get the story out, the vaults would be cleansed, the victims would learn their identities, the story would become part of history, and the people who had been injured could seek recompense. Instead, what happened was the great void."[34] Seeking to explain why the CIA's "accomplices in torture" had escaped closer examination, author A. J. Langguth concluded: "Senator Frank Church tried to force some admissions but his witnesses sidestepped his staff's sketchy allegations. Given the willingness of Congress to accept the C.I.A.'s alibis about national security, I don't think any other public hearing would fare better."[35]

Even after revelations about the Phoenix program, there was still a deep, almost inexplicable silence, in Congress and the press, over the issue of torture. In 1977, for example, former CIA agent Frank Snepp published a bestselling memoir of his Vietnam experience. With graphic detail reminiscent of George Orwell's *1984*, Snepp's first chapter described the months he spent torturing a captured North Vietnamese cadre, Nguyen Van Tai. Just as Orwell's fictional interrogator broke the antihero Wilson by discovering his greatest fear, rats, so CIA and Vietnamese interrogators found that this dedicated Communist had one "psychic-physical flaw"—a dread of the cold. For over four years, the CIA, using its technique of sensory deprivation, kept Tai in solitary confinement inside an all-white, windowless room with just one feature— "heavy-duty air conditioners." Even so, the Vietnamese inquisitors failed. Next, an "American specialist" made little progress. Finally, Snepp himself, assigned to the case as lead interrogator, maintained the frigid air conditioning and probed, through two or three sessions daily, to discover "only two discernibly exploitable flaws" in Tai's personality—most important, a longing to return to his wife and child. Playing on this weakness "to drive the wedge deeper," Snepp varied Tai's interview times randomly "so as to throw off his internal clock" and tantalized him with the hope of reunion with his family. These techniques finally worked, and the dossier began to grow as Tai, enticed by Snepp's hints of release, started talking. Just before Saigon fell, however, a "senior CIA official" suggested that Tai should be "disappeared," and he was "loaded onto an airplane and thrown out over the South China Sea."[36]

By his references to an "American specialist" in interrogation, the elaborate sensory deprivation, and psychological probing to produce personality regression, Snepp provided unmistakable clues that the CIA was, by this point, applying sophisticated techniques. But the media focused on his tales of political intrigue and ignored these revelations that the agency was engaged in torture.[37]

In retrospect, Phoenix proved a seminal experience for the U.S. intelligence community, combining both physical and psychological techniques in an extreme method that would serve as a model for later counterinsurgency training in South and Central America. In 1965–66, Army Intelligence launched Project X, which was designed, according to a confidential Pentagon memo, "to develop an exportable foreign intelligence package to provide counterinsurgency techniques learned in Vietnam to Latin American countries."[38] According to a Pentagon counterintelligence staffer, Linda Matthews, the team of Army officers drafting one of the project's training manuals, "Intelligence for Stability Operations," in 1967–68, was in contact with "a resident instruction course . . . in the Phoenix program" at the Army Intelligence School, and thus "some offending material from the Phoenix program may have found its way into the Project X materials."[39] One of these manuals, in the Pentagon's words, "provided training regarding use of sodiopentathol compound in interrogation, abduction of adversary family members to influence the adversary, prioritization of adversary personalities for abduction, exile, physical beatings and execution"—in short, the trademark Phoenix techniques.[40] For the next quarter of a century, the Army would transmit these extreme tactics, by both direct training and mailings of manuals, to the armies of at least ten Latin American nations. By the mid-1980s, counterguerrilla operations in Colombia and Central America would thus bear an eerie but explicable resemblance to South Vietnam.

Although the Phoenix program was the largest and bloodiest CIA interrogation effort, it was the OPS police training in Latin America that prompted a Senate attempt to end torture training altogether. Ironically, it was the murder of an American police adviser in Uruguay that exposed Public Safety's involvement in torture and precipitated the program's abolition.

The story broke in August 1970 when the *New York Times* reported that an American police adviser, Dan A. Mitrione, had been kidnapped by Tupamaro guerrillas in Montevideo. The first dispatches described him as an ordinary family man from Indiana who was heading the Public Safety program in Uruguay to encourage "responsible and humane police administration." In an inadvertent hint of Mitrione's actual mission, the account added that he "unquestionably knew more about the Tupamaro operations than any other United States official."[41] Ten days later, in its story of his point-blank execution, the *Times* noted that he "was considered to have contributed materially to the Government's anti-guerrilla campaign." Nonetheless, an accompanying editorial expressed the paper's "shock and horror": "Only diseased minds could see in the gunning down of this father of nine from Indiana the weakening of the capitalist system or the advancement of social revolution in the Americas."[42]

Mitrione's burial, in Richmond, Indiana, was an emotional tribute to an American hero. Nine thousand people paid their respects. A cavalcade of 125 cars moved through a city decorated with black-bowed roses to the cemetery. There Secretary of State William Rogers and President Nixon's son-in-law David Eisenhower listened as the Uruguayan ambassador, Hector Luisi, promised that the "masterminds" of this crime would "reap the wrath of civilized people everywhere." Only days after the funeral, the truth of Mitrione's role began to emerge. A senior Uruguayan police official, Alejandro Otero, told the *Jornal do Brasil* that Mitrione had used "violent techniques of torture and repression." On August 15, a U.S. embassy spokesman in Montevideo called the charge "absolutely false."[43]

Eight years later, however, a Cuban double agent, Manuel Hevia Cosculluela, who had joined the CIA and worked with Mitrione in Montevideo, published a book with a very different picture of this American hero. In the Cuban's account, Mitrione had tortured four beggars to death with electric shocks at a 1970 seminar to demonstrate his techniques for Uruguayan police trainees. "The special horror of the course," Hevia added, "was its academic, almost clinical atmosphere. Mitrione's motto was: 'The right pain in the right place at the right time.' A premature death, he would say, meant that the technique had failed." Over drinks at his home, Mitrione had given Hevia a summary of his methods that showed the influence of the CIA's psychological paradigm: "He said he considered interrogation to be a complex art . . .

The objective was to humiliate the victim, separating him from reality, making him feel defenseless. No questions, just blows and insults. Then silent blows." Significantly, the Cuban charged that Mitrione's deputy in the Public Safety office was William Cantrell, a CIA agent.[44]

Only three months before Mitrione's death in Uruguay, the unsettling coincidence of U.S. police training in Brazil and evidence of torture finally raised questions in the U.S. Congress. In May 1971, the Senate Foreign Relations Committee summoned the chief public safety adviser for Brazil, Theodore D. Brown, and scrutinized his program. Brown's statement that OPS taught "minimum use of force, humane methods" sparked a dialogue that led to an affirmation by all, senators and police adviser alike, that America would not, could not, train torturers. In his questioning of Brown, Senator Claiborne Pell (Democrat, Rhode Island) had the uncommon insight to recognize the delegitimizing impact of torture on the regimes it was designed to defend: "Why is it the Brazilians . . . use torture as a police method when it will alienate their friends and allies around the world?" Yet Pell followed up with a question revealing the mistaken assumption that psychological torture was not really torture: "But from a police viewpoint, you would agree that psychological, nonphysical methods of interrogation can be just as effective as the physical, as torture?"[45]

It took another four years for Congress to curtail the OPS's operations. Led by Senator Abourezk of South Dakota, congressional investigators found widespread allegations that the program was training Latin American police to torture.[46] Concerned about these persistent, disturbing charges, Congress finally cut all funds effective July 1975 for "training or advice to police, prisons, or other law enforcement"—in effect, abolishing the Office of Public Safety. Many of the U.S. AID public safety officers soon found themselves disavowed, discredited, and unemployed.[47]

Although these reforms were well intentioned, Congress had failed to probe for the source of the training. The investigations had exposed some elements of the CIA's mind-control project, but there was no public pressure to restrain the agency's propagation of psychological torture. Furthermore, by the time Congress began investigating the OPS, the

CIA had already stopped using it as a cover for its foreign operations, shifting its torture training to the Army's Military Adviser Program.[48]

Among Washington's torture training programs, few were as disastrous as the CIA effort in Iran. In the turmoil of the late 1970s, Iran showed the long-term instability fostered by U.S. tolerance of an ally's torture and human rights abuse. After launching a coup in 1953 that restored the shah to direct rule, the CIA, in the decades that followed, helped consolidate his control. By 1959, American and Israeli advisers were involved in the reorganization of the "Iranian secret police." Most important, the agency helped establish the most lethal of the shah's secret police units, the Savak, and even trained its interrogators.[49]

In 1962, for example, the Kennedy administration's top-level Special Group–Counter Insurgency, which included CIA director John McCone, approved $500,000 for riot control equipment to expand the Iranian capital's contingent from 350 to 500 men.[50] Consequently, in early 1964, the State Department reported that "with the arrival of most of the AID-programmed riot-control equipment for the Tehran police," training was now starting that would allow the Gendarmerie "to deal with any likely and foreseeable civil disturbance in Tehran."[51] According to a former CIA analyst, Jesse Leaf, senior agency officials were training Savak in interrogation methods "based on German torture techniques from World War II." Although no Americans participated in the actual torture, Leaf recalled "people who were there seeing the rooms and being told of torture. And I know that the torture rooms were toured and it was all paid for by the U.S.A."[52]

As opposition to the shah grew in the 1970s, Savak tortured dissidents cruelly and indiscriminately, fueling angry Iranian student protests in Europe and the United States against the brutality of the shah's police and their detention of fifty thousand political prisoners.[53] Defending his regime in an interview with *Le Monde,* the shah spoke candidly: "Why should we not employ the same methods as you Europeans? We have learned sophisticated methods of torture from you. You use psychological methods to extract the truth: we do the same."[54]

After the shah fell from power in 1979, Savak's torture and the CIA's role were heavily publicized, both in Iran and in the United

States. One former CIA analyst told the *New York Times* matter-of-factly that the agency had sanctioned the torture.[55] Writing in *The Nation,* the Iranian poet Reza Baraheni claimed that "at least half a million people have . . . been beaten, whipped, or tortured by Savak"—a cruelty that he illustrated with gruesome autopsy photos of mangled bodies, scabbed and scarred.[56]

The Islamic revolutionary government's prosecution of former Savak agents for torture and murder also received extensive international coverage, including several reports in the *New York Times.* At his trial in June 1979, a former Savak interrogator, Bahman Naderipour, confessed in "excruciating detail" to years of "interrogation, torture, and killing." While his story was gripping, Naderipour was just number 300 among the shah's secret police tried by the Islamic revolutionary courts.[57] Despite such sordid detail, there was little public reaction in the United States to revelations about the CIA's ties to the shah's secret police.

Yet Iran provided an important cautionary tale. By buttressing the shah's rule with riot police and ruthless interrogation, the CIA unwittingly contributed to the rising opposition that eventually toppled his regime. After training his police, Washington underestimated the stigma attached to torture and stood by, confused, while its key Persian Gulf ally slowly lost legitimacy. The lesson was clear: Torture introduced to defend the shah had instead destroyed the shah.

The Philippines provides the most poignant lesson about the consequences of CIA psychological torture, particularly its violent post-Phoenix variant. From 1972 to 1986, torture was a key instrument in President Ferdinand Marcos's martial-law rule, creating a cohort of young officers who demonstrated, more than any, the corrosive effects of torture training on a nation's military. In a sense, these Filipino interrogators carried the agency's paradigm to its ultimate level, combining an expansive psychological theatricality with a lurid physical brutality to terrorize, not just their many victims, but an entire society. As they probed human consciousness in the ad hoc laboratory of thousands of torture sessions over a span of fourteen years, these officers discovered the capacity of sexual humiliation to damage the psyche. As they stretched the CIA's methods into a latter-day *Théâtre du Grand-Guignol* of psychological torture, they revealed the extraordinary power of this paradigm to damage military discipline and destabilize the very regime the officers were supposed to uphold.[58]

Among the authoritarian regimes of the 1970s, the Marcos government was exceptionally lethal. Films such as *Missing, State of Siege,* and *Kiss of the Spider Woman* lend an aura of ruthlessness to Latin American dictatorships that overshadows the Philippines. But statistics tell another story. Marcos's tally of 3,257 killed exceeds, for example, or the 266 dead and missing during the Brazilian junta's most brutal period (1964–79) and even the 2,115 extrajudicial deaths under General Augusto Pinochet in Chile (1973–90). Under Marcos, moreover, military murder was the apex of a pyramid of terror—in addition to the 3,257 killed, an estimated 35,000 were tortured.[59] In a distinctive twist, some 2,520 victims, an overwhelming 77 percent of the Filipinos killed were "salvaged"—that is, tortured, murdered, and their remains dumped for display.[60]

The torture cell thus became a play within the larger play. Inside the safe house, Filipino interrogators acted out their script before the victim, an audience of one. If the plot, through various turns, ended with a victim's death, then interrogators discarded the mangled corpse in a public place, a roadside or busy intersection, to be seen by passersby. Every road or plaza, indeed all public space, then became a proscenium of psychological terror. Indeed, this practice had such a disturbing resonance within the country's collective consciousness that the Filipino-English dialect coined the neologism "salvaging" to capture its aura of terror.[61] Seeing the marks on the victim's body, or simply hearing of them, Filipinos could read, in an instant, the entire drama acted out inside the safe house.

The officers who administered the torture were not impersonal cogs in a military machine, but actors who embodied the violent capacities of Marcos's authoritarian rule. Whether through mass arrests or targeted reprisals, it was the armed forces, particularly younger officers, many of them recent graduates of the Philippine Military Academy, who carried out these orders. Gradually, these experiences made Marcos's military interrogators a destabilizing element within the

Army, repeating patterns seen earlier in France as well as in Brazil. After a decade of harsh martial rule, ending in 1975, senior Brazilian military purged the torturers from its ranks, in the words of one observer,
"so as to save the Army." Torture was becoming "a sort of gangrene," as
security agencies "working extralegally inevitably start behaving ille-
gally as well," turning the torturers into "smugglers, blackmailers, and
extortionists" who represented an implicit challenge to the chain of
command and threatened to split the Brazilian military into warring
factions.[62]

Through a similar dynamic, the Philippines suffered more coup attempts during the 1980s than any other country in the world. After
twelve years of Marcos's authoritarian rule, a group of middle-echelon
officers, hardened by their extralegal duties, formed a volatile clique,
the Reform the Armed Forces Movement, or RAM. With singular determination, these colonels spent a decade plotting to seize the state.
Led largely by officers experienced in torture, RAM attempted its first
coup d'état against Marcos in 1986 and, failing to take power,
launched five more against his successor, President Corazon Aquino.
After the collapse of their largest coup attempt in 1989, the RAM
leaders then took their disaffected comrades underground for a revolt against civil authority that continued, with terror bombings and
abortive coups, until rebels and government finally concluded a peace
accord in 1995.

The RAM leaders had acquired an overweening will to power,
gained largely through the omnipotent role they had played during the
Marcos regime's many torture sessions. Their theatrical variant of the
practice seems wholly lifted from CIA interrogation manuals. Indeed,
the Philippine methods appear so similar to the agency's that we must
ask: Did the CIA train Marcos's interrogators? The answer may well be
yes. During the Cold War's final, bitter phase after the fall of Saigon in
1975, Washington intensified its counterinsurgency operations among
Third World allies, stepping up its dissemination of CIA torture techniques. Much of this transmission was done through training. In 1978,
a Philippine human rights newsletter reported that the Marcos regime's
top torturer, Lieutenant Colonel Rolando Abadilla, was studying at the
Command and General Staff College in Fort Leavenworth, Kansas.

A year later, another human rights group claimed that his understudy, Lieutenant Rodolfo "Rudy" Aguinaldo, was on his way to the United States "for six months to one year for additional training under the Central Intelligence Agency."[63] Were the Filipino officers, like those from Latin America, given some secret training in either tactical interrogation or torture? Because both have since been assassinated by Communist guerrillas for their "heinous crimes against the people"—Abadilla in 1996 and Aguinaldo in 2001—definitive answers must await future release of classified American documents.

These torture techniques were also spread by simply mailing out manuals. Under "Project X," the U.S. Army Intelligence Center and School in Arizona sent thousands of counterinsurgency-training handbooks to all "nonresident foreign students" nominated by "Missions, Military Groups, Attaches, and other US Military agencies in the US advisory-training efforts in friendly foreign countries"—criteria that fit the Philippines perfectly and language that hints at CIA involvement as one of those "other US . . . agencies."[64] As of 1977, the center's curriculum for "Interrogation of Prisoners of War" included a publication, *Handling of Sources,* with instructions that, in the Pentagon's words, included "beatings, false imprisonment, executions and the use of truth serum."[65] But there is no list of the hundreds of foreign agencies and individuals who received these manuals over the twenty-six-year life of the mail-order program. Even absent such documentation, however, the Filipino interrogators seemed to rely on brutal methods detailed in manuals distributed throughout Latin America.

A rural Filipino priest tortured by Marcos's interrogators offers uncommon insight into the impact of these psychological tactics. Arrested for subversion in October 1982, Father Edgardo Kangleon was subjected to two months of constant interrogation before succumbing. In his confession, he admitted to being a Communist agent and named fellow clergy as subversives—charges that the Marcos regime then seized on to harass the Roman Catholic Church.[66] Throughout his long confinement, the priest suffered only limited physical abuse and was instead broken psychologically by his chief interrogator, Lieutenant Colonel Hernani Figueroa, a Constabulary commander who later became chairman of the RAM rebel faction.

A week after his release from military custody, Father Kangleon composed a twenty-five-page memoir revealing the phenomenology of psychological torture from the victim's perspective. Although he reviles himself as a "stinking coward" and "traitor" who broke under interrogation, his letter provides an astute analysis of the theatricality of psychological torture: the cell becomes a studio, the inquisitors actors, and the detainees their audience. Most significantly, Kangleon's interrogation echoes techniques in the CIA's *Human Resource Exploitation Training Manual—1983,* then being used to train Honduran officers on the other side of the Pacific. As prescribed in the manual, discussed in detail below, the Filipino colonel entered Father Kangleon's cell with bulging files and maintained a controlling calm.[67]

> The entry of the dreaded chief intelligence officer, who came in with a thick pile of documents, dashed to the ground the last bit of my hopes to get out of there "unscathed." His initial declaration: "Father, the general has decided that we start interrogating you tonight" was enough to unleash that fear that was building up inside me for these past two months. I felt cold sweat, sweat broke all over my body and I thought I was going to faint.
>
> For several hours, predator and prey fenced around verbally, one sizing up the other. Questions were posed and answers of innocence were given. Suddenly the "chairman" changed his approach. He said that since I would not answer his questions without my lawyer's presence, it would suffice if I would just give my biodata. And readily I fall for it. . . . I had fallen into a trap. I was already talking. Hastily, I tried to correct it by sticking to innocent or safe answers.
>
> Sensing that I had caught up to what he was up to and, irritated with the futility of that encounter, Ltc. Figueroa finally said: "Since you refused to cooperate, Father, we will be forced to use other means. We cannot allow ourselves to be taken for fools."[68]

At the colonel's command, the priest was blindfolded and taken to the nearby offices of the Military Intelligence Group where his new interrogators added physical abuse to compound the effect of sensory disorientation and sexual humiliation.

> Inside I was made to sit on a stool. I felt a small table being placed in front of me. Then, I heard voices—new voices! Three or four of

these voices—the more commanding ones—took their places around me. And with actors in their places, the most crucial stage of my detention started to unfold.

"Now, Father, you are going to answer our questions!"

"As the [Communist] NPA utilizes terrorism, we are also willing to use counter-terror. . . . Every time you preached against us, I wished at that time to just shoot you there at the altar."

"What's the name of that sister you used to visit at the Sacred Heart College? She is your girlfriend, *ano*? You are fucking her? How does it feel? . . ."

"For me, he is not a priest. Yes, your kind is not worthy of a respect of a priest."

"OK, take off his shirt. Oh, look at that body. You look sexy. Even the women here think you are macho. You are a homosexual, *ano*?"

"Let's see if you are that macho after one of my punches." A short jab below my ribs.

"Hey, don't lean on the table. Place your arms beside you. That's it." Another jab.

"You, take that stool away from him." I stood up. A blow landed behind my ears. I started to plead that they stop what they are doing to me. I started to cower. More blows.

"You better answer our questions or else you will get more of this." With that, a short blow landed in my solar plexus.

I was already quaking with fear. The psychological and physical aspect . . . of my interrogation had finally taken its toll. I finally broke down. "Yes. Go call Ltc. Figueroa. I am now willing to cooperate."[69]

As Father Kangleon implies by calling the interrogators "actors," his torture is a perverse theater in which he is compelled to play the lead in a drama of his own humiliation. After blindfolding, stripping, and insulting the priest, the soldiers communicate their dominion by beating him, almost playfully, forcing him to assist in his own degradation. He is beyond the help of courts and the law.[70] And, in the end, as the CIA's Honduran handbook would have predicted, the priest capitulates and calls out the name of his torturer as his savior.

Other future RAM leaders spent the early, formative years of their military careers engaged in similar tortures that proved profoundly corrosive of military discipline. Lieutenant Victor "Vic" Batac, later known as "the brains of RAM," emerges from victims' affidavits as a persistent torturer in his role as a leader of Marcos's elite anti-subversion squad, the 5th Constabulary Security Unit. While the unit's most aggressive interrogator, Lieutenant Aguinaldo, sometimes assaulted his victims with a relentless physical energy, Batac grew too obese for such activity and instead posed as all-powerful inquisitor, ordering sexual humiliation and theatrical torment.[71]

In 1974, only three years after his graduation from the military academy, Batac participated in the torture of a senior officer due, in normal times, the greatest deference. "I was picked up at my residence in Makati at about 9 p.m. on 25 May 1974 by 5th CSU . . . intelligence led by 1st Lt. Batac," recalled Navy Captain Danilo Vizmanos, who had recently retired as inspector general of the armed forces. After being blindfolded and driven to a safe house, this senior officer "heard the metallic click of an automatic pistol being loaded" and then felt "the muzzle pressed at the back of my head . . . for at least one minute [that] seemed like an eternity." Under "threat of liquidation," he was "ordered to identify certain names." When he refused, the captain was locked in "a tomblike cell made of concrete with a solid steel door" for sixty days of solitary confinement. During his 808 days of detention, Captain Vizmanos noted that the "RAM officers who participated in my arrest, detention, & torture were Lt. Batac, Lt. Aguinaldo, Lt. [Billy] Bibit."[72] For young lieutenants, trained to obey superiors without question, these acts—breaking into a senior officer's home, arresting him at night without a warrant, putting a pistol to his head, detaining him endlessly—represent a serious rupture in their military socialization into subordination.

Among Batac's many victims, it was a journalism student, Maria Elena Ang, who provided the most detailed description of his methods. In her account, Batac and his men practiced tortures inspired by metaphors, even conceits, of inverted production and reproduction, assaulting her sexual organs while administering a water torture they called the "NAWASA session" (a reference to the national waterworks) and electrical shocks they styled the "MERALCO treatment" (after the city's power utility). Even in its most extreme physical aspects, her torture was aimed ultimately, as she tells us with an insightful reference to "psywar tactics," at effecting a psychological breakdown by sexual humiliation.

I am Maria Elena Ang, 23 years old, a senior journalism student and research aide at the University of the Philippines. On the morning of August 5, 1976, I was on my way to Lourdes Church in Quezon City when unidentified military authorities pounced on me. . . . and dumped me into the car. . . .

It was about a five-minute trip from my place of arrest to the secret headquarters of ISAFP [Intelligence Service, AFP]. . . . Immediately, I was subjected to a most degrading, inhuman and humiliating experience I would never want to relive again. But the memories keep coming back. Up to now in detention, I still have recurrent nightmares.

I remember that while being restrained in a high-backed chair, several men, about 10 to 20, swelled the ranks of those already in the room. Immediately, they swamped me with a battery of questions and psywar tactics. They threatened to kill me, get my relatives and friends and torture them in front of me. They kept telling me nobody saw them taking me in.

Failing to answer one of their questions, I immediately received a slap in the face and a blow in the thighs.

By this time, I was able to remove my blindfold and identify two of the officers in the rooms as Lazaro Castillo of the National Intelligence Security Authority and Lt. Victor Batac of the 5th CSU or Constabulary Security Unit . . .

Then, several agents began clamoring that I be given what they called the MERALCO treatment—MERALCO being the supplier of electricity in Manila.

An agent then forcibly removed my blouse and bra and unzipped my fly. Another brought in a hand-cranked electric generator used in military telephone . . .

Two exposed wires were then tied around . . . my right hand foot. Castillo, with a sneer on his face, started cranking the generator and fired another barrage of questions. Suddenly, the current shot painfully through my body. I could do nothing but scream and plead and scream but he only turned the crank until I was screaming continuously . . . The electric-shock session lasted for nearly two hours and was repeated in the evening . . .

After the electric-shock session, the military authorities still were not satisfied . . . This time I was stripped naked and forced to lie on a short table.

At this instance, Major Arsenio Esguerra of the 5th MIG ISAFP entered the room and signaled the start of the water cure, which they laughingly called the NAWASA session—NAWASA being the supplier of water in Manila . . . This time, besides four men restraining my hands and feet, another formed my hair into a bun and pulled my head down so that it kept hanging [in] the air until I felt that the water was racing through my brains. I passed out twice but they kept pouring water until I thought I would die.

Besides pouring water, several agents mashed my breasts while another contented himself by inserting his fingers in my vagina after failing to make me masturbate.[73]

Of the RAM leaders, only Batac has been forced to respond to allegations of torture. While speaking at the University of Wisconsin–Madison in October 1986, he was confronted by the local Amnesty chapter with the 5th CSU's record of torture. "Yes," he answered, "we were aware of abuses in the unit." Admitting that his comrades "may have been guilty," Batac explained that torture arose from "individual initiatives to get information in a short time." Although he denied any role in Maria Elena Ang's torture, claiming that he was asleep at the time, Batac insisted, like other defenders of these practices, on the state's sovereign right to do "anything necessary" to protect itself.[74]

Maria Elena Ang nonetheless insists it was Lieutenant Batac who directed her torture. "Batac ordered me stripped naked and tied to a chair," she stated in a 1989 interview. As soldiers gave her electrical shocks with a crank radio, "Batac . . . sat there, leaning back in his chair with his feet on the table facing me with a smirk on his face. At one point I can recall him saying 'give her the NAWASA treatment.' And they filled me up with water." As she sank into a sea of water and vomit, Batac was "leaning back with arms behind his head with that smirk on his face."[75]

Many of these torture sessions share a similar plot. The interrogator begins with a few questions, meets resistance, and next applies coercion, psychological then physical, to elicit cooperation. Thespians all, the torturers assume the role of omnipotent inquisitor, using the theatricality of the torture chamber to heighten the victim's pain and disorientation. Within this script, there is ample room for improvisation.

Each interrogator seems to extemporize around a guiding image that becomes imbedded in the victim's recollection of the event.

Though these Filipino victims clearly understand, even as their torture transpires, the psychological techniques being used to attack their consciousness, they are ultimately defenseless against their power. In accounts written right after their torture, the victims both identify and analyze these techniques with great insight. Father Kangleon describes the "psychological and physical aspect" of his interrogators' theatricality, Maria Ang their tactics of psychosexual humiliation, and Captain Vizmanos the pain of protracted isolation. To grasp fully the devastating force of these CIA-inspired methods, we cannot distance and dismiss with our usual defenses, thinking these victims somehow less educated, less intelligent, or less resilient than we. Captain Vizmanos is a graduate of the U.S. Merchant Marine Academy at Kings Point, New York, and later topped the Navy's anti-submarine warfare course in San Diego; Maria Ang is an alumna of the elite University of the Philippines whose graduates now fill senior professional posts in institutions across America; and Father Kangleon was a member of a Catholic clergy that ranks among the most erudite in Christendom.[76] Their texts, quoted above, are not translations, but were told in their own words in flawless, idiomatic English. They are us. What they suffered, we would suffer. What they could not resist, we could not and cannot. No human, none of us, is capable of blocking the life-destroying effects of psychological torture.

But what is the impact of this behavior on the torturer? For young lieutenants to degrade and dominate society's leaders—priests, professors, and senior officers—may have induced a sense of mastery, even omnipotence. By breaking their superiors through psychological manipulation, the young officers gained a sense of their society's plasticity, fostering an illusion that they could destroy and remake the social order at will. Through their years of torturing priests and senior officers for Marcos, the officers slowly gained the daring to attack Marcos himself. Clearly, their training in psychological techniques, rather than more obvious physical methods, had important political implications for the Philippines.

During the fourteen years of the Marcos dictatorship, these young lieutenants learned, in the most formative stage of their military careers, to regard their own society as the enemy and to use espionage, surveillance, arrest, and torture against people who, in normal circumstances, they would have been defending from foreign attack. Rather than fight for their country in battle, the officers violated lifelong sanctions, familial and military, by torturing helpless victims drawn, in many cases, from their nation's elites. Such experience armed the RAM leaders for future political warfare. Through their extraordinary duties in the service of dictatorship, they acquired an almost unimaginable arrogance, a sense of themselves as supermen who could capture the state. Instead of rejecting their experiences in the safe houses, these rebel officers invested the violence with a romantic power, making them the main force in a protracted military revolt against the Philippine state.

In retrospect, psychological torture played a catalytic role in the rupture of military socialization, investing the RAM leaders with a self-image as protean creator/destroyers, lords of life and death, creation and destruction. Instead of the self-effacing manner of the modern soldier, they embraced a warrior ethos of limitless violence and untrammeled will profoundly disruptive of military discipline. In July 1986, four months after Marcos's ouster, I visited RAM's overall leader, Colonel Gregorio "Gringo" Honasan, at his security compound inside the Philippine Defense Department, there finding an atmosphere akin to Q's laboratory in a James Bond film. A tank of pet piranhas greeted visitors to his office. A personal statement was plastered to the door: "My Wife Yes, My Dog Maybe, But My Gun Never." He wore custom-tailored combat fatigues, and his military name patch read "GRINGO." Instead of standard-issue weapons, his officers were toying with crossbows, Israeli assault rifles, and rapid-fire pistols. Instead of dress uniforms for headquarters duty, the RAM boys marched down air-conditioned corridors in jungle camouflage. In place of short haircuts, they sported manes, beards, and mustaches. It was as if these rebel officers had erupted out of their regulation uniforms into costumes of lethal masculinity—a seductive aura that inspired a ten-year military revolt against the Philippine state.

As in Brazil, torture's complex pathology had led to its uncontrolled spread among the Philippine armed forces, weakening discipline and threatening the chain of command. As in France after Algeria, this long experience of torture, of an empowering illegality, encouraged a key military echelon to rise in revolt against the state it was supposed to defend. And like his friend the shah of Iran, Marcos, through his tolerance of torture, gradually eroded the legitimacy of his regime. If the Philippine experience is any guide, CIA psychological torture can do long-term damage to any army that practices it, corroding military discipline and fostering protracted political instability.

During the last decade of the Cold War, in the 1980s, media probes and congressional pressure led to surprising revelations about the extent of CIA torture training in Latin America. While the Senate's inquiries in the 1970s had been inconclusive, the later investigations established unequivocally that the agency had coached military interrogators throughout the region, propagating the systematic tortures that became the hallmark of its military dictatorships. As we have seen, denied access to Latin American police after the abolition of OPS in 1975, the CIA worked primarily through U.S. military advisers to train allied armies.

At a deeper level, the year 1975 is doubly significant, marking not only the dissolution of OPS but the defeat of the United States in Vietnam. Amid these traumatic transitions, the CIA, in collaboration with the Defense Department, intensified its efforts in Latin America where Washington was determined to hold the line against communism. Thanks to freedom of information, we can now track the paper trail of these changes through once-classified Pentagon memos about Project X, the Army's top-secret program for transmitting Vietnam's lessons to South America.[77]

During its quarter-century of operation, 1966 to 1991, Project X developed a complete counterinsurgency curriculum based on seven training manuals, all in Spanish, that addressed key tactical problems—including *Handling of Sources, Interrogation, Combat Intelligence,* and *Terrorism and the Urban Guerrilla.* Among these seven handbooks, at least five contained violent counterterror tactics far beyond anything in the CIA's 1963 *Kubark* manual. For example, the Project X handbook on *Handling of Sources,* mentioned earlier, refers, in the words of a Pentagon review, "to motivation by fear, payment of bounties for enemy dead, beatings, false imprisonment, executions and the use of truth serum."[78]

Upon closer reading, the 1989 edition of this *Handling of Sources* handbook has some chilling lessons about control of assets in counterinsurgency, applying past examples from the Philippines and Malaysia to ongoing Latin American operations. By appealing to "mercenary motivations" or using "fear as a weapon," the counterintelligence agent should recruit an "employee" for infiltration into a guerrilla zone, taking care to psychologically manipulate the employee's every emotion and thus "maintain the necessary control." To establish this asset's credibility as a "guerrilla recruit," the agent, the manual says, "could cause the arrest or detention of the employee's parents, imprison the employee or give him a beating." After successful insertion, the agent "could increase the employee's value" by destroying the surrounding guerrilla organization through "arrests, executions or pacification." And if regular scrutiny of this employee's reports reveals "possible deception," then the agent begins with "friendly character interrogations," checking all answers against an operational archive and preparing a "new Declaration of Personal History." In one case, says the manual's anonymous author, this latter method elicited the innocent admission that an employee, while a P.O.W. in the Soviet Union in 1944, had been "moved to Tallin" where "the Soviets transferred . . . only prisoners selected to be trained in brain washing" and a "number . . . were recruited by the Soviet Intelligence Service to serve as clandestine informants." If this friendly approach fails to produce a similar breakthrough, then the agent should move to the "mental test," waking the employee from a deep sleep for questioning, and next escalate to the "mechanical test" with hypnotism and injection of sodium pentathol (truth serum). If the employee turns out to be an "information trafficker" or a guerrilla "penetration agent," then our operative should "initiate termination proceedings" on "bad terms" through means "which are only limited by the agent's imagination." Although "threats of physical violence or true physical abuse" should, if possible, be avoided, the agent can effect an erring employee's "removal by means of imprisonment" after setting him up "to commit an illegal act." Or, in the ultimate twist, the agent can send "him in a specially dangerous mission for which he has been inadequately prepared . . . [and] pass information to guerrilla security elements"—thus, saving his government the cost of the bullet.[79] Apart from these cold-blooded tactics of kidnapping, murder, beatings, and betrayal, the manual evidences, in its 144 single-spaced pages, an amorality, a studied willingness to exploit an ally without restraint or compunction, hardened on the anvil of the Vietnam conflict.

For over twenty years, Project X was energetic, even determined, in its dissemination of these techniques. From 1966 to 1976, the U.S. Army's School of the Americas, then based in Panama, taught these methods to hundreds of Latin officers in its military intelligence course. After President Jimmy Carter's human rights concerns forced a four-year hiatus in the training—and famously produced a suspension in CIA covert operations—the Army's Southern Command resumed distribution of revised editions of the manuals during the 1980s, using them as handouts for its training programs in Colombia, Peru, Ecuador, El Salvador, and Guatemala.[80] Between 1989 and 1991, moreover, the School of the Americas, now relocated to Georgia, issued 693 copies of the handbook as texts in intelligence courses for students from ten nations, including Bolivia, Colombia, Peru, Venezuela, Guatemala, and Honduras.[81]

Simultaneously, the Army Intelligence Center at Fort Huachuca, Arizona, ran a mail-order operation under the rubric of Project X, sending complete training packets to foreign officers nominated by their U.S. counterparts. Interrogation was central to this curriculum. In the "annual list of instructional material" for 1977, there were eight basic academic subjects, divided into some 240 units, including a course on "Interrogation of Prisoners of War" with a three-tier structure of escalating sophistication—first, "introduction of the art of interrogation" and "introduction to counterintelligence"; next, the "process of interrogation" and "interrogation and document exploitation center"; and, finally, "interrogation practical exercise I" and "interrogation practical exercise II."[82]

Although the intelligence community operated in this way across Latin America, our detailed knowledge of the actual training comes from a single surviving document, from the agency's Honduras *Human Resource Exploitation Training Manual—1983*. In comparison to the Army's Project X handbooks, with their lurid, post-Phoenix methods of kidnapping and murder, this CIA manual emphasizes the nonviolent psychological techniques defined in the original *Kubark* doctrine—a reason, perhaps, that it survived the Pentagon's later destruction of almost all Project X documents. After completing a training session for Honduran interrogators in early 1983, an anonymous CIA instructor evidently combined his field experience with the agency's psychological doctrine to produce a full statement of its methods.[83]

At the outset of the Honduran training session, the anonymous instructor emphasizes that he will explain two types of psychological approaches, the coercive and the noncoercive. "While we do not stress the use of coercive techniques," the agent tells his students, "we do want to make you aware of them and the proper way to use them."[84] In his review of noncoercive methods, the agent says that they "are based on the principle of generating pressure inside the subject without application of outside force. This is accomplished by manipulating the victim psychologically until resistance is broken and an urge to yield is fortified."[85] When a questioner uses threats, "it should always be implied that the subject himself is to blame by using words such as, 'You leave me no other choice but to. . . .' He should never be told to comply or else."[86]

To establish control from the start, the questioner should, the instructor notes, "manipulate the subject's environment, to create unpleasant or intolerable situations, to disrupt patterns of time, space, and sensory perception. The subject is very much aware that the 'questioner' controls his ultimate disposition." In these manipulations, "the number of variations in techniques is limited only by the experience and imagination of the 'questioner.'"[87] Among many possible techniques, the subject can be arrested at a time selected to "achieve surprise and the maximum amount of mental discomfort," particularly in the early morning when "most subjects experience intense feelings of shock, insecurity, and psychological stress."[88] Once in custody, a subject should be immediately placed in "isolation, both physical and psychological," "completely stripped and told to take a shower" while blindfolded before a guard, and "provided with ill-fitting clothing (familiar clothing reinforces identity and thus the capacity for resistance)."[89] To convince the subject that much is already known and resistance is futile, the questioner should enter with a thick dossier, "padded with extra paper, if necessary, to give the illusion that it contains more data than is actually there."[90] If the subject proves resistant, then an interrogator can employ a "few non-coercive techniques which can be used to induce regression"—practices that would reappear twenty years later at Abu Ghraib and Guantánamo, including:

A. Persistent manipulation of time
B. Retarding and advancing clocks
C. Serving meals at odd times
D. Disrupting sleep schedules
E. Disorientation regarding day and night
F. Unpatterned "questioning" sessions
G. Nonsensical questioning
H. Ignoring half-hearted attempts to cooperate
I. Rewarding non-cooperation.[91]

Although the manual's overall approach is psychological, the trainer points out that coercion still plays an important role in effective interrogation. "The purpose of all coercive techniques," he explains, "is to induce psychological regression in the subject by bringing a superior outside force to bear on his will to resist." As coercion is applied, the subject suffers "a loss of autonomy, a reversion to an earlier behavioral level."[92]

There are, the manual states, three basic coercive techniques— debility, disorientation, and dread. "For centuries," according to the trainer, "'questioners' have employed various methods of inducing physical weakness . . . [on the] assumption that lowering the subject's physiological resistance will lower his psychological capacity for resistance."[93] While disorientation can "destroy his capacity to resist," sustained dread also "induces regression."[94] Thus, the trainer explains, in words that emphasize the primacy of the psychological over the physical: "The threat of coercion usually weakens or destroys resistance more effectively than coercion itself. For example, the threat to inflict pain can trigger fears more damaging than the immediate sensation of pain."[95]

But even within the CIA's psychological paradigm, there are times when threats of physical pain are necessary. "Threat is basically a means for establishing a bargaining position by inducing fear in the subject," the trainer says. "A threat should never be made unless it is part of the plan and the 'questioner' has the approval to carry out the threat."[96] In his conclusion, however, the trainer reiterates his emphasis on the psychological. "The torture situation is an external conflict, a contest between the subject and his tormentor," he explains. Pain inflicted on the victim "from outside himself may actually . . . intensify his will to resist," but pain that "he feels he is inflicting upon himself is more likely to sap his resistance."[97] The success of these techniques relies ultimately on the psychological empowerment of the interrogator. "Remember," the trainer writes, "the 'questioner' always has the advantage in a 'questioning' . . . He creates, modifies, amplifies, and terminates the subject's environment. He selects the emotional keys upon which the 'questioning' will proceed."[98]

Restating the defining tenet of CIA doctrine, the manual warns that crude physical torture weakens the "moral caliber of the [security] organization and corrupts those that rely on it." But the agency missed an important point evident from its experience in Iran and the Philippines: psychological torture has a far more corrupting impact on perpetrators than its physical variant.[99]

Comparing the 1983 Honduran handbook with the CIA's original 1963 *Kubark* manual reveals, in ten key passages, almost verbatim language for both conceptual design and technical detail. After describing psychological techniques to induce "regression" in the subject, both documents emphasize the elimination of "sensory stimuli" through solitary confinement; both warn that pain inflicted externally, by an interrogator, can actually strengthen a subject's resistance; and both itemize the particular methods that will effect a devastating assault on individual identity—disorienting arrest, isolation, manipulation of time, threats of physical pain or drug injection, and careful staging of the interrogation room. (See Table 1.)

TABLE 1

Comparison of CIA Interrogation Manuals, 1963 and 1983

	Kubark Interrogation, 1963, Langley, Virginia	*Human Resources Manual*, 1983, Honduras
Psychological Design	"[S]ound interrogation nevertheless rests upon a knowledge of the subject matter and on certain broad principles, chiefly psychological." (p. 1)	"Successful 'questioning' is based upon a knowledge of the subject matter and upon the use of psychological techniques." (I-D)
Regression	"Manipulative techniques . . . are in essence methods of inducing regression of the personality . . . regression is basically a loss of autonomy." (p. 41)	"Regression is basically a loss of autonomy, a reversion to an earlier behavioral level." (L–2)
Self-inflicted Pain	"[W]hereas pain inflicted on a person from outside himself may actually focus or intensify his will to resist, his resistance is likelier to be sapped by pain which he seems to inflict upon himself." (p. 94)	"The pain which is being inflicted upon him [subject] from outside himself may actually intensify his will to resist. . . . [P]ain which he feels he is inflicting upon himself is more likely to sap his resistance." (L–12)
Sensory Deprivation	"The more completely . . . confinement eliminates sensory stimuli, the more rapidly and deeply will the interrogatee be affected. Results produced only after weeks or months of imprisonment in an ordinary cell can be duplicated in hours or days in a cell which has no light." (p. 90)	"Solitary confinement acts on most persons as a powerful stress. . . . The symptoms most commonly produced by solitary confinement are superstition, intense love of any other living thing, perceiving inanimate objects as alive, hallucinations, and delusions." (L–10)

Isolation	"Separation permits . . . techniques . . . not be possible otherwise. It also intensifies in the source the feeling of being cut off from friendly aid." (p. 47)	"Prisoners should be segregated immediately. Isolation, both physical and psychological, must be maintained from the moment of apprehension." (F–5)
Manipulation	"Some interrogatees can be regressed by persistent manipulation of time, by retarding and advancing clocks and serving meals at odd times. . . . [This] is likely to drive him deeper and deeper into himself, until he is no longer able to control his responses in adult fashion." (p. 77)	"The 'questioner' should be careful to manipulate the subject's environment to disrupt patterns, not to create them. Meals and sleep should be granted irregularly, in more than abundance or less than adequacy, on no discernible pattern. This is done to disorient the subject and destroy his capacity to resist." (L–3)
Environment	"The room in which the interrogation is to be conducted should be free of distractions. The colors of walls, ceiling, rugs, and furniture should not be startling." (p. 45)	"The 'questioning' room is the battlefield upon which the 'questioner' and the subject meet. However, the 'questioner' has the advantage in that he has total control over the subject and his environment." (E–33).
Arrest	"What we aim to do is to ensure that the manner of arrest achieves, if possible, surprise, and the maximum amount of mental discomfort in order to catch the suspect off balance and to deprive him of the initiative." (p. 85)	"When arrested [early in the morning], most subjects experience intense feelings of shock, insecurity, and psychological stress, and for the most part have great difficulty adjusting to the situation." (F–1).

TABLE 1 (continued)

	Kubark, 1963	Human Resources, 1983
Threats and Fear	"The threat of coercion usually weakens or destroys resistance more effectively than coercion itself. The threat to inflict pain, for example, can trigger fears more damaging than the immediate sensation of pain." (p. 90)	"A threat is basically a means for establishing a bargaining position by inducing fear in the subject. . . . It should always be implied that the subject himself is to blame by using words such as, 'You leave me no other choice but to. . . .'" (I–22)
Drugs	"Just as the threat of pain may more effectively induce compliance than its infliction, so an interrogatee's mistaken belief that he has been drugged may make him a more useful interrogation subject than he would be under narcosis." (p. 98)	"There is no drug which can force every subject to divulge all the information he has . . . It is possible to create a mistaken belief that a subject has been drugged by using the 'placebo' technique." (L–15)

Sources: *KUBARK Counterintelligence Interrogation* (July 1963), File: Kubark, Box 1: CIA Training Manuals, National Security Archive, Washington; *Human Resources Exploitation Training Manual—1983*, Box 1, CIA Training Manuals, National Security Archive, Washington, D.C.

In 1988, only five years after the Honduran manual was produced, reporter James LeMoyne, writing in the *New York Times Magazine,* uncovered the CIA's role in the country's brutal counterinsurgency, producing another cycle of public shock and official indifference. Most important, the *Times* revealed both the extent of agency torture training and its impact on military operations. As civil war had intensified in Honduras during the late 1970s, the CIA imported Argentine officers, veterans of that nation's "dirty war," to train local interrogators, and also sent Honduran soldiers to the United States for instruction by its own experts. "I was taken to Texas with 24 others for six months between 1979 and 1980," Sergeant Florencio Caballero told the *Times* reporter. "There was an American Army captain there and men from the CIA." The sergeant knew the chief agency instructor only as a "Mr. Bill" who had served in Vietnam. As Caballero recalled, the officers "taught me interrogation in order to end physical torture in Honduras. They taught us psychological methods—to study the fears and weaknesses of a prisoner. Make him stand up, don't let him sleep, keep him naked and isolated, put rats and cockroaches in his cell, give him bad food, serve him dead animals, throw cold water on him, change the temperature."[100]

After their training, these soldiers joined Battalion 316, a special Honduran army intelligence unit supported by the CIA and organized by Colonel Gustavo Alvarez Martinez, a "vitriolic, anti-communist . . . trained in Argentina" who commanded both the national police and a private death squad. One person tortured by Caballero's unit, Ines Murillo, a young Marxist, described her eighty days of torture in an interview with the *Times* from exile in Mexico. Following her capture in 1983, she was taken to an army safe house in the town of San Pedro Sula where she was stripped naked and subjected to electrical shocks for thirty-five days. Then, she was moved to a second, secret prison near Tegucigalpa where her questioners, following the CIA's more refined methods, "gave her raw dead birds and rats for dinner, threw freezing water on her naked body every half hour for extended periods, and made her stand for hours without sleep and without being allowed to urinate." Although CIA agents visited both prisons and interrogated the prisoners, it is not clear whether they knew of these abusive practices and tolerated them as an acceptable level of coercion. Caballero said the "Americans didn't accept physical torture," but the CIA nonetheless backed the rise of Colonel Alvarez to command the army even though another local colonel had denounced him as a killer at a press conference in 1982. Indeed, U.S. ambassador John D. Negroponte told the *Times* that Colonel Alvarez was "a hard man but an effective officer" needed in a country where "Marxist guerillas are organizing." And regarding torture, one U.S. official added: "The C.I.A. knew what was going on, and the Ambassador complained sometimes. But most of the time they'd look the other way."[101]

The *New York Times* exposé of the CIA's role in Honduras prompted a congressional inquiry that, though somewhat cursory, did reveal, for the first time, the existence of the agency's torture training handbooks. When the Senate's Select Committee on Intelligence, responsible for legislative oversight of the CIA, met in closed session to review the *Times* allegations, its chair, Senator David Boren (Democrat, Oklahoma), stated that in the course of the agency's internal review "several interrogation training manuals, including one used to train the Hondurans, had been uncovered." The techniques in these manuals were, in Boren's view, "completely contrary to the principles and policies of the United States."[102]

In secret testimony before the committee, the CIA's deputy director for operations, Richard Stolz, confirmed the essential accuracy of the *Times* story: "[Sergeant] Caballero did indeed attend a CIA human resources exploitation or interrogation course [deletion] from February 8th to March 13th, 1983." This five-week course, held in Honduras, featured "two weeks of practical exercises which included the questioning of actual prisoners by the students."[103] The chief instructor, Senator Boren reported, was "an experienced CIA trainer" and, some months later, one of his colleagues drew upon "this man's accumulated materials and compiled the manual," evidently producing the *Human Resource Exploitation Training Manual—1983*. This trainer, Stolz explained, had prepared "the course lesson plan . . . based on his own experience in the U.S. Army . . . and on various other material [deletion] acquired over the course of [deletion] career," but the basic techniques were "assembled back in March of 1964"—an apparent reference to the original *Kubark* manual.[104]

Suddenly, Senator Frank H. Murkowski (Republican, Alaska), reflecting the reluctance of Congress to explore CIA operations during the Cold War, objected to the entire line of questioning. "Mr. Chairman, I feel very uneasy about getting into these areas," the senator said, challenging the wisdom of treating a mere newspaper article so seriously. "I mean this is the report and we're going through it. . . . I really question the propriety. I mean, hell, there's a million reports." When Senator William S. Cohen (Republican, Maine) replied that this was no mere press report but an actual CIA manual, Murkowski repeated, "I just want to note that this Senator feels very uncomfortable."[105]

Deftly evading any discussion of past CIA research into interrogation, Stolz explained that, in 1985, senior agency officers had ordered revisions to the manual and related training policies. The new text banned "interrogation which results in the use of force, mental or physical torture, demeaning indignities or exposure to inhumane treatment of any kind as an aid to interrogation."[106]

But Senator Alan Cranston (Democrat, California) pointed out that the manual stated explicitly that "there are times when you should use coercive methods." Nonetheless, Stolz insisted that "we were not talking anything about the kind of coercive methods that was alleged" in the *Times* article. In defense of his explanation, Stolz added, "we are talking about . . . sitting in a chair or a stool for a long period of time, some sensory deprivations, sounds . . . and some techniques that while it might appear harsh were certainly not anything like what was alleged in the article." Then Senator Bill Bradley (Democrat, New Jersey) launched into an aggressive cross-examination of the witness about the article's accuracy, ultimately revealing the committee's complete unawareness of the CIA's long involvement in torture research and training.[107]

SENATOR BRADLEY: Denying sleep?
MR. STOLZ: Yes, there was some denied sleep.
SENATOR BRADLEY: Making them stand up?
MR. STOLZ: Yes.
SENATOR BRADLEY: So making him stand up, denying him
    sleep—keeping him naked?

MR. STOLZ: No. Definitely not.

SENATOR BRADLEY: Rats?

MR. STOLZ: No rats.

SENATOR BRADLEY: Where it says: the CIA taught us psychological methods, to study the fears and weaknesses of the prisoner, make him stand up, yes; don't let him sleep, yes. Keep him naked and isolated—

MR. STOLZ: No.

SENATOR BRADLEY: Isolated?

MR. STOLZ: Well, yes—the answer is yes.

SENATOR BRADLEY: Naked no. Isolated yes.

MR. STOLZ: Right.

SENATOR BRADLEY: Put rats and cockroaches in the cell, no. Give him bad food?

MR. STOLZ: No. Bland food but not bad food . . .

SENATOR BRADLEY: Serve him dead animals.

MR. STOLZ: No.

SENATOR BRADLEY: Throw cold water on him.

MR. STOLZ: No, sir.

SENATOR BRADLEY: Changed the temperature?

MR. STOLZ: I don't know the answer to that. That's not impossible.

A moment later, apparently aware that he had stumbled onto something larger than a few training manuals, Bradley interjected: "Who was in charge of all this? Prior to 1984?" Stolz's four-line reply is blacked out.[108]

In a follow-up question, Senator Cohen, again revealing the committee's ignorance, said, "I am not sure why in 1983 it became necessary to have such a manual." More pointedly, Cohen asked "why the word 'questioning' is always in quotes in the manual itself," and suggested that the CIA might be "sending subliminal signals that say this [coercion] is improper, but by the way, you ought to be aware of it." Nonetheless, the senator, seemingly unaware that Stolz was offering minimal replies to conceal the CIA's long years of mind-control research, praised the agency for being "most cooperative." In his closing remarks, Stolz assured the senators that the CIA's inspector general would conduct a prompt review of these allegations—a review that, if ever completed, has not been released.[109]

Significantly, a fact sheet prepared for the committee showed that Army Special Forces had conducted at least seven "human resources exploitation" courses in Latin America between 1982 and 1987—a frequency confirming that the CIA had indeed shifted its interrogation training from police advisers to Army instructors after Congress had abolished OPS in 1975.[110]

Although the country's leading newspaper had published a detailed report of CIA torture training, Congress was, as this committee showed, unwilling to expose the agency's human rights violations. Under the pressures of the Cold War, torture training had again eluded serious reform.

While Washington tacitly tolerated torture by its Third World allies, several European civil-society groups launched a global movement to check the epidemic of human rights abuse. Responding to the proliferation of military regimes reliant on torture, the international community proposed treaties to ban the practice and therapy to treat its victims. In 1972, Amnesty International, realizing the limitations of its lawyerly approaches of documentation and petition, appealed to the medical profession for support. A group of Danish doctors responded by examining Greek and Chilean refugees for "forensic medical evidence about the after-effects of torture," discovering a pernicious form of post-traumatic stress disorder. Of the 200 victims examined, Danish doctors found nearly 70 percent still had "mental symptoms at the time of examination," even many years after their torture, including nightmares, depression, panic attacks, and low energy. "When you've been tortured," explained one of the Danish researchers, Dr. Inge Genefke, "the private hell stays with you through your life if it's not treated." But the victims could recover, the doctors learned, with the right therapy. By 1982, these discoveries inspired the founding of Copenhagen's Rehabilitation and Research Centre for Torture Victims (RCT). Within a decade, the RCT built a global network of ninety-nine treatment centers in forty-nine countries, developing a therapy regimen that in one year, 1992, treated 48,000 victims.[111]

These efforts broadened medical understanding of torture and built international support for its abolition. In December 1984, after years of global grass-roots agitation, the UN General Assembly finally adopted the Convention Against Torture, defining the practice broadly, under Article I, as "any act by which severe pain or suffering, whether physical or mental, is intentionally inflicted on a person for such purpose as obtaining from him or a third person information or a confession."[112] Approved by a unanimous UN vote, the convention created enormous international pressure for compliance. President Ronald Reagan sent it to Congress in 1988 with a ringing invocation of "our desire to bring an end to the abhorrent practice of torture." Simultaneously, however, the administration proposed a record nineteen reservations that stalled the convention's ratification in the Senate for the next six years.[113]

Among the many reservations, the Reagan administration focused, above all, on the issue of psychological torture. As Assistant Attorney General Mark Richard explained, both the State and the Justice Departments had found an "unacceptable level of vagueness" in the UN convention's definition of mental pain. To correct this problem, the State Department drafted a four-part diplomatic reservation, or exception, to U.S. approval of the convention, by defining psychological torture specifically to mean just "prolonged mental harm caused by . . . (1) the intentional infliction or threatened infliction of severe physical pain or suffering; (2) the administration . . . of mind-altering substances . . . ; (3) the threat of imminent death; or (4) the threat that another person will imminently be subjected to death . . . or other procedures calculated to disrupt profoundly the senses or personality."[114] Strikingly, Washington's narrow redefinition of "mental harm" excluded sensory deprivation (hooding), self-inflicted pain (stress positions), and disorientation (isolation and sleep denial)—the very techniques the CIA had refined at such great cost over several decades.

Why this impassioned concern, with just one word, "mental," in a UN convention filling twenty-six printed pages? Was the objection a response to some Reagan-era ideological concerns, or, more likely, the result of the CIA's clandestine maneuvering, through the State and Justice Departments, to protect its torture paradigm from international sanction?

Whatever the cause, the State Department's four-part redefinition of torture did, if narrowly interpreted, exempt the agency's psychological methods from the UN convention—at least as it was recognized and ratified by the United States. Once drafted, the narrow redefinition soon found its way, verbatim, into two later U.S. criminal laws and thus became the basis for Washington's policy on prisoner interrogation during the war on terror fifteen years later. Through this process, the United States, in effect, accepted just half the UN Convention Against Torture—affirming only the ban on physical methods. This decision, unnoticed when Congress finally ratified the convention in 1994, would effectively exempt the CIA's interrogation methods from international law. This clever diplomatic maneuvering meant that U.S. practice could diverge, even dangerously so, from international standards.

At the same time, with the end of the Cold War, the United States also resumed its active participation in the global human rights movement through both diplomacy and domestic legislation. In 1991, Congress passed the Protection for Victims of Torture Act, to allow civil suits in U.S. courts against foreign perpetrators who enter American jurisdiction—using the same narrow definition of "mental pain" that the State and Justice Departments had drafted for the Reagan administration back in 1988.[115] And at the 1993 Vienna human rights conference, Washington revived its vigorous advocacy of a universal humanitarian standard, opposing the idea of exceptions for "regional peculiarities" advocated by dictatorships of the left and the right, China and Indonesia.[116] A year later, while responding to President Clinton's appeal for ratification of the UN anti-torture convention, Congress also amended the U.S. criminal code, under Section 2340–2340A, to make torture, again as narrowly redefined by the Reagan administration in 1988, a crime punishable by twenty years' imprisonment.[117]

Ironically, it was the liberal Clinton administration that, in approving the UN convention, acceded to the conservative language of Reagan-era reservations, in essence legitimating torture as an open, accepted practice in the U.S. intelligence community. Through their ignorance of CIA covert practices, Congress and the Clinton White House had granted psychological torture a qualified legality in the very legislation designed to ban its practice.

Capping the process, President Bill Clinton announced that he was "pleased to sign into law" the War Crimes Act of 1996 as "an important reaffirmation of American leadership in the development of law for the protection of victims of war." Indeed, this law provides that any American, civilian or military, who "commits a grave breach of the Geneva Conventions," including all later protocols ratified by the United States, shall be punished by imprisonment or even death "if death results to the victim."[118]

Ironically, amid this ambiguous legislative process, the military moved decisively to make its interrogation doctrine fully compliant with the Geneva Conventions. In September 1992, the Army Intelligence Center at Fort Huachuca issued a revised field manual, *FM 34–52: Intelligence Interrogation,* using its recent experience in the Gulf War to "move interrogation into the 21st century." Taking full cognizance of international law, the manual cited the Geneva Conventions on both prisoners and civilians to state, categorically, that "physical or mental torture and coercion revolve around eliminating the source's free will, and are expressly prohibited." Not only was torture illegal, but it was, the Army advised, both impractical and immoral. As interrogators had learned since the days of imperial Rome, the U.S. Army had found that torture "yields unreliable results, may damage subsequent collection efforts, and can induce the source to say what he thinks the interrogator wants to hear." Not only is the yield low, but the consequences are grave. "Revelation of use of torture by US personnel will," the Army manual warns, "bring discredit upon the US and its armed forces while undermining domestic and international support for the war effort." So serious are the ramifications that even "knowing the enemy has abused US and allied PWs [prisoners of war] does not justify using methods of interrogation specifically prohibited."[119]

Defining torture broadly as "the infliction of intense pain to body or mind to extract a confession or information," the Army's field manual barred the most common forms of physical abuse, including electric shock, food deprivation, beating of any kind, "infliction of pain through chemicals or bondage," and, significantly, "forcing an individual to stand, sit or kneel in abnormal positions for prolonged periods of time." In marked contrast to the sanctioning of psychological torture under U.S. criminal law, the military guidelines banned "mental torture," including such specific practices as mock executions, "chemically induced psychosis," and importantly, "abnormal sleep deprivation." In a broad-brush prohibition, the Army warned that the "psychological techniques . . . in this manual should neither be confused with, nor construed to be synonymous with, unauthorized techniques such as brainwashing, physical or mental torture, or any other form of mental coercion."[120]

Although strict in its ban on any sort of torture, the Army's new guidelines did allow for interrogation procedures that were essentially psychological and thus showed clear traces of the CIA's influence. Yet these methods were, at the same time, restrained by clear warnings against crossing an invisible line. Just as the agency's 1983 Honduran torture training handbook said "subjects experience intense feelings of shock, insecurity, and psychological stress" at the time of their arrest, so the Army manual states most prisoners "indicated extreme disorientation immediately after capture" that increases their "susceptibility to interrogation." Coordinating closely with the military police to determine "what types of behavior . . . will facilitate the screenings," Army interrogators are advised to set the physical stage carefully and then assess all available information for "indicators of psychological or physical weakness that might make the source susceptible to one or more approaches." Recognizing that every detainee "does possess weakness which . . . can be exploited," the interrogator should combine seventeen basic psychological techniques—including the "direct approach" for those deemed cooperative; "emotional love" and "emotional hate" for those passionately patriotic or deeply embittered; and "fear-up" or "fear-down" to exploit "preexisting fear during the period of capture."[121]

Beyond these broad emotional strategies, Army interrogators could employ specific tactics such as feigning "we know all," by reading from a carefully assembled "file and dossier" to "give the illusion it contains more data than actually there," or insisting the "source has been correctly identified as an infamous individual" and then challenging the target to "establish [his] identity." To give force to the questioning, delivery should range from rapid-fire and repetition to silence. Among these approaches, only "fear-up" seemed a potential gateway to abuse, since interrogators were to "behave in an overpowering manner with a loud and threatening voice," and may "feel the need to throw objects across the room to heighten the source's implanted feelings of fear." Even here, however, interrogators were warned not to "violate the prohibition on coercion and threats contained in the GPW [Geneva Convention on Prisoners of War], Article 17." To drive the point home, the manual warned interrogators that any violations would "subject them to prosecution" under ten separate articles of the Uniform Code of Military Justice.[122]

The sum of these reforms, civil and military, amounted to a contradictory conclusion of the Cold War. Civil authorities had ratified the UN antitorture convention in ways that legitimated psychological torture within U.S. criminal law; the Army, by contrast, was complying fully with the Geneva Conventions by making all torture, physical and psychological, crimes under the Uniform Code of Military Justice. In effect, Washington had, by the late 1990s, buried this bundle of contradictions—American civil law versus military justice, U.S. criminal code versus UN convention—only to have them erupt with phenomenal force, just a few years later, in the Abu Ghraib controversy.

Although most citizens could not fully grasp these anomalies, the country's dwindling community of peace activists sensed something amiss in Washington's emergence from half a century of continuous global conflict. Throughout the 1990s, an ad hoc alliance of press and peace activists engaged this paradox in a fitful, even flawed manner as civil society struggled to correct excesses remaining from the Cold War. Through the combined failings of state and civil society, America would thus end the twentieth century with these contradictions ultimately unresolved.

Public advocacy of human rights and official secrecy over their violation collided most notably in a long-running controversy about torture instruction at the School of the Americas, the training facility for the Latin American military that the U.S. Army had operated in Panama since 1949.[123] As part of the U.S. withdrawal from the Canal Zone, the school moved to Fort Benning, Georgia, in 1984, bringing the facility, for the first time, within striking distance of the U.S. peace movement. Critics, who branded this facility the "School of Assassins," pressed for its abolition throughout the 1990s by mounting an annual demonstration outside the base each November. These swelling protests were led by Catholic activists, Hollywood stars like Martin Sheen, and Washington liberals like Representative Joseph P. Kennedy II (Democrat, Massachusetts). Adding to the criticism of U.S. relations with Latin militaries, the Harvard-trained lawyer Jennifer Harbury mounted a well-publicized campaign for truth about the disappearance of her husband, a Guatemalan activist last seen in a military jail with the marks of torture. Her quiet eloquence and long fast outside the White House reduced this complex issue to a single, comprehensible human loss.[124]

With its mix of idealism and celebrity, the movement served as the catalyst for further disclosures about torture training. After Representative Robert Torricelli (Democrat, New Jersey) charged that Harbury's husband had been murdered by a Guatemalan colonel in the CIA's employ, President Clinton's Intelligence Oversight Board investigated and, in June 1996, produced an inadvertently revealing report. Deep inside this fifty-three-page document, the board admitted, without any detail, that "the School of the Americas and U.S. Southern Command had used improper instruction materials in training Latin American officers, including Guatemalans, from 1982 to 1991." The training materials, the board said, had passages that condoned "executions of guerrillas, extortion, physical abuse, coercion, and false imprisonment."[125]

As both the media and the activists seized on this brief passage to file Freedom of Information lawsuits, the national security bureaucracy gradually declassified more detailed documentation. The released papers showed that the CIA's methods had spread beyond the intelligence community and been transmitted, through Army training teams, to military forces throughout Latin America. In a memo dated March 1992, the assistant secretary for intelligence oversight advised the U.S. defense secretary that a review of the department's files had found seven training manuals, all compiled during the mid-1980s, containing "material that either was not or could be interpreted not to be consistent with U.S. policy." These manuals, the assistant secretary added, "were based in part, on material dating back to the 1960s from the Army's Foreign Intelligence Assistance Program, entitled 'Project X.'" The 1992 memo indicates that the Defense Department had somehow lost control of this program, and Army trainers were operating in clear violation of military regulations. Had the CIA detached military officers from the chain of command and integrated them into a covert program with its own extralegal procedures? Significantly, the assistant defense secretary noted: "It is incredible that the use of the lesson plans since 1982, and the manuals since 1987, evaded the established system of doctrinal controls." Interviews with Army intelligence personnel who had used the manuals found they operated under the false impression that regulations on "legal and proper" interrogation "were applicable only to U.S. persons and thus did not apply to the training of foreign personnel." As a corrective, the assistant secretary's office had tried to recover all copies of these manuals from Latin American governments and recommended that, with the exception of a single file copy, the rest "should be destroyed."[126]

The explicitness of the CIA's torture training was finally exposed to public scrutiny eight years after the Cold War's end. In January 1997, the *Baltimore Sun, Washington Post,* and *New York Times* published extracts from the agency's Honduran handbook, the *Human Resource Exploitation Training Manual—1983,* describing it as the latest edition of a thousand-page manual distributed to Latin American armies for twenty years. Under the damning headline "Torture Was Taught by CIA," one press account began: "A newly declassified CIA training manual details torture methods used against suspected subversives in Central America during the 1980s, refuting claims by the Agency that no such methods were taught there."[127]

Although these press descriptions of torture were chilling, the public reaction was muted. Citizens and civic groups remained silent. Editorials did not call for an investigation. Congress did not react. Above all, there was no pressure on the CIA to repudiate or reform the techniques revealed in its training manual. Throughout this decade of media exposé, congressional criticism, and public protest, attention focused on sensational post-Phoenix excesses such as assassination and physical abuse, leaving the more complex issue of psychological torture largely unexamined. In effect, this public debate complemented the national security bureaucracy's own resolution of the torture question after the Cold War—purging the Phoenix-style physical abuse but preserving the original psychological paradigm as legal and even necessary.

Indeed, at its fiftieth anniversary, in 1997, the agency's central role in national security was affirmed and its budget has since continued to grow. While other covert agencies synonymous with the Cold War, such as the Securitate, Stasi, and KGB, had disappeared, the CIA survived—its archives sealed, its officers decorated, its crimes forgotten, and its torture techniques effectively legalized.

As victors in the Cold War, Americans in the 1990s seemed to view the new world order that followed in its wake with a certain self-satisfaction, reaching out into troubled regions beyond their borders to support the global transition to democracy with funds for electoral reform, press freedom, and human rights. Although they applauded these efforts abroad, Americans proved reluctant to examine their own excesses. They did not, perhaps could not, ask if fighting the Cold War abroad might not have damaged democracy at home. Absent any searching examination, absent any reforms to restrain the intelligence community, the torture doctrines developed during the Cold War lay fallow in this decade of peace, ready to be revived in any future crisis—as indeed they would be in the traumatic aftermath of 9/11.

4

WAR ON TERROR

AFTER THE ATTACKS on September 11, 2001, the White House made torture its secret weapon in the war on terror. Although Washington mobilized its regular military forces for conventional combat in Afghanistan and Iraq, the main challenge in this new kind of warfare was a covert campaign against "nonstate actors," terrorists who move easily, elusively across the Muslim world, from Morocco to Manila, in "ad hoc networks that dissolve as soon as the mission is accomplished." With its countless Cold War victories, overthrowing enemies on four continents by coups and covert operations, the CIA had an aura of invincibility and soon became Washington's chosen instrument for the fight against Al Qaeda. Yet, in truth, the agency's reputation for clandestine derring-do was grossly inflated and its qualifications for this new mission were few indeed.[1]

In any war against an underground movement, Communist or terrorist, global or local, accurate intelligence is the key to victory. The CIA, though brilliant against states or state agencies, is a centralized Washington bureaucracy often lacking the specific knowledge, languages, or street smarts for effective intelligence gathering on nonstate actors. Whether in France, Italy, Iran, Guatemala, Congo, or Chile, most of the CIA's legendary Cold War successes came, even at its peak in the 1950s, as a U.S. government agency penetrating foreign government agencies, civil and military, to carry out coups or clandestine operations. Similarly, the CIA fought larger, longer covert wars in Greece, Laos, and Afghanistan essentially as the lead U.S. agency in alliance with foreign states.

Only once before in its history had the agency tried to amass tactical intelligence, and it had failed, defaulting to torture in the process. By manipulating South Vietnam's military, the CIA installed and then toppled President Ngo Dinh Diem with consummate skill. But it then proved impotent against the country's underground movement, the Vietcong. In this its first major campaign against a non-state actor, the CIA tried a range of tactics—psychological warfare and paramilitary forces—without success. Desperate for intelligence about its invisible enemy, the agency soon descended into systematic torture of suspected Vietcong. Then, forty years later, confronted with a second, similar campaign against another nonstate actor, the CIA found it had few, if any, assets inside Al Qaeda or militant Muslim circles, forcing the agency to revive the torture techniques it had once used in South Vietnam. With surprising speed, Washington's recourse to torture in the hunt for Al Qaeda replicated the same outcome first seen during its "dirty war" in Vietnam—anger among the local population and alienation of the American people from the larger war effort.[2]

In the ten-year hiatus between the last known use of torture training manuals, in the early 1990s, and the declaration of war on Al Qaeda, in September 2001, torture had been out-sourced to U.S. allies. At the start of President Clinton's covert campaign against Al Qaeda in the mid-1990s, the CIA lacked the skills to translate raw intelligence into real results and so, in frustration and desperation, formed covert alliances with Third World security services known for torture. In 1995, CIA agents kidnapped terror suspects in the Balkans, some of them Egyptian nationals, and shipped them to Cairo for brutal interrogation. Former CIA director George Tenet later testified that, in the years before 9/11, the CIA was involved in the transport of some seventy individuals to foreign countries without formal extradition—a process called "extraordinary rendition" that was banned under international conventions.[3]

Such secondhand torture was evident at Manila in 1995 when the

Philippine National Police, working with the CIA, discovered plans for a wave of trans-Pacific aircraft bombings. As the successor to the Philippine Constabulary, the PNP was a natural CIA ally, with clandestine ties dating back to the 1950s, including some exposure to agency torture training. In the post-9/11 media, this Manila incident, albeit distorted, was cited repeatedly to justify the use of torture—making it worth recounting in some detail.

In a security sweep before the pope's 1995 visit, Manila police found bomb-making materials in the apartment of an Arab tourist, Abdul Hakim Murad. For two days, Murad "taunted his captors" at the PNP Intelligence Command until the police, in the words of a Filipino journalist, "racing for time" to protect the pope, did "what they did best to a prisoner at crunch time." After weeks of physical and psychological torture by beating, water boarding, holding "lighted cigarettes to his private parts," and threats of rape, all while he was blindfolded, Murad supposedly cracked and confessed to a plot to blow up eleven trans-Pacific aircraft and kill their four thousand passengers and crew members. Although advised of the arrest, U.S. embassy officials delayed Murad's extradition for months while, as one Filipino officer put it, "we did the dirty job for them." After three months in the hands of the Filipino police, Murad, who evidently had been implicated in the 1993 World Trade Center bombing, was finally sent to New York City to face trial.[4]

After September 2001, a growing public consensus emerged in favor of torture. In October, the *Washington Post* reported impatience at the Federal Bureau of Investigation over the interrogation of four suspected terrorists arrested after 9/11. "We're into this thing for 35 days and nobody is talking," said a senior FBI official, adding that "frustration has begun to appear." With surprising frankness, the agent admitted that the FBI was considering torture: "We are known for humanitarian treatment. . . . But it could get to that spot where we could go to pressure . . . where we won't have a choice, and we are probably getting there." One "law enforcement official" suggested that suspects be extradited to Morocco, where, as everyone knew, the king's

CIA-trained interrogators were notorious.[5] A week later, the *Los Angeles Times* reported serious discussion of torture in intelligence circles. "A lot of people are saying we need someone at the agency who can pull fingernails out," said one thirty-year CIA veteran. "Others are saying, 'Let others use interrogation methods that we don't use.' The only question then is, do you want to have CIA people in the room?"[6]

These musings inspired support for torture by media commentators spanning the political spectrum. Writing in the *Wall Street Journal*, the historian Jay Winnick, twisting the facts of Hakim Murad's Manila torture to portray the results as timely and valuable, asked: "What would have happened if Murad had been in American custody?"[7] In *Newsweek*, the columnist Jonathan Alter wrote: "In this autumn of anger, even a liberal can find his thoughts turning to . . . torture." Citing the Filipino success with Murad, he added, "some torture clearly works." Alter advocated psychological techniques or the transfer of suspects to "our less squeamish allies."[8] When a panelist on PBS Television's *McLaughlin Group* asked fellow columnists where they would send Al Qaeda suspects for torture, the *National Review* editor Rich Lowry bellowed, "The Turks!" Host John McLaughlin shouted out, "The Filipinos!"[9]

Adding academic gravitas to the media swagger, Harvard law professor Alan M. Dershowitz told CBS Television's popular *60 Minutes* that torture was inevitable: "If you've got the ticking bomb case, the case of the terrorist who knew precisely where and when the bomb would go off, and it was the only way of saving 500 or 1,000 lives, every democratic society would, have, and will use torture." Writing in the *Los Angeles Times,* Dershowitz argued that judges should be allowed to issue "torture warrants" for "non-lethal pressure" in a "ticking bomb" case when "a captured terrorist who knows of an imminent large-scale threat refuses to disclose it." Elaborating on these views in a book several months later, Dershowitz cited the "lifesaving information" that Manila police beat out of Murad to argue that torture can sometimes "prevent harm to civilians."[10] Reviewing the book for the *New Republic,* federal Judge Richard A. Posner cited this "telling example" from Manila to argue that civil liberties are no more than a "point of balance between public safety and personal liberty." When the balance is tipped by a ticking nuclear bomb in Times Square, then, the judge ruled, "torture should be used."[11] But Dershowitz's Harvard colleague Philip B. Heymann, a former deputy attorney general, challenged the chimera of limited, judicially controlled torture, saying judges would prove indiscriminate and "torture will spread," compromising international "support of our beliefs."[12] In retrospect, the public silence greeting this media chatter suggests that the American people were willing to consider and then quietly condone torture as a weapon in the war on terror.

Yet this enthusiasm for harsh methods seems founded on misinformation and, more deeply, on an ignorance of torture's complex trajectory. In fact, as the *Washington Post* reported in the midst of the media debate, the Manila police got all the important information from Murad in the first few minutes, when they seized his laptop with the bomb plot and evidence that led the FBI to World Trade Center bomber Ramzi Ahmed Yousef in Pakistan. Most of the supposed details gained from the sixty-seven days of torture that followed were, as one Filipino officer testified in New York, police fabrications that Murad mimed to end the pain.[13] In weighing personal liberty versus public safety, the "pro-pain pundits" were also ignorant of torture's perverse pathology, which leads to both the uncontrolled proliferation of the practice and long-term damage to the perpetrator society. In advocating torture, moreover, these American commentators seemed utterly unaware of the CIA's long history of torture and thus had no inkling that they were reactivating a ruthless apparatus that had only recently been restrained.

Even while the pundits and professors fantasized about limited, surgical torture, the administration of George W. Bush was secretly sanctioning harsh interrogation that would spread, in just months, from a few top Al Qaeda suspects in CIA custody to hundreds of ordinary Afghans and thousands of innocent Iraqis. More significantly, this very public discussion and its consensus for tough methods was taking place at the same time the White House was quietly rescinding legal restraints on brutal interrogation, and may well have contributed to a climate conducive to covert, yet officially sanctioned, torture.

On September 11, 2001, right after his evening address to a shaken nation, President Bush gave his White House counterterrorism staff wide latitude for retribution, saying "any barriers in your way, they are gone." When Defense Secretary Donald Rumsfeld interjected that there were legal restraints on such action, the president shouted back, "I don't care what the international lawyers say, we are going to kick some ass."[14]

Within six days, Bush gave the CIA broad powers to attack terrorists, including transfer of suspects to nations notorious for torture. Two months later, on November 13, he issued a sweeping order, drafted by the vice president's counsel, David S. Addington, for detention of Al Qaeda suspects under "such other conditions as the Secretary of Defense may prescribe"—thus denying these detainees access to any court, whether U.S. or international, and instead relegating their cases to military tribunals which, he said, would be "full and fair." Finally, on January 8, 2002, the president decided to "suspend" the Geneva Conventions for his war on terror.[15] Just as Soviet leaders turned to torture in times of crisis, as the CIA had once reported, so President Bush, on that fateful day of 9/11, moved from fear in the morning, to flight in the afternoon, to tough talk and torture orders in the evening.

Conservative administration lawyers quickly translated the president's directive into policy. In late 2001, the Justice Department gave the CIA a narrow interpretation of the UN antitorture convention that sanctioned use of "sleep deprivation . . . and deployment of 'stress factors'" for interrogating Al Qaeda suspects—as long as they did not reach "severe physical or mental pain." On January 9, 2002, John Yoo of the Justice Department's Office of Legal Counsel wrote a forty-two-page memo asserting that the Geneva Conventions and the U.S. War Crimes Act did not apply to the Afghanistan conflict. Arguing Afghanistan was a "failed state," Yoo's memo swept Al Qaeda and the entire Taliban regime into a new category, beyond soldier and civilian, called "illegal enemy combatants," thus placing them outside the Geneva Conventions. Even Article 3, common to all four of the Geneva Conventions, barring "cruel treatment and torture" or "humiliating and degrading treatment," did not, Yoo argued, apply to this conflict "between a State and a transnational terrorist group." This radical view sparked a strong rebuttal from the State Department. "In previous conflicts," wrote State's legal adviser William H. Taft IV, "the United States has dealt with tens of thousands of detainees without repudiating its obligations under the Conventions." Specifically, Taft insisted that Yoo's argument about Afghanistan contravened national policy, and his contention that the president could ignore Geneva was "incorrect" and "confused."[16]

Significantly, on January 11, 2002, when the first Afghan captives started arriving at the Pentagon's prison in Guantánamo Bay, Cuba, Rumsfeld denied them legal status as prisoners of war: "Unlawful combatants do not have any rights under the Geneva Convention." As one of the few U.S. bases "not officially on American territory," Guantánamo was, in the Pentagon's view, beyond the reach of the courts and their requirements of due process. Rumsfeld called it "the least-worst place we could have selected" to house rising numbers of captives packed into the brigs of Navy ships.[17] Indeed, just two weeks before this decision, the Justice Department had sent Rumsfeld's general counsel a detailed memo, again drafted by John Yoo, arguing that "a federal district court could not properly exercise habeas jurisdiction over an alien detained" at Guantánamo. But, hinting at the litigation that would indeed follow, Yoo warned that because the "issue has not yet been definitively resolved by the courts . . . there is some possibility that a district court would entertain such an application."[18]

Then, on January 18, 2002, White House legal counsel Alberto R. Gonzales informed President Bush that the Justice Department "had issued a formal legal opinion concluding that the Geneva Convention III on the Treatment of Prisoners of War (GPW) does not apply to the conflict with Al Qaeda." That same day, the president decided that "the war against terrorism is a new kind of war" that "places a high premium on . . . the ability to quickly obtain information from captured terrorists . . . to avoid further atrocities against American civilians." Accordingly, the president ordered that the Geneva Convention "does not apply to al Qaeda and the Taliban," and their members "are not prisoners of war" under the convention.[19] Consequently, the next day, January 19, Defense Secretary Rumsfeld advised all his combat commanders that "Al Qaeda and Taliban individuals under the control of the Department of Defense are not entitled to prisoner of war status for purposes of the Geneva Conventions of 1949."[20]

Four days later, on January 22, Assistant Attorney General Jay S. Bybee sent Gonzales a detailed, thirty-seven-page legal road map for practicing coercive interrogation without legal complications, arguing that "neither the federal War Crimes Act nor the Geneva Conventions would apply to the detention conditions of al Qaeda prisoners." More important, Bybee added that the president has "the plenary constitutional power to suspend our treaty obligations toward Afghanistan during the period of the conflict." On February 2, 2002, the administration's top lawyers, with the exception of those at State and the Pentagon, approved Justice's position that the Geneva Conventions did not apply to the Afghan war. This same memo noted, said the *New York Times,* the CIA asked for assurances that the administration's public pledge to abide by the spirit of the conventions did not apply to its operatives"; and it was allowed ten "enhanced" interrogation methods, including "waterboarding" designed by "agency psychologists."[21]

Responding to a strong protest from Secretary of State Colin Powell over the decision to waive the Geneva Conventions, Gonzales advised the president that "this new paradigm renders obsolete Geneva's strict limitations on questioning of enemy prisoners and renders quaint some of its provisions." The president's formal waiver of the convention, Gonzales continued, "substantially reduces the threat of criminal prosecution under the [U.S.] War Crimes Act," particularly for violations of Geneva's ban on "outrages against personal dignity" and "inhuman treatment."[22] But on February 7, Secretary Powell, after warning that setting the conventions aside would "have a high cost in terms of negative international reaction" and "undermine public support among critical allies," won a very limited victory. The White House announced that Geneva would apply to the Afghan war but not to Taliban or Al Qaeda prisoners—a large loophole that would, in fact, allow torture. The next day in a Pentagon briefing, Secretary Rumsfeld reiterated his position that "the current war on terrorism is not a conflict envisioned by the framers of the Geneva Convention," and that members of the

Taliban do not "qualify for POW status." In sum, the White House policy, in *Newsweek*'s assessment, "set the stage for the new interrogation procedures ungoverned by international law."[23]

Less visibly, the administration began building a global gulag for the CIA. Sometime in late 2001, Rumsfeld, working with the CIA and allied agencies, launched a "special-access program" under the "most stringent level of security" to pursue Al Qaeda's leadership. As the most secret protocol in U.S. security parlance, a SAP is known only to a few top officials, and those "read in" at lower levels are barred from even saying its name or admitting its existence. Indeed, one of the few public acknowledgments of this kind of protocol came in June 2002 when the president grudgingly signed Pentagon budget legislation with a congressional notification requirement for SAPs that read: "Situations may arise especially in wartime in which the President must promptly establish special access controls on classified national security information." To assure the success of this particular SAP, Rumsfeld armed it with some extraordinary weapons—prior authorization for kidnapping, assassination, and torture; elite troops from the Navy Seals and Army Delta Force; and a network of secret CIA detention centers. According to the journalist Seymour M. Hersh, the program was authorized by President Bush, known to fewer than two hundred operatives and officials, and directed by Rumsfeld's trusted aide, Stephen Cambone, later the undersecretary of defense for intelligence.[24]

After the president signed a classifed order on September 17 giving the agency "new powers," Washington negotiated supporting agreements with eight nations for secret CIA prisons in Thailand, Diego Garcia Island, Afghanistan, and Eastern Europe. Inside the long-established U.S. base at Guantánamo, the CIA operated "Camp Echo"—an off-limits cluster of a dozen concrete-block houses, each with a "steel cage, a restroom, and a table for interviews." To keep these prisoners beyond the reach of the International Red Cross, Rumsfeld agreed, at the request of CIA director George Tenet, to create a special category for "ghost detainees"—arrested in Pakistan, Indonesia, Thailand, Iraq, and elsewhere—by holding them without the registration numbers required by the Geneva Conventions. By mid-2004, the *New York Times* estimated that the CIA was holding, in its nascent gulag, some twelve to twenty-four top Al Qaeda suspects who had never been visited by "a lawyer or a human rights organization." Lesser suspects were, at this stage, left to the regular U.S. Army. By the end of 2004, the number of CIA ghost detainees had risen to an estimated thirty-six, including the Al Qaeda leaders Khalid Sheik Mohammed, Abu Zubaydah, and Nurjaman Riduan Isamuddin (a.k.a. "Hambali"). In later congressional testimony, General Paul Kern noted that the CIA may have hidden up to one hundred ghost detainees in prisons around the globe.[25]

The agency's global gulag was inextricably interwoven with secret-police prisons across Asia and the Middle East. In June 2004, the respected British newspaper *The Observer* estimated that three thousand terror suspects were being held both in CIA centers and allied prisons throughout the Middle East—a figure also claimed by the CIA's counterterrorism chief at Langley, Cofer Black. In this same period, the CIA, under President Bush's direct orders, engaged in the extraordinary rendition of some 150 Al Qaeda suspects, sending them to nations whose secret police were, in the view of the State Department, synonymous with torture—Egypt, Jordan, Morocco, Saudi Arabia, Syria, and Pakistan. "We don't kick the [expletive] out of them," said one U.S. official involved in the renditions. "We send them to other countries so they can kick the [expletive] out of them." In somewhat more decorous language, a senior Moroccan intelligence officer explained: "I am allowed to use all means in my possession. . . . We break them yes. And when they are weakened, they realize that they are wrong." To avoid using Air Force planes that might reveal its role in these prisoner transfers, the agency expanded its secret cluster of charter airlines to a fleet of twenty-six aircraft, including several jets that made hundreds of clandestine flights over the next few years, many of them originating at Washington-area airports. With these aircraft, the CIA shuttled prisoners invisibly around the globe to its own secret prisons and to allied agencies in Egypt, Syria, Jordan, Morocco, and Uzbekistan—most with long ties to the CIA. In early 2005, after nearly four years of such rendition, American reporters began documenting moving accounts of individual victimization within this web. One retired agency official called the rapid expansion of the rendition program after 9/11 "an abomination."[26]

The sum of these actions, overt and covert, soon invested the CIA with operational command over the war on terror and insured the use of its more extreme methods—effectively marginalizing the FBI, Army, and Navy, whose rigid guidelines required humane interrogation within the bounds of law. In November 2001, when the Pakistanis turned over the head of an Al Qaeda training camp, Ibn al-Sheikh al-Libi, a decisive bureaucratic battle erupted between CIA and FBI teams in Kabul over control of this trophy captive and others who would follow. At the start, the FBI, in keeping with its long-standing lead role in counterintelligence, had control of the Al Qaeda interrogations. Speaking over a secure line from New York, veteran FBI agent Jack Cloonan instructed his field agents in Kabul to work by the book in ways that would allow later prosecution. "Do yourself a favor," Cloonan said, "read the guy his rights. It may be old-fashioned, but this will come out if we don't. It may take ten years, but it will hurt you, and the bureau's reputation, if you don't. Have it stand as a shining example of what we feel is right." So the FBI operatives went to work using their standard procedures. "And they start building rapport," Cloonan continued. "And he starts talking about [shoe-bomber Richard] Reid and Moussaoui. They're getting good stuff, and everyone's getting the raw 302s [interview summaries]—the agency, the military, the director. But for some reason, the CIA chief of station in Kabul is taking issue with our approach." In fact, the Kabul station head was firing off complaints to Cofer Black at Langley, sending Director Tenet to the White House, where the CIA won control. Back in Kabul, Cloonan recalled, "CIA officers come in, start shackling al-Libi up. Right before they duct tape his mouth, he tells our guys, 'I know this isn't your fault.'" Shackled and gagged, al-Libi was taken to Kabul's airport where a CIA case officer put him on a charter jet, saying, as one FBI man recalled, "You're going to Cairo, you know. Before you get there I'm going to find your mother and I'm going to f—— her."[27]

The problematic nature of intelligence gained by the CIA's methods was evident from the start. Addressing the UN in February 2003, Secretary of State Powell famously cited a terrorist source, who "was responsible for one of Al Qaeda's training camps in Afghanistan," to charge that Saddam Hussein had offered terrorists instruction in

"chemical or biological weapons"—an embarrassingly erroneous assertion that Powell later retracted. In mid-2004, *Newsweek* reported that
al-Libi was the source of this false intelligence. "It was ridiculous for
interrogators to think Libi would have known anything about Iraq,"
said retired FBI agent Dan Coleman, Cloonan's longtime colleague in
counterterrorism. "The reason they got bad information is that they
beat it out of him. You never get good information from someone that
way." Another FBI agent told *Newsweek* that the CIA, used to dealing
with a handful of spies or Russian defectors, were unfamiliar with routine interrogation, and so, once they won this mission, were "searching
for effective techniques . . . and in their inexperience were floundering
for a while." In effect, the FBI's slow-but-sure method of gaining trust
had now lost out to the CIA's extralegal methods, which matched the
mind-set of Bush's war on terror. "All you need to know" about "very
highly classified . . . operational flexibility," Cofer Black told Congress
in September 2002, in words powerfully evocative of the agency's
covert ethos, "is that there was a 'before 9/11' and there was an 'after
9/11.' After 9/11, the gloves came off."[28]

From a pragmatic perspective, the choice of the CIA as lead
agency was ill-advised. The war on terror was a hybrid mission, spanning domestic and international jurisdictions, legal and extralegal
methods. As members of an undercover agency long exempted from
U.S. law, the CIA's agents, unlike the FBI's, had little legal training
and less experience in taking custody of suspects with procedures that
would allow their later prosecution. Indeed, the agency's institutional
cloak-and-dagger culture was antithetical to the bureaucratic systems
needed in collecting evidence that could stand scrutiny in an open
court. In the Vietnam War, the CIA had solved this problem by keeping its Phoenix program under wraps and avoiding the formalities of
prosecution with pump and dump—pumping suspects for information
by torture and then dumping the bodies, more than twenty thousand
of them between 1968 and 1971.[29]

Before 9/11, during President Clinton's early campaign against Al
Qaeda, CIA operatives had mediated the boundary between the overt
and covert by shipping a few dozen captives to allied foreign agencies.
"They loved that these guys would just disappear off the books, and never

be heard of again," said FBI agent Coleman, who collaborated with CIA operatives in this period. "They were proud of it."[30] Compounding the CIA's post-9/11 problems, detainee numbers soon soared beyond dozens into the hundreds. In Germany and the United States, moreover, trials of terrorists were complicated by CIA refusal to deliver detainees when their evidence, incriminating or exculpatory, was required. In 2003, a Virginia court dismissed some charges against the alleged 9/11 plotter Zacarias Moussaoui on the grounds that the White House had refused to provide information from a CIA captive, Ramzi bin al-Shibh. And in early 2004, German courts released two alleged confederates of the lead 9/11 hijacker Mohamed Atta, Hamburg residents Mounir el-Motassadeq and Abdelghani Mzoudi, on the same grounds—though one of the accused, el-Motassadeq, was later convicted on reduced charges.[31] Observers have noted that once interrogations are done and information extracted, the CIA, no longer able to pump and dump, has found itself stuck with hundreds of detainees, who will remain in legal limbo for the rest of their lives. "Are we going to hold these people forever?" asked a retired CIA agent, Michael Scheuer. After a detainee's rights have been violated, he explained, you cannot put him on trial and "you can't kill him," creating "a nightmare."[32]

Initially, only top Al Qaeda leaders were subject to this legal limbo. In Pakistan in April 2002, the agency captured one of its first targets, Abu Zubaydah, chief recruiter for Al Qaeda, and flew him to its secret base in Thailand for interrogation. Although he had been shot in the groin during his capture, the CIA denied him painkillers during interrogation. In general, the Bush administration was pleased with the yield from Zubaydah's torture, since he helped identify Khalid Sheikh Mohammed as a principal in the 9/11 attacks, and also served as the main source for the discovery of a supposed "dirty bomb" plot in Chicago manned by Jose Padilla. In June, moreover, Indonesian agents, working with the CIA, caught Al Qaeda's foremost Southeast Asian operative, Omar al-Faruq, and the agency flew him to its Bagram base for interrogation. In the words of the New York Times, Faruq was, for three full months, "left naked most of the time, his hands and feet bound," while "subjected to sleep and light deprivation, prolonged isolation, and room temperatures that varied from 100 degrees to 10 degrees." One Western intelligence official called this treatment "not quite torture, but about as close as you can get." In the end, Faruq gave some information about Al Qaeda members and their projected operations in Southeast Asia. But CIA agents, frustrated at this limited yield, wanted tougher techniques to extract more information from, for example, Zubaydah, who "refused to bend to CIA interrogation." These early efforts sparked a serious debate among counterterror officials, with some wanting to go further and others worried they had already gone too far. Such concerns about the limits of antitorture laws prompted a correspondence between the agency and the Justice Department "over the legality of specific techniques."[33]

In response to the CIA request for clarification, the Justice Department launched what the *Washington Post* called the "first ever" government review of just "how much pain and suffering" U.S. interrogators could inflict. White House counsel Gonzales chaired these meetings, which included detailed discussions of methods such as "open-handed slapping, the threat of live burial and 'waterboarding.'"[34]

In August 2002, as a way to legalize such questionable techniques, Assistant Attorney General Bybee, aided by his deputy Yoo and vice presidential counsel Addington, delivered a fifty-page memo to Gonzales providing "sweeping legal authority" for harsh interrogation. By carefully interpreting key words in the UN antitorture convention and its parallel congressional legislation, USC §§ 2340–2340A, Bybee concluded that federal law limited the crime of torture to "acts inflicting, and . . . specifically intended to inflict, severe pain or suffering, whether mental or physical." To constitute torture under U.S. statute, the physical pain must, he said, "be equivalent in intensity to the pain accompanying serious physical injury, such as organ failure, impairment of bodily function, or even death." Invoking both President Reagan's original four-part reservation to the UN antitorture convention from 1988 and the Clinton administration's ratification and enabling legislation six years later, Bybee found his primary grounds for exculpating CIA practices in a clause that emphasized the agent's intention. Thus, an interrogator who tortured but later claimed that his aim was to gain information rather than inflict pain, was not, in Bybee's twisted logic, guilty of abuse. Further limiting the ambit of CIA culpability, Bybee observed that psychological torture could become a crime only if there were three tightly linked conditions: (1) the "specific intent" to cause (2) "prolonged mental harm . . . such as post-traumatic stress disorder" solely by (3) committing one of the four forms of mental torture (with threats or drugs) specified in the 1994 law. Thus, the statute, in Bybee's analysis, "prohibits only extreme acts." In particular, the "sensory deprivation techniques" central to the CIA's paradigm did not, in his view, "produce pain or suffering of the necessary intensity to meet the definition of torture." More broadly, he concluded that any limitation on commander-in-chief powers to order interrogations would "represent an unconstitutional infringement of the President's authority to conduct war."[35]

By emphasizing "specific intent" as a necessary condition for criminal torture, Bybee narrowed the definition of psychological torture as stated in the 1994 legislation, which had already muddled the clear prohibition on physical and psychological abuse in the UN's original language. Through this linguistic legerdemain, the Justice Department granted the CIA de facto authority to use torture techniques, excepting only "the most heinous acts" that brought maiming or death. When the White House released the text of the August 2002 memo two years later, prominent legal scholars mocked its transparently tendentious reading of the law. "If the president has commander-in-chief power to commit torture," said the Yale law dean, Harold Hongju Koh, "he has the power to commit genocide, to sanction slavery, to promote apartheid, to license summary execution." But, back in the summer of 2002, there was no such criticism inside the Bush administration. Bybee's logic, although clearly flawed, became national policy.[36]

At the same time that Bybee's memo began circulating in August 2002, the Justice Department issued a set of instructions, still classified, for permissible CIA behavior. According to the New York Times, the directive allowed "specific interrogation techniques more coercive than those permitted for use by the military." Among these methods was "water boarding," which, as we know, inflicts intense physical and psychological pain by pouring water down the victim's throat to simulate, with terrifying reality, the sensation of drowning.[37]

Both the implications and the impact of Bybee's memo were profound. By misinterpreting U.S. law, Bybee issued a virtual license for torture that would remain in effect during two years of the most aggressive counterterror operations, August 2002 to June 2004. By inventing a new defense for torture, the memo encouraged the CIA to sanction extreme measures by its agents, who had been nervous about possible prosecution since Congress had enacted antitorture laws in the 1990s. If a defense based on a looser definition did not work, then, in Bybee's view, an interrogator charged with torture could walk free by claiming that the "intent" was information and not pain. Moreover, by raising the bar of acceptable physical pain to the level of "organ failure" and broadening the bounds of psychological methods, Bybee had expanded the range of U.S. interrogation techniques. Above all, he had exposed CIA and military interrogators to possible criminal charges and certain international opprobrium. Washington's original ratification of the UN antitorture convention, by exempting most forms of psychological torture, had already placed American interrogators, even when following the letter of U.S. law, at or beyond the bounds of international law. But now, by reaching his extraordinary definition of "severe pain," Bybee had, remarkably, breached many of the relevant military regulations—the Army field manual and the Uniform Code of Military Justice.[38]

As executive directives percolated from the Pentagon to prisons in Guantánamo and Iraq, American soldiers were, by orders derived from Bybee's memo, encouraged to use interrogation techniques that would lead, almost automatically, to their military prosecution and imprisonment. In effect, the White House had passed the word quietly down the chain of command that torture was an acceptable weapon in the war on terror, even though military courts insisted that it was still a crime under the UCMJ—a contradiction that some soldiers, sadly, did not discover until they were charged. But beyond these legal implications, Bybee's memo claimed that the president, as commander in chief, could defy Congress and criminal law to order whatever interrogation techniques he deemed necessary. In making this sweeping assertion for executive power, Bybee overlooked the landmark 1952 Supreme Court case *Youngstown Sheet & Tube Co. et al. v. Sawyer,* which had barred President Harry Truman from seizing the steel industry, and established, in the words of Justice Robert Jackson, that it is "obvious from the Constitution and from elementary American history" the president's military powers "do not supersede" the law.[39]

In March 2003, nine months after Bybee's memo and the Justice Department's directives were distributed, the agency apprehended Khalid Sheikh Mohammed in Pakistan, where he was carrying a letter from Osama bin Laden, and shipped him to an undisclosed location for coercive interrogation. According to the *New York Times*, Mohammed was "water-boarded"—"strapped to a board and immersed in water . . . to make the subject believe that he might be drowned." Frustrated that Mohammed was not forthcoming about bin Laden's location, CIA officials "then authorized even harsher techniques."[40]

The Justice Department memos, and the administration consensus they reflected, would lead, in the coming months, to widespread use of more brutal methods by both CIA and military interrogators. As Iraq erupted in revolt and Guantánamo prisoners proved recalcitrant, pressures began building that made the memos a subtle signal throughout the intelligence community that the gloves were indeed off. "Every impulse tugs downward," explains Army interrogator Chris Mackey from his Afghan service after 9/11. "The prohibition on the use of stress positions early in the war gave way to policies allowing their use to punish prisoners for disrespectful behavior. The rules were relaxed further by those who followed us at Bagram, and within a year stress positions were a formally authorized interrogation technique by the command in Iraq." And he added, "Rules regarding sleep deprivation, isolation, meal manipulation, and sensory deprivation followed similar trajectories."[41]

In the next few years of the war on terror, the toll from President Bush's orders, as conveyed in these memos and others still secret, would be chilling—some 14,000 Iraqi "security detainees" subjected to harsh interrogation, often with torture; 1,100 "high-value" prisoners interrogated, with systematic torture, at Guantánamo and Bagram; 150 extraordinary, extralegal renditions of terror suspects to nations notorious for brutality; 68 detainees dead under suspicious circumstances; some 36 top Al Qaeda detainees held for years of sustained CIA torture; and 26 detainees murdered under questioning, at least 4 of them by the

CIA.[42] Adding to the casualties from this covert war, Bush hinted at torture and extrajudicial execution during his State of the Union address in January 2003, when he spoke about the "3,000 suspected terrorists . . . arrested in many countries. And many others have met a different fate. They are no longer a problem for the United States."[43] To all these statistics, we should add another casualty—one great nation's international reputation.

As its clandestine gulag grew, the CIA's Cold War torture techniques resurfaced first at the agency's Bagram Collection Point, near Kabul, in December 2002. There in a sprawling, dungeon-like hangar replete with "chains jangling between prisoners' ankles; gates and latches slamming and locking; violent shouts from interrogators," the United States held many of its two hundred to three hundred high-value Afghan detainees. Shattering the media silence over interrogation, the Washington Post reported, in December 2002, that prisoners inside Bagram were subjected to "standing or kneeling for hours in black hoods or spray-painted goggles," and were forced into "awkward, painful positions and deprived of sleep with a twenty-four-hour bombardment of lights." According to American eyewitnesses, captives were "softened up" by Army military police and Special Forces, "who beat them up and confine them to tiny rooms." In response to this information, Human Rights Watch warned that Washington was violating "the most fundamental prohibitions of international human rights law." From London, the conservative Economist magazine chided the American media for "only a desultory discussion" of the Washington Post story: "there is a line which democracies cross at their peril: threatening or inflicting actual bodily harm. On one side of that line stand societies sure of their civilized values."[44]

Even more disturbing, that December two Afghan prisoners were found dead in their cells at Bagram. For months, the military command in Kabul insisted that one of the deceased, a twenty-two-year-old farmer named Dilawar, had died of a heart attack. But in February 2003, New York Times correspondent Carlotta Gall learned from two other prisoners jailed with Dilawar that they had all been short-shackled, arms up and feet immobile, for days on end until their ankles tightened painfully, constricting blood flow. This reporter then tracked Dilawar's family to a remote village in eastern Afghanistan and there found his U.S. military death certificate with an X in the box for "homicide." Under "cause of death," a Pentagon pathologist, Major Elizabeth A. Rouse, had written "blunt force injuries to lower extremities." Back in Kabul, the reporter asked the commander, Lieutenant General Daniel K. McNeil, if the prisoners had suffered injuries in custody, and he replied, "Presently, I have no indication of that." Questioned about the shackling, the general replied, "We are not chaining people to the ceilings." But the Army's legal adviser at Bagram, Major Jeff A. Bovarnick, later told the *Times* that, on arrival in November 2002, he had inquired whether this sort of shackling was "humane" and was advised, by the military and CIA officials in charge, that "it was not inhumane." In fairness, General McNeil deferred his final judgment to an ongoing investigation that, two years later, brought charges against Sergeant James P. Boland and recommended additional charges against two dozen members of the 519th Military Intelligence Battalion. According to Army evidence in these cases, one of the accused, Pfc. Willie V. Brand, had slowly killed Dilawar during a five-day period by "destroying his leg muscle tissue with repeated unlawful knee strikes" so brutal that even if the victim had survived "both legs would have had to be amputated." Significantly, the initial investigation had been slowed, in part, because the battalion and its commander, Captain Carolyn A. Wood, had been transferred to Iraq, where they were setting up the interrogation procedures at Abu Ghraib prison.[45]

Just as the details of Bagram's detention center began to emerge, the Defense Department authorized harsher tactics at Guantánamo Bay, Cuba. In October 2002, the Pentagon had removed Brigadier General Rick Baccus as base commander after complaints from military interrogators that he "coddled" detainees by allowing copies of the Koran and disciplining abusive guards. Appointed in November with orders to get tough and get information, Major General Geoffrey D. Miller would hold this post during a critical year, developing new military doctrines for coercive interrogation. Among his early innovations, Miller authorized creation of the Behavioral Science Consultation

Team with a psychologist and psychiatrist whose mission was to "engineer the camp experiences of 'priority' detainees to make interrogation more productive." To facilitate their work, BSCT members were given unauthorized access to detainee medical records. Guantánamo commanders also asked the Pentagon for more latitude to interrogate potential assets like the camp's most valuable prisoner, Mohamed al-Kahtani, a twenty-six-year-old Saudi branded "the twentieth hijacker"—claiming, in the words of the Southern Command chief General James T. Hill, that "some detainees have tenaciously resisted our current interrogation methods." In support of his request, General Hill attached a memo from Guantánamo's Joint Task Force 170, recommending, first, "stress positions (like standing) for a maximum of four hours"; next, "isolation facility for up to 30 days"; third, "deprivation of light and auditory stimuli"; fourth, hooding; fifth, "use of 20-hour interrogations"; and, finally, "wet towel and dripping water to induce the misperception of suffocation"—in sum, the CIA's established combination of sensory deprivation and self-inflicted pain.[46]

Consequently, in early December 2002, Secretary Rumsfeld "approved" sixteen techniques beyond the seventeen already allowed in the Army's standard interrogation manual, *FM 34–52*, which used only moderate psychological methods in compliance with the Geneva Conventions. The defense secretary, referring to the standing "designer desk" in his office, added a jocular handwritten note signaling his tolerance for a tough interpretation of these guidelines: "However, I stand for 8–10 hours a day. Why is standing limited to 4 hours?"[47]

The devastating impact of this decision on its first target, al-Kahtani, was recorded in Guantánamo's interrogation logs, later published by *Time* magazine. In entries for fifty days, from late November 2002 to early January 2003, the official log described sessions that ran for twenty unbroken hours, and were often spiked by novel psychological pressures. After guards filled al-Kahtani's bladder with over three bags of intravenous fluid, they denied him a toilet break until he answered questions. When his replies proved unsatisfactory, interrogators made him urinate in his pants. Playing upon Arab attitudes toward dogs, the Guantánamo guards, in their entry for December 20,

2002, wrote: "Began teaching the detainee lessons such as stay, come, and bark to elevate his social status up to that of a dog. Detainee became very agitated."[48]

In the following weeks, however, some officials reported that the new methods extracted little information from al-Kahtani, who "had been most forthcoming under more subtle persuasion." Of equal importance, Navy lawyers at Guantánamo objected, through the Navy Department in Washington, that such techniques might be criminal. In December 2002, Dr. Michael Gelles, chief psychologist at the Naval Criminal Investigative Service, told the Navy's general counsel, Alberto J. Mora, that Guantánamo interrogators were using "abusive techniques" and "coercive psychological procedures" on al-Kahtani. Gelles warned, moreover, of "force drift"—a natural inclination to uncontrolled abuse when interrogators encounter resistance. In turn, Mora told his Pentagon superiors, including senior counsel William J. Haynes, that these methods were "unlawful and unworthy of the military services," and the use of "coercive techniques" placed all involved at risk of prosecution.[49]

Consequently, in mid-January 2003, Rumsfeld suspended the procedures while his subordinates debated. Starting this process, an internal Defense Department Working Group circulated a draft document with a narrow definition of torture and a broad interpretation of executive power, similar to Bybee's August 2002 Justice Department memo. In response, senior military lawyers were unanimous in advocating strict adherence to law and treaty. The deputy judge advocate general for the Air Force, Major General Jack Rives, warned that the "more extreme interrogation techniques, on their face, amount to violations of domestic criminal law and the UCMJ" and placed "interrogators . . . at risk of criminal accusations" at home and abroad. More broadly, these executive guidelines could do long-term damage to the military. "U.S. Armed Forces culture and self-image, which suffered during the Vietnam conflict . . . due to perceived law of armed conflict violations," had been repaired starting in 1979, Rives recalled, "by establishing high benchmarks of compliance with the principles and spirit of the law of war, and humane treatment of all persons." While the detainees' status as "unlawful belligerents may not entitle them to protections of the Geneva Conventions," this subtle "legal distinction . . . may be lost on the members of the armed forces," and may be seen as "giving official approval and legal sanction" for techniques that are "unlawful." Of equal concern, should information about "the more extreme interrogation techniques become public," it will, the general predicted, attract press coverage that "could have a negative impact on international, and perhaps even domestic, support for the war on terrorism."[50]

The other top judge advocate generals seconded these views. The Navy's chief lawyer, Rear Admiral Michael F. Lohr, expressed concern that the American people would condemn the military for "condoning practices that, while technically legal, are inconsistent with our most fundamental values." The Army's senior law officer, Major General Thomas J. Romig, added that the Justice Department's approach "will open us up to criticism that the 'U.S. is a law unto itself.'" Since Bybee's view that the president's powers as commander in chief override "any existing federal statutory provision or international obligation" would not convince the courts, then, the general warned, "soldiers ordered to use otherwise illegal techniques run a substantial risk of criminal prosecution."[51] All these warnings by senior service lawyers were informed by decades of military experience. All would prove unerringly prescient. All were ignored.

Setting aside the many objections, the Defense Working Group produced a final memo, in early March, that affirmed the White House decision to use extreme interrogation. In April, therefore, Rumsfeld restored the wide latitude, albeit with a few new restrictions, for Guantánamo interrogators, sanctioning seven methods beyond the basic sixteen techniques in the Army's interrogation manual—including "environmental manipulation," "reversing sleep cycles from night to day," and isolation for up to thirty days. Under General Miller, military intelligence units at Guantánamo adopted a "72-point matrix for stress and duress" strikingly similar to the CIA's original paradigm, using "harsh heat or cold; withholding food; hooding for days at a time; naked isolation in cold, dark cells for more than 30 days; and . . . 'stress positions' designed to subject detainees to rising levels of pain."[52]

Beyond the matrix, Guantánamo's command began to probe Muslim cultural and sexual sensitivities, using women interrogators to humiliate Arab males. Just as the Phoenix program had added the physical violence of extrajudicial executions to U.S. interrogation doctrine, so the war on terror would develop a conscious strategy of sexual humiliation as an adjunct to the CIA's paradigm. According to a sergeant who served under General Miller, female interrogators regularly removed their shirts and one wiped red ink on a detainee's face saying she was menstruating, leaving him to "cry like a baby." Singled out for tough treatment, al-Kahtani was subjected to a "special interrogation plan" that mixed old and new techniques. He was given a particularly rigorous form of sensory deprivation—including 160 days of isolation; temperature reduction so extreme he twice required hospitalization for a slowed heart; exposure to a working dog "directed to growl, bark, and show his teeth"; water poured over his head seventeen times in one month; being blasted with "loud music during interrogation"; and being required to stand in "forced positions." These methods were buttressed with novel applications of psychological tactics called "ego down," "futility," and "gender coercion via some domination." During forty-eight days of interrogation, often with only four hours of sleep, al-Kahtani was "told his mother and sister were whores"; taunted over his "homosexual tendencies. . . . that other detainees knew" about; "forced to dance with a male interrogator"; "forced to wear a bra and a thong . . . on his head"; "led around by a leash tied to chains"; "forced to stand naked in front of a female interrogator"; and held down while a female interrogator "straddled" his groin. By mid-2004, over seven hundred detainees from forty-four nations, some as young as thirteen, would pass through Guantánamo, with still uncounted numbers subjected to variations of such illegal interrogation.[53]

When the Pentagon Working Group's March 2003 memo became military policy, a delegation of "very senior uniformed military lawyers" from the Judge Advocate General's (JAG) Corps paid an unofficial visit to Scott Horton, then head of the Human Rights Committee of the New York City Bar Association. Concerned that their exemplary, fifty-year history with the Geneva Conventions was ending, the JAG officers warned that "important policy decisions had been taken in the office of secretary of defense . . . which would lead to the abuse of detainees held in the Global War on Terror"—specifically, what they called "the disengagement of military lawyers from a watchdog role in the interrogation facilities," a new procedure, they said, that "served no legitimate policy purpose." As the interrogation techniques were implemented, military lawyers found themselves "being continuously circumvented in the process of policy analysis, presumably because they had consistently raised objection to initiatives of Rumsfeld on grounds that they . . . would violate the law of armed conflict." These military lawyers urged Horton's committee "to challenge the Bush administration about its standards for detentions and interrogation." Others outside the military also felt that the March document constituted a turning point. "We believe that this memo," said Jamie Fellner of Human Rights Watch, "shows that at the highest levels of the Pentagon, there was an interest in using torture as well as a desire to evade the criminal consequences of doing so."[54]

Under the pressure of the Iraq occupation, these brutal interrogation policies quickly proliferated. In August 2003, Iraq suffered a wave of terror bombings that rocked the Jordanian embassy with nineteen deaths and blasted UN headquarters, leaving twenty-three dead, including its head, the Brazilian diplomat Sergio Vieira de Mello. According to a U.S. military study, the lethal bombings were "the result of painstaking surveillance and reconnaissance" and the rebels were drawing their intelligence from sympathizers in both the Iraqi police and inside the Green Zone, the heavily guarded American compound in downtown Baghdad. In striking contrast to the rebels, the U.S. command realized, in this study's words, that its own "human intelligence is poor or lacking . . . due to the dearth of competence and expertise." As American casualties surged and violence spread, U.S. headquarters in Baghdad ordered sweeps of civilian neighborhoods, rounding up suspects and filling up military prisons whose populations quickly swelled from 3,500 to 18,000. "The gloves are coming off gentlemen regarding these detainees," a U.S. Army captain emailed his Military Intelligence (MI) comrades in mid-August. "Casualties are mounting and we need to start gathering info to help protect our fellow soldiers from any further attacks. I thank you for your hard work and dedication. MI ALWAYS OUT FRONT!"[55]

This pacification effort transformed Abu Ghraib prison into a hell-hole. In July 2003, Brigadier General Janis Karpinski, the military police commander for Iraq, had walked through Abu Ghraib's knee-deep rubble left by looters to inspect just twenty-five remaining prisoners; three months later the prison, only twenty kilometers from Baghdad, became the epicenter in the military's interrogation campaign, with some fourteen thousand "security detainees," over half of them crowded into this single prison. Inside Abu Ghraib's sprawling 280 acres, surrounded by a twenty-foot concrete wall extending four kilometers and spiked with twenty-four guard towers, the central compound housed three distinct areas—a cluster of minimum-security tents ringed with concertina wire, ordinary lockups, and the maximum-security cell blocks, 1-A and 1-B. As Abu Ghraib's population soared, General Karpinski came to see the prison's selection as a serious error—situated near hostile communities, subjected to incoming mortar rounds at night, and suffering oppressive 140-degree heat during the day. And the 3,400 soldiers of Karpinski's 800th Military Police Brigade were under enormous pressure: though vast, Abu Ghraib was but one in a military gulag of seventeen prisons whose population soon reached about 20,000, putting enormous strain on the guards.[56]

As the Iraqi insurgency erupted in August, Secretary Rumsfeld reportedly acted with characteristic decisiveness by ordering his special-access program operatives into Iraq, inserting them into military prisons with the authority for harsh interrogation beyond Army regulations.[57] Operating under code name Copper Green, Rumsfeld's SAP, which included the CIA, soon ran into serious problems. The team focused, in part, on interrogations at Abu Ghraib, where, over Karpinski's objections, the CIA concealed some thirty ghost detainees who were not logged into the system. Whether they were SAP or ordinary CIA, Karpinski began seeing mysterious operatives, whom she called "disappearing ghosts," around the prison in late 2003, who masked their identities with aliases and civilian clothes. Besides employing the usual psychological tactics, these interrogators reportedly introduced the practice of forced nudity and explicit photography, on the theory that "Arabs are particularly vulnerable to sexual humiliation." But by late fall of 2003, senior CIA officials were recoiling from abuses at Abu Ghraib, saying, in the words of a former intelligence officer, "No way. We signed up for the core program in Afghanistan—pre-approved for operations against high-value terrorist targets—and now you want to use it on cabdrivers, brothers-in-law, and people pulled off the streets." And in a reference to the Vietnam War's Phoenix program, the source added, "We're not going to use our guys to do this. We've been there before." As the CIA quit the SAP on advice of its lawyers, others in the intelligence community became concerned that the Abu Ghraib interrogations might compromise what they viewed as an effective covert operation. "This was stupidity," a security consultant told reporter Seymour Hersh. "You're taking a program that was operating in the chaos of Afghanistan against Al Qaeda, a stateless terror group, and bringing it into a structured, traditional war zone."[58]

Beyond the SAP's activities, military intelligence and the CIA were, after August 2003, engaging in harsh interrogation at Abu Ghraib and other camps with high-value detainees—despite President Bush's assurances that the Geneva Conventions applied to Iraq. That summer, at a Pentagon briefing on the growing insurgency, Rumsfeld "complained loudly" about poor intelligence from Iraq, contrasting it with the yield from the new "extreme" interrogation practices at Guantánamo. Voicing "anger and frustration" over the application of the Geneva Conventions in Iraq, Rumsfeld gave oral orders for the Guantánamo commander, Major General Miller, to "Gitmoize" Iraqi intelligence. Consequently, in early September 2003, the general, who had spent the past nine months developing Guantánamo's regimen, inspected Iraqi prisons with "a team of personnel experienced in strategic interrogation." In a classified report for Army headquarters in Baghdad, Miller observed that "it is essential that the guard force be actively engaged in setting the conditions for successful exploitation of internees." The general also urged a radical restructuring of detainee policy, to make Iraq's prisons the front line for information warfare, saying: "Detention operations must act as an enabler for interrogation . . . to provide a safe, secure and humane environment that supports the expeditious collection of intelligence." In expansive, almost visionary rhetoric, Miller wrote that his program would allow Abu

Ghraib to "drive the rapid exploitation of internees to answer . . . theater and national level counter terrorism requirements," thus meeting the "needs of the global war on terrorism." If implemented immediately, the plan would, he said, produce "a significant improvement in actionable intelligence . . . within thirty days."[59]

During a meeting with Karpinski, Miller began "dictating" the new procedures, waving his arms aggressively and invoking the name of the U.S. commander for Iraq: "Ric Sanchez said I could have whatever facility I wanted, and I want Abu Ghraib, and we're going to train the MPs to work with the interrogators." Explaining his plan to Gitmoize Abu Ghraib, Miller added: "We're going to select the MPs who can do this, and they're going to work specifically with the interrogation team." Miller left an interrogation manual and compact disk with what he called "training information" to facilitate integration of the MPs into the procedure. In one of his internal reports that September, Miller also advised that "teams, comprised of operational behavioral psychologists and psychiatrists, are essential in developing integrated interrogation strategies and assessing interrogation intelligence."[60]

Indeed, on September 14, 2003, just five days after Miller's departure, the commander for Iraq, Lieutenant General Ricardo S. Sanchez, signed a remarkable memo authorizing, in the words of a later inquiry, "a dozen interrogation techniques beyond [Army] Field Manual 34–52—[and] five beyond those applied at Guantánamo."[61] In his instructions, Sanchez explained that his "Interrogation and Counter-Resistance Policy" was "modeled on the one . . . for interrogations conducted at Guantánamo Bay, but modified for applicability to a theater of war in which the Geneva Conventions apply." In a very restricted distribution, Sanchez provided copies of his guidelines only to military intelligence, denying knowledge of the radical measures to Karpinski or her MP officers. This memo, which remained in effect for a month, ordered sophisticated psychological torture, derived from the CIA's basic methods of sensory disorientation and self-inflicted pain, and exemplified by ten techniques:

T. Dietary Manipulation: Changing the diet of a detainee . . .
U. Environmental Manipulation: Altering the environment to

create moderate discomfort (e.g. adjusting temperatures or introducing an unpleasant smell) . . .

   V. Sleep Adjustment: Adjusting the sleeping times of the detainee (e.g. reversing the sleeping cycles from night to day). This technique is NOT sleep deprivation.

   W. False Flag: Convincing the detainee that individuals from a country other than the United States are interrogating him.

   X. Isolation: Isolating the detainee from other detainees while still complying with basic standards of treatment. . . . Use of this technique for more than 30 days . . . must be briefed to 205th MI BDE Commander prior to implementation.

   Y. Presence of Military Working Dogs: Exploits Arab fear of dogs while maintaining security during interrogations . . .

   Z. Sleep Management: Detainee provided minimum 4 hours of sleep per 24 hour period, not to exceed 72 continuous hours.

AA. Yelling, Loud Music, and Light Control: Used to create fear, disorient detainee and prolong capture shock. Volume controlled to prevent injury.

BB. Deception: Use of falsified representations, including documents and reports.

CC. Stress Positions: Use of physical posturing (sitting, standing, kneeling, prone, etc.) for no more than 1 hour per use. Use of technique(s) will not exceed 4 hours and adequate rest between use of each position will be provided.

So extreme was the sum of these methods that military lawyers objected and, a month later, Sanchez rescinded some of the "harshest techniques." Nonetheless, the force of these memos was soon felt at remote Army outposts and inside Abu Ghraib prison. "On 15 Oct 2003," one prisoner told investigators, "they started punishing me in all sorts of ways . . . and they cuffed me high for 7 or 8 hours. And that caused a rupture to my right hand . . . And in the following days, they also put a bag over my head, and of course, this whole time I was without clothes and without anything to sleep on." That September as well, the 82nd Airborne Division started torturing Iraqi captives with

"beatings, exposure to extremes of heat and cold, . . . and sleep deprivation." Of particular note, the *New York Times* reported the soldiers
had learned these "stress techniques" in Afghanistan "watching Central Intelligence Agency operatives interrogating prisoners."[62]

Significantly, General Sanchez, although trained as an ordinary
combat commander, had issued orders for a multifaceted assault on
the human psyche. The synergy of the techniques produced, in sum, a
systematic attack on all human receptors, psychological and biological, similar to the practices outlined in the CIA's 1983 Honduran
training manual. Indeed, a line-by-line comparison of Sanchez's memo
with the CIA's Honduran handbook reveals six key points of correspondence, both in broad principles and in particular methods.

The Honduran handbook says "successful 'questioning' is based
upon . . . psychological techniques"; in similar language, General
Sanchez advises that "interrogation approaches are designed to manipulate the detainee's emotions and weaknesses to gain his willing cooperation." Just as the 1963 *Kubark* manual and the 1983 Honduran
handbook emphasize that "isolation, both physical and psychological,
must be maintained" to effect sensory disorientation, so Sanchez orders "isolating the detainee from other detainees," "reversing the sleeping cycles from night to day," and "dietary Manipulation." Moreover,
the Honduran handbook teaches that "pain which he [the subject]
feels he is inflicting upon himself is more likely to sap his resistance."
Sanchez gives comparable instructions by authorizing "stress Positions: use of physical postures (sitting, standing, kneeling, prone,
etc.)." In their lists of specific techniques, the two documents, as well
as the CIA's *Kubark* manual, create an environment that elevates the
interrogator, by making him, as Sanchez puts it, "appear to be the one
who controls all aspects of the interrogation," while simultaneously
breaking down the detainee by "significantly increasing the fear level."
The general's use of extreme psychological techniques indicates the
agency's methods had, in fact, spread to become the conceptual foundation for U.S. interrogation doctrine, even within the regular military.
Clearly, in both its design and detail, General Sanchez's memo was influenced by past CIA interrogation research.[63]

The sum of all these command initiatives was a climate of harsh interrogation at Abu Ghraib that descended, by degrees, into brutality, even depravity. To improve the intelligence yield, veteran interrogators from the 519th Military Intelligence Battalion, led by Captain Wood, had arrived from service at the CIA's Bagram center in July 2003 and were, as the insurgency intensified, preparing to introduce aggressive methods—including some that had already led to several Afghan fatalities. From October to December 2003, moreover, a six-person team traveled from Cuba to Iraq, bringing the "lessons learned" at Guantánamo Bay, notably the use of military dogs. One team member, Staff Sergeant James Vincent Lucas, later testified that they introduced Abu Ghraib interrogators to Guantánamo's aggressive, innovative techniques, including "short chaining" and "clothing removal." Apparently building upon these procedures, as well as on orders from Miller and Sanchez, military police in the security blocks at Abu Ghraib began to soften up detainees for CIA and MI interrogation with techniques documented, in the words of an Army report, by "numerous photos and videos portraying in graphic detail detainee abuse by Military Police." One of the MPs later convicted of abuse, Private Ivan L. Frederick, recalled that an interrogator gave him lists of prisoners he wanted dog handlers to visit, and guards then used the animals to "intimidate inmates." Significantly, cell blocks 1-A and 1-B, the sites of the notorious Abu Ghraib photographs, had been informally removed from Karpinski's command and were now controlled by two intelligence officers who reported directly to Sanchez's headquarters in Baghdad—Colonel Thomas M. Pappas and Lieutenant Colonel Steve Jordan.[64]

Then, on November 19, 2003, Sanchez issued orders removing all of Abu Ghraib prison from Karpinski's command and assigning it, along with the top-secret facility near Baghdad airport known as Camp Cropper, to the 205th Military Intelligence Brigade under Pappas—a division of authority that Army investigators later called "not doctrinally sound," since it exacerbated an "ambiguous command relationship." As a by-the-book MP chief, Karpinski had told Sanchez that she opposed any restrictions on Red Cross access to cell blocks 1-A and 1-B during interrogation. After she was ousted from Abu Ghraib,

Karpinski met with Sanchez's intelligence chief, General Barbara Fast, who told her, "We're going to run interrogations the way we want them run." In the period of most intense abuse, in late 2003, Sanchez summoned Pappas for periodic grillings and pressed him, forcefully, to deliver more intelligence.[65]

Under Pappas, the military police at Abu Ghraib were responsible for an initial phase of intensive disorientation to prepare detainees for interrogation by the CIA, military intelligence, and private contractors. The result was what the Army's investigation would call "numerous incidents of sadistic, blatant, and wanton criminal abuses . . . on several detainees." In the words of Major General Antonio Taguba's investigation, the abuse involved "punching, slapping, and kicking detainees" and "keeping them naked for several days at a time." In the escalation that often comes with psychological torture, this treatment soon moved beyond sleep and sensory deprivation to sexual humiliation marked by "photographing naked male and female detainees; forcibly arranging detainees in various sexually explicit positions . . . ; forcing groups of male detainees to masturbate while being photographed." Dismissing the idea of such behavior as simply aberrant, Taguba's inquiry found that "Military Intelligence (MI) interrogators and Other U.S. Government Agency's (OGA) [CIA] actively requested that MP guards set physical and mental conditions for favorable interrogation."[66]

In making the latter charge, Taguba cited a revealing statement by one of the MPs later accused of abuse, Sabrina Harman. She was, she said, ordered to stop prisoners from sleeping, including one famously photographed on a box with wires to his hands and feet. "MI wanted them to talk," she observed, then implicating two of her fellow MPs. "It is Graner and Frederick's job to do things for MI and OGA [CIA] to get these people to talk."[67]

As part of Taguba's investigation, the MI chief at Abu Ghraib, Colonel Pappas, drew up a memo, "Interrogation and Counter-Resistance Policy," in January 2004 outlining the procedures he had been using in cell blocks 1-A and 1-B. His orders required MI interrogators, in cooperation with physicians and the military police, to employ a method whose design seems derived from the CIA's trademark fusion of sensory deprivation and self-inflicted pain. "Typically," Pappas wrote, interrogators give MP guards "a copy of the interrogation plan and a written note as to how to execute [it] . . . The doctor and psychiatrist also look at the files to see what the interrogation plan recommends." The policy, Pappas contends, followed innovations at Guantánamo Bay, where teams of psychologists and psychiatrists helped tailor harsh techniques to break individual prisoners. At Abu Ghraib, Pappas's interrogators used seven sensory disorientation techniques to soften up the prisoners:

1. "dietary manipulation—minimum bread and water, monitored by medics";
2. "environmental manipulation—i.e. reducing A.C. [air conditioning] in summer, lower[ing] heat in winter";
3. "sleep management—for 72-hour time period maximum, monitored by medics";
4. "sensory deprivation—for 72-hour time period maximum, monitored by medics";
5. "isolation—for longer than 30 days";
6. "stress positions"; and
7. "presence of working dogs."[68]

Then, in the second phase of Pappas's program, trained MI and CIA operatives administered the requisite mix of interrogation and self-inflicted pain—a process that evidently took place outside the frame of the now-famous photographs. Under the 205th Military Intelligence Brigade, forced nudity became a standard procedure to humiliate and break prisoners at Abu Ghraib, in a search for answers to seven key questions, among them: "Who and where are the mid-level Baathists?" "Which organizations or groups . . . will conduct high payoff attacks?" "What organizations are Baathist surrogates?" and "Who are the saboteurs against infrastructure?" Amidst this harsh regimen, there were, moreover, increasing incidents of capricious cruelty. In November 2003, for example, five Iraqi generals suspected of instigating a small prison riot were manacled, blindfolded, and beaten by guards "until they were covered in blood." Although the prison's Detainee Assessment Branch filed at least twenty reports of serious abuse with Sanchez and Fast, headquarters did not intervene. Taguba later found that Pappas and his deputy, Lieutenant Colonel Jordan, chief of the Joint Interrogation and Debriefing Center, were "directly or indirectly responsible" for the abuse at Abu Ghraib.[69]

In contrast to Taguba's succinct, dispassionate descriptions, a February 2004 Red Cross report offers explicit, even chilling details of interrogation techniques. By late 2003, the International Committee of the Red Cross had made twenty-nine visits to U.S. detention facilities across Iraq, exercising its right to arrive unannounced for unrestricted inspections. While conditions for most detainees were, the Red Cross found, satisfactory, those "under supervision of Military Intelligence were at high risk of being subjected to a variety of harsh treatments ranging from insults, threats and humiliation to both physical and psychological coercion, which in some cases was tantamount to torture." Some military intelligence officers from allied nations told the ICRC that "between 70 percent and 90 percent" of detainees in Iraq, totaling over 41,000 by mid-2004, "had been arrested by mistake." In their visits to Abu Ghraib's military intelligence section, several U.S. officers told the ICRC that "it was part of the military intelligence process to hold a person . . . naked in a completely dark and empty cell for a prolonged period [and] to use inhumane and degrading treatment, including physical and psychological coercion." In words that could have been lifted almost verbatim from CIA interrogation manuals, the ICRC detailed the forms of "ill treatment" that military intelligence used "in a systematic way to . . . extract information" from detainees:

- Hooding, used to prevent people from seeing and to disorient them, and also to prevent them from breathing freely . . . ;
- Beatings with hard objects (including pistols and rifles) . . . ;
- Threats (of ill-treatment, reprisals against family members, imminent execution . . .);

- Being stripped naked for several days while held in solitary confinement . . . ;
- Being paraded naked outside their cells in front of other persons . . . ;
- Being attached repeatedly over several days, for several hours each time, with handcuffs to the bars of their cell door in humiliating (i.e., naked or in underwear) and/or uncomfortable position causing physical pain;
- Being forced to remain for prolonged periods in stress positions such as squatting or standing with or without the arms lifted.[70]

During a visit to Abu Ghraib in October 2003, the height of General Sanchez's extreme regimen, the ICRC discovered detainees "completely naked in totally empty concrete cells and in total darkness, allegedly for several days." The Red Cross medical staff determined that prisoners so treated were suffering from "memory problems, verbal expression difficulties, incoherent speech, acute anxiety reactions, . . . and suicidal tendencies." The ICRC concluded that military intelligence was engaged in practices that "are prohibited under International Humanitarian Law."[71]

Although these methods were harsh, military interrogators apparently applied them, in some cases, with even greater intensity. After Saddam Hussein's dramatic capture on December 13, 2003, U.S. headquarters in Baghdad sent a dozen of the aides arrested with him to Abu Ghraib, creating new pressures for tough questioning. To exploit these assets in the apparent absence of CIA interrogators, who had since quit Rumsfeld's top-secret SAP, General Fast authorized a "special projects team" to use tactics beyond those in the Army manual, including reduced diet, sleep deprivation, confinement in isolation cells for thirty days, and the presence of military dogs. The yield from Saddam's entourage was reportedly rich, leading to the arrest of Baath Party officials, former generals, and tribal leaders involved with the resistance.[72]

By December as well, military stockades were overloaded with detainees from the Army's incessant sweeps and arbitrary arrests. As they filled Abu Ghraib, spilling out of the cell blocks into concertina-wire corrals, Karpinski, no longer in charge of the prison though still a member of the Security Detainee Release Board, pressed for accelerated discharges. But Major General Walter Wodjakowski, deputy commander for Iraq, insisted: "I don't care if we're holding 15,000 innocent people. We're winning the war." Forgetting the deference due a superior, Karpinski shot back: "Not inside the wire you're not, sir. Every one of them is our enemy when they get out."[73]

Then the photos leaked and everything changed. On the night of January 13, 2004, a young MP guard, specialist Joseph M. Darby, slipped a compact disk with the notorious photographs under the door of the Criminal Investigation Division at Abu Ghraib—setting in motion Taguba's investigation in February, the explosive scandal, and, far less visibly, bitter intrigues within the Army to avoid responsibility.[74]

Just four days later, on January 17, Sanchez pinned the blame on Karpinski by reprimanding her formally for "poor leadership" of the MP brigade that had produced these "incidents over the preceding six months." Five days after that, Karpinski was finally shown the images. "I was shocked. I felt sick to my stomach," she recalled. "And not that they were torturing these people, but this was absolute humiliation of a sexual nature, and their faces [the MPs'] seemed to reveal that they were enjoying it." As she studied the photos, Karpinski concluded "they were staged and set up to be used to show to a detainee," allowing interrogation teams "to get information quickly, more quickly and more efficiently, from a new detainee." She did not see "six or seven bad apples" among her MPs but "six or seven individuals who may have been specifically selected." Indeed, one former intelligence official could not believe that these reserve MPs, these "recycled hillbillies from Cumberland, Maryland," were capable of such sophisticated psychocultural techniques, instead attributing them to top-secret SAP operatives inside that cell block. And from her six years in the United Arab Emirates as a training officer, Karpinski was appalled at the impact that the photos might have in the Middle East. In an imaginary dialogue with the MI interrogators she said: "Do you know what this does in an Arab culture? Do you know what you are doing? This is the equivalent of castrating them in public."[75]

When Taguba's team arrived in Baghdad on February 8, 2004, with Pentagon orders to investigate the 800th Military Police Brigade, Karpinski's command, Sanchez was sharply critical of her work in closed-door meetings with investigators. Sanchez blamed her even though he had given control of Abu Ghraib cell blocks 1-A and 1-B to military intelligence in September, before the abuse began, and personally ordered brutal, possibly illegal interrogation methods. Accordingly, in his report dated February 26, Taguba stated, as he assigned responsibility, "I totally concur with LTG Sanchez's opinion regarding the performance of BG Karpinski." In the weeks before this investigation made her the scapegoat, Karpinski could sense, as she intruded into "the last masculine, male domain" of combat command, strong hostility from her superior officer. "Sanchez and his crew," she recalled, "didn't like me because I was a female, I was a general officer, I was a reservist, and I was commanding soldiers successfully in his theater of war. And Sanchez didn't want that rose pinned on him for the rest of his life."[76]

As investigations into Abu Ghraib continued, the CIA apparently maneuvered to minimize its exposure to prosecution. On March 19, 2004, the Justice Department's Office of Legal Counsel drew up a memo, at the CIA's behest, enabling the agency to remove prisoners from Iraq for "facilitating interrogation." Although Article 49 of the Fourth Geneva Convention bars all such transfers "regardless of their motive," the memo parsed the convention's language to allow such extraordinary rendition. During the eleven months prior to this memo, the CIA had already flown a dozen of its ghost detainees out of Iraq. One of these prisoners, Hiwa Abdul Rahman Rashul, had been captured in Iraq in mid-2003 and flown to Afghanistan for interrogation. Following the Justice Department's objections in October, the CIA was forced to return him to Iraq and hide him, with Rumsfeld's permission, in the military prison system for seven months. After this incident, the agency extracted the March memo from the Justice Department to legalize the renditions retroactively. From his investigation of the incident, Senator Edward Kennedy concluded that the CIA had sought the memo "to protect their agents from being prosecuted."[77]

*   *   *

On April 28, 2004, the CBS Television news program *60 Minutes II* scored a major media coup by broadcasting the Abu Ghraib prison photos showing Iraqis stripped naked and subjected to humiliation by American soldiers. When Brigadier General Mark Kimmitt, speaking for Sanchez, appeared on camera to blame "leadership, supervision" for the failings of the military police, he pointed an accusing finger at just one officer—Janis Karpinski.[78] With the Iraq war going badly and a burst of color-coded terror warnings fostering a sense of fear across America, the political climate was not conducive to such an exposé. Public response to the CBS broadcast was, at best, muted.[79]

Nonetheless, the Abu Ghraib scandal intensified over the following weeks and months, as the undeniable power of these photos unleashed a complex interplay among autonomous American institutions that drove the controversy relentlessly forward. Just hours before the CBS exposé aired on April 28, the Supreme Court had assembled for oral arguments in the detainee rights cases and had heard solemn assurances by the U.S. solicitor general that the government could be trusted not to torture—a coincidence that would soon have far-reaching consequences.[80]

Following the broadcast, the press also published leaked copies of secret Bush administration documents, including Bybee's August 2002 memo. And, above all, those indelible images and horrific stories from Abu Ghraib began circulating worldwide over the Internet.

Among the most gruesome of these revelations was the murder of Major General Abed Hamed Mowhoush, the former Iraqi air defense chief, whose demise the Pentagon had long attributed to "natural causes." But when the *Denver Post* published the findings of a U.S. military autopsy just weeks after the CBS exposé, the Pentagon admitted that he had, in fact, died from suffocation and "blunt force trauma"—wounds whose real cause would only be revealed by a long criminal prosecution. After months of delays, moreover, the Pentagon suddenly issued death certificates for twenty former Iraqi prisoners, twelve of them cases of homicide or unexplained death—including one for Mowhoush stating that he had suffocated "during interrogation by military intelligence, after having been interrogated by C.I.A." Of even greater import, General Mowhoush's death also produced the first major revelations about the agency's Iraqi operations when the *Denver Post* won a court order to break the national-security seal on pre-trial hearings for soldiers charged with his murder. According to these records, Mowhoush had walked into Forward Base "Tiger" at Al Qaim in the Iraqi desert on November 10, 2003, asking to see U.S. officers about the release of his son. Instead, troops detained him as well. When he ended up in the interrogation room, the general at first cooperated, telling interrogators he was "commander of the al Quds Golden Division," a network of Saddam loyalists supplying the insurgents. After soldiers tried tough tactics to get more information and the general grew silent, he was transferred to the nearby "Blacksmith Hotel," a ramshackle desert prison where CIA and Special Forces were doing tactical interrogation. There he was worked over by an agency operative named "Brian," a Special Forces veteran, and his four-man squad of "Scorpions," Iraqi mercenaries the CIA had formed for sabotage but were now using for counterguerrilla operations—just as the Phoenix program had once used similar units, called PRUs, in South Vietnam. "When he didn't answer or provided an answer that they didn't like, at first [redacted] would slap Mowhoush, and then after a few slaps, it turned into punches," Army investigator Curtis Ryan told the military court. "And then from punches, it turned into [redacted] using a piece of hose." When the CIA team was done, two military interrogators used a "claustrophobic technique," zipping the general into a sleeping bag and beating the bundled body—in this case, until the victim was dead. The former commander, Colonel David A. Teeples, told the court that this technique was "approved and effective," used both before and after Mowhoush's death.[81]

Responding to the deepening scandal in May and June 2004, the Bush White House issued pro forma apologies while still insisting that events at Abu Ghraib involved "abuse," not systematic torture. At a Pentagon press conference on May 4, Rumsfeld stated that "what has been charged thus far is abuse, which I believe technically is different from torture." When pressed, the secretary said, "I'm not going to address the 'torture' word." And in a curious ritual, the Pentagon held closed-door screenings for Congress, with hundreds of classified Abu

Ghraib photos flashing by. Legislators emerged grim and shaken. "I saw cruel, sadistic torture," said Senate majority leader Bill Frist (Republican, Tennessee). "It felt like you were descending into one of the rings of hell," stated Senator Richard J. Durbin (Democrat, Illinois), "and sadly it was our own creation." On May 10, after the Senate condemned the violence against detainees by a 92 to 0 vote, Bush offered an oblique apology, noting that there would be "a full accounting for the cruel and disgraceful abuse of Iraqi detainees." Four days later, Sanchez announced an end to all coercive interrogation in Iraq, although, on questioning by reporters, his spokesman admitted that the general reserved the right to hold prisoners in isolation cells for more than thirty days. Speaking to the Army War College on May 24, Bush promised to demolish Abu Ghraib as "a symbol of disgraceful conduct by a few American troops who dishonored our country and dishonored our values," and replace it with "a modern, maximum security prison . . . as a fitting symbol of Iraq's new beginning." But the move was soon blocked by an Army judge, who ordered the prison preserved as a "crime scene" for prosecution of accused MPs, and the White House quickly dropped this gesture.[82]

Despite these efforts at damage control, a torrent of leaked executive documents would show that officials up and down the chain of command had condoned the brutality—from White House lawyers who defined torture narrowly to allow abuse; to Assistant Attorney General Bybee who argued that the president had the legal authority to torture; to Rumsfeld, who ordered the harsh measures; to senior military personnel, who pressed subordinates for better intelligence; all the way down to field-grade officers and ordinary soldiers who carried out these commands, often with a steely professionalism, occasionally with psychopathic abandon. As Congress probed the scandal, the Bush administration, in the words of the *New York Times*, "spent nearly two months obstructing investigations and . . . stonewalled senators over dozens of Red Cross reports that document the horrible mistreatment of Iraqis at American military prisons." In particular, the newspaper branded Rumsfeld's prevarication over the release of Red Cross reports as "the most outrageous example of the administration's bad faith on the prison scandal."[83]

World opinion was unanimously and sharply critical. In early June, the UN Office of the High Commissioner for Human Rights, in Geneva, condemned the "willful killing, torture and inhuman treatment" in Iraq, calling it a "grave breach" of international law that "might be designated as war crimes by a competent tribunal." The scandal was, the commissioner added, recognized by even coalition leaders as "a stain upon the effort to bring freedom to Iraq." When Bush visited the Vatican on June 4, Pope John Paul II, referring to the Abu Ghraib scandal, spoke publicly of "deplorable events . . . which have troubled the civic and religious conscience of all."[84] Two weeks later, UN Secretary General Kofi Annan responded negatively when the United States asked for the immunity of its troops from actions taken by the International Criminal Court, calling the request unacceptable, "given the prisoner abuse in Iraq." Faced with certain defeat in the UN Security Council, Washington was forced to withdraw its request for immunity; among other reasons, former backers of the move, like China, were, in the words of its ambassador, "under pressure because of the scandals and the news coverage." As international outrage mounted, Attorney General John Ashcroft, long a strong supporter of more severe interrogation, announced the indictment of a CIA contract employee, David A. Passaro, who had "brutally" beaten an Afghan detainee to death with his hands, feet, and flashlight for two days in June 2003.[85] At the same time, the Bush administration repudiated the August 2002 memo, prepared by Jay Bybee, that had allowed wide latitude for interrogations—leaving the military and the CIA politically exposed to take the fall for the administration's own decisions.[86]

Closing a month of rapid-fire criticism of White House policy toward detainees, the Supreme Court affirmed, in a landmark decision handed down on June 28, 2004, the right of "enemy combatants" held at Guantánamo to due process under law, flatly rejecting the White House's insistence on unchecked, unlimited detention of all prisoners in the war on terror, whether aliens or citizens. Abu Ghraib, although not mentioned explicitly, cast a heavy shadow over the Court's deliberations. In oral arguments for *Rumsfeld v. Padilla* on April 28, Justice Ruth Bader Ginsburg had challenged the executive's claim to exemption from judicial oversight: "So what is it that would be a check against torture?" When the deputy solicitor general, Paul D. Clement, tried to evade the question with a bland assurance that military violators would be prosecuted, the justice pressed harder: "Suppose the executive says mild torture, we think, will help get this information." To quiet her concern, the deputy solicitor general insisted that "our executive" would never tolerate torture. In wartime, he added, "you have to trust the executive to make the kind of quintessential military judgments that are involved in things like that."[87]

Now, in handing down its decisions about the rights of "enemy combatants," the Court ruled, in sum, that "war is not a blank check when it comes to the rights of the Nation's citizens." Writing for the plurality in a 6 to 3 decision that Yaser Esam Hamdi, a Saudi American arrested in Afghanistan, was entitled to due process, Justice Sandra Day O'Connor said that "indefinite detention for the purpose of interrogation is not authorized." And, extending these concerns to foreigners held at Guantánamo, she warned that "an unchecked system of detention carries the potential to become a means for oppression and abuse of others." Dissenting from the court's finding that it had no jurisdiction over Jose Padilla, a U.S. citizen then confined in a Navy brig on suspicion of plotting to detonate a nuclear "dirty bomb" in Chicago, Justice John Paul Stevens argued that it was of "no consequence" whether information extracted from indefinite detention "is more or less reliable than that acquired by more extreme forms of torture." In a minority opinion joined by three justices, Justice Stevens added pointedly: "For if this nation is to remain true to the ideals symbolized by its flag, it must not wield the tools of tyrants even to resist an assault by the forces of tyranny." Suddenly, the Pentagon's plans for open-ended detention of six hundred Guantánamo detainees, without judicial oversight, were thrown into disarray, and the Bush administration was faced with a possible mass transfer of hundreds of cases to the federal courts.[88]

To block that eventuality, the Pentagon quickly convened, just nine days later, an ad hoc military court at Guantánamo Bay, the Combatant Status Review Tribunal, and pushed hundreds of detainees through hasty hearings by three-member military panels within six months. Although the White House thus claimed full compliance with these Supreme Court decisions, the tribunal denied detainees legal representation and made their military jailers both judge and jury. In this star-chamber setting, prisoners were not given access to the evidence against them, an imbalance that would lead to the release, as of March 2005, of just 33 of the 558 detainees. These procedures—which mocked the usual meaning of due process and opened a new legal battleground—were suddenly stopped when U.S. District Judge James Robertson ruled, in a suit filed by a Guantánamo detainee, that the military courts had violated defendants' rights and failed to handle the prisoners in compliance with the Geneva Conventions. In effect, Robertson's decision rejected the legality of the president's original order denying POW status to Al Qaeda detainees. In another challenge to the military panels, nearly one hundred prisoners, most of them represented by lawyers working pro bono, began papering the federal courts with habeas corpus petitions. In January 2005, District Judge Joyce Hens Green, reviewing petitions from fifty of the detainees, affirmed the right of federal courts to issue habeas corpus writs for Guantánamo prisoners, ruling that the evidence in the military tribunals might well be tainted by torture.[89]

With each twist in this confrontation, the battle between the Bush White House and civil society over issues of human rights and civil liberties deepened. Though the Court of Appeals reversed Judge Robertson's decision in July 2005, allowing the special military tribunal to resume detainee trials, New York's leading law firms had by then made Guantánamo Bay their preferred pro bono destination. As top lawyers from corporate powerhouses like Clifford Chance and Allen and Overy began shuttling to Cuba for regular meetings with their clients, the isolation and lack of publicity, once the military's most powerful psychological weapons, were shattered. Indicative of this shifting balance of power, volunteer lawyers from Allen and Overy even filed an ethics complaint with the California medical licensing board, asking that the head of Guantánamo's hospital, Captain John S. Edmonson, be disciplined for allegedly withholding medication from detainees deemed uncooperative with their interrogators.[90] Clearly, after three years of the war on terror, the struggle over civil liberties and executive power was just beginning.

In its first months, the Abu Ghraib scandal was thus a serious blow to U.S. prestige, sparking strong domestic and international pressures for both reform and punishment. Even in the face of mounting evidence of systematic abuse, the Pentagon and the White House continued to reject any suggestion that the low-ranking soldiers involved were following orders, or that their cruelties sprang from standard interrogation procedures. Yet instead of dissolving into the typical media frisson quickly superseded by the next sensation, the issue of torture and treatment of detainees became the subject of a serious nationwide political debate.

The White House, with the support of its allies in Congress and in the conservative movement, maneuvered, with desperate determination, to preserve executive prerogatives of arbitrary arrest, unrestrained interrogation, and endless incarceration. Concerned, by contrast, about the implications of these practices for the rule of law, an ad hoc coalition of the federal courts, the legal profession, the human rights community, and the national press mounted a sustained campaign to end prisoner abuse in Afghanistan, Iraq, and, above all, Guantánamo Bay. Rather reluctantly, the Senate also joined this campaign. The result was an epic political struggle and a substantive public discussion over the Constitution, civil liberties, and international law—a discussion marked by nuance, passion, and even, at times, erudition; and one with profound significance for the future of the Republic.

5

IMPUNITY IN AMERICA

THE LANDMARK POLITICAL struggle sparked by the broadcast of photos from Abu Ghraib prison moved through two distinct phases marked by high political drama. During the first phase, from June to November 2004, the White House slowly ground down critics with its formidable powers of persuasion, moving the country, by degrees, toward a blanket "impunity" for all implicated in the torture scandal. Indeed, two months after release of the Abu Ghraib images, an ABC News/*Washington Post* poll found that 35 percent of Americans felt that torture was acceptable in some circumstances.[1] But in the second, more intense phase that followed the November presidential elections, an ad hoc civil-society coalition of courts, press, civil libertarians, and the Senate redoubled its efforts, scoring some surprising successes in slowing the country's inexorable slide into impunity.

Deployed with characteristic skill, the White House's stonewall strategy combined cosmetic gestures to placate critics, official investigations that assigned blame to a few low-ranking soldiers, and, less directly, a defense of torture as necessary to save American lives. In this damage-control effort, the administration made full use of its vast resources—particularly, congressional allies, command over the military, and a cooperative silence from the television networks. While there were soon half a dozen Pentagon inquiries into military interrogation, the CIA, as an executive unit subject to direct presidential orders, was spared the spotlight and allowed to conduct a slow-paced internal investigation that was still not complete a full year after release of the first Abu Ghraib photos. In a less visible parallel move, however, the White House seemed to be holding the agency in reserve as a potential scapegoat should the controversy spin out of control.

The bitter debate over torture was not without precedent. Strong democracies, far more than post-authoritarian societies, have difficulty dealing with torture. While nations emerging from dictatorship can purge and punish perpetrators as part of a sweeping change of regime, democracies, by their nature, usually decorate the illegality of torture with a nominal legality from the start and have the continuity of governance that protects loyal perpetrators inside the national-security apparatus. In the months following release of the prison photos, the United States moved quickly through the same stages, as defined by John Conroy, that the United Kingdom traversed after revelations of its torture in Northern Ireland during the early 1970s—first, minimizing the abuse with euphemisms such as "interrogation in depth"; next, justifying it on the grounds that it was necessary or effective; and, finally, burying the issue by blaming "a few bad apples."[2]

In the aftermath of the scandal, the Bush administration and much of the media studiously avoided the word "torture" and focused the blame on those bad apples, the nine military police subsequently accused. In the year after CBS broadcast those chilling Dantean images in April 2004, the Pentagon conducted six inquiries into almost every aspect of military culpability—in the end, exonerating all save one senior officer and blaming the bad apples, but also producing, buried in the reports' back pages, some important revelations. In July, the Army's inspector general, Paul T. Mikolashek, delivered the first of these findings, a 321-page report attributing ninety-four incidents of abuse, including twenty homicides, not to "system failures" but to "an individual failure to uphold Army Values." The inspector general concluded that all "observed commanders, leaders, and Soldiers treated detainees humanely"; he even recommended that regulations be loosened to allow "commanders to more effectively conduct intelligence exploitation in a non-linear battlespace."[3]

These exculpatory conclusions were echoed in an emerging conservative consensus. "Interrogation is not a Sunday-school class," said Senator Trent Lott (Republican, Mississippi). "You don't get information that will save American lives by withholding pancakes."[4] Nonetheless, during Mikolashek's appearance before Congress, several senators faulted him for failing to investigate Major General Antonio Taguba's earlier findings of "systemic and illegal abuse of detainees"—a conclusion corroborated by the Red Cross report that humiliating sex acts at Abu Ghraib were done "in a systematic way." The *New York Times* called Mikolashek statements "comical" and his report a "whitewash," but his approach proved a fair indicator of the military findings that would follow.[5]

In their rush to exonerate everyone except those nine bad apples, General Mikolashek and most congressional investigators failed to explore an obvious line of inquiry. Between White House decisions allowing torture and the ordinary soldiers who practiced it, there was a chain of command that transmitted the methods, potentially implicating everyone from Defense Secretary Donald Rumsfeld to General Ricardo Sanchez in Iraq and his deputies. Although equally evasive about assigning blame, the two that followed in this procession of official reports, one by the Defense Department and another by the Army, provided information that, when read closely, revealed the links between Rumsfeld and the soldiers at Abu Ghraib.

Next in this double-time investigative parade, on August 24 an independent Defense Department panel headed by James R. Schlesinger, a former defense secretary, found that institutional sins of omission—such as inadequate training and insufficient forces—were largely responsible for problems at the prison. The most egregious abuses in the photographs were, Schlesinger said, simply "free-lance activities on the part of the night shift." But the panel did show the migration of abusive techniques down the hierarchy and across the globe. After Rumsfeld had expanded the range of approved techniques for interrogation at Guantánamo Bay in April 2003, the methods, which included the use of nudity, dogs, and stress positions,

traveled first to Afghanistan and then to Abu Ghraib. Moreover, the
panel found, General Geoffrey Miller's August 2003 visit to Iraq
played a seminal role in convincing Sanchez to authorize brutality toward detainees. Then, as the Iraqi insurgency intensified and pressure
for intelligence grew, some of the military police gave "vent to latent
sadistic urges," while "many well-intentioned professionals, attempt-
ing to resolve the inherent moral conflict between using harsh techniques to gain information to save lives and treating detainees
humanely, found themselves in uncharted ethical ground." Overall,
about one-third of the sixty-six documented cases of abuse at Guantánamo, Afghanistan, and Iraq were what the panel called "interrogation related." To his credit, Schlesinger stated that "the abuses were
not just the failure of some individuals to follow known standards,
and they are more than the failure of a few leaders to enforce proper
discipline." There was, he concluded, "both institutional and personal
responsibility at higher levels." In addition, his report hinted at a new
direction in the overall inquiry by noting a lack of "full access to information" about the CIA's role and recommending "further investigation and review."[6]

Also in August, Major General George R. Fay released his report
with some stunning revelations, often obscured in opaque bureaucratic
prose, on the role of military intelligence. His account blamed not the
nine bad apples but the interrogation procedures at Abu Ghraib. After
finding prior Army interrogation doctrine sound, the general was forced
to confront a central, uncomfortable question: What, then, was the
source of the aberrant practices at Abu Ghraib?

In its short answer to this critical question, General Fay's report
traced the "non-doctrinal" interrogation methods back to the CIA. He
charged that a flouting of military procedures by agency interrogators
"eroded the necessity in the minds of Soldiers and civilians for them to
follow Army rules." Specifically, because the Army "allowed CIA to
house 'Ghost Detainees' who were unidentified and unaccounted for
in Abu Ghraib," it encouraged violations of "reporting requirements
under the Geneva Conventions." Freed from military regulations, CIA
interrogators moved about the prison with a corrupting "mystique" and
extreme methods that "fascinated" some Army interrogators. In sum,

General Fay seemed to say that the CIA had compromised the integrity and effectiveness of the military. Had he gone further, the general might have noted that the techniques of sensory deprivation, stress positions, and cultural shock, created by the use of dogs and nudity, were plucked from the pages of past CIA torture manuals.[7]

Scattered through Fay's report are the dots, politely left unconnected, leading from the White House to that cell block at Abu Ghraib—unconnected, and with certain questions unasked and unanswered, in large part because Fay, a reserve officer on active duty for just five years, was a political general and former fund-raiser, in civilian life, for the Republican Party. Through interviews with soldiers at Hessen and Baden-Württemberg, Germany, in May 2004, Scott Horton of the New York City Bar Association learned that Fay had told a meeting of military intelligence soldiers formerly stationed at Abu Ghraib "that any non-commissioned officer who observed the abuse of detainees . . . and who failed to intervene or stop it was guilty of an infraction and could be brought up on charges." Horton inferred that the aim of this announcement was to silence potential witnesses and sustain "a preconceived theory that the abuse . . . was the result of a handful of 'rotten apples' rather than systematic instructions." Consequently, Fay's initial draft report lacked credibility. Indeed, even Sanchez reportedly dismissed it as "such a whitewash of the role of military intelligence personnel that it stood no chance of gaining acceptance and would only subject the Army to further ridicule." To heal the breach, General Anthony R. Jones was brought in suddenly to supervise the investigation, and the final Fay-Jones report of July 2004 was so "broadly rewritten" that it "bears little similarity to the original draft Fay report and reflects a notably more professional attempt to address the issue of liability down the chain of command." Yet even this revised document, in Horton's view, was drafted in ways that explicitly "protected" or "shielded" key architects of Rumsfeld's hard-interrogation policy, notably "MG Geoffrey Miller, MG Barbara Fast, COL Marc Warren, COL Steven Bolz, LTG Sanchez and LTG William ('Jerry') Boykin."[8]

Despite these limitations, Fay and Jones, while corroborating Schlesinger's conclusions about the migration of harsh techniques, offered a far franker assessment of the causes for the most spectacular abuse. Under Rumsfeld's original December 2002 "Counter-Resistance" memo, Guantánamo interrogators began using "stress positions, isolation for up to thirty days, removal of clothing, and the use of detainees' phobias (such as the use of dogs)." In Afghanistan, military interrogators, employing many similar techniques, all seemingly drawn from the CIA's canon, were "removing clothing, isolating people for long periods . . . , using stress positions, exploiting fear of dogs and implementing sleep and light deprivation." By July 2003, the tough measures approved by Rumsfeld for Guantánamo and Afghanistan, both exempted from Geneva by the Bush White House, had reached Iraq via two routes, one overt and the other covert. After working with the CIA in Afghanistan—deploying methods "neither limited nor safeguarded," which killed one prisoner—the 519th Military Intelligence Battalion became, in July 2003, the first interrogators at Abu Ghraib, setting policies for the military police and MI units that followed.[9]

Then in early September, the aggressive General Miller arrived directly from Guantánamo, with three of his tough Tiger Teams of interrogators. Under the pressure of the Iraqi revolt and chaotic conditions inside the prison, the techniques grew even more brutal as "both MP and MI stretched the bounds into further abuse"—using "sensory deprivation and unsafe or unhealthy living conditions"; "exploiting the Arab fear of dogs"; combining "sleep adjustment" with "stripping [prisoners] and giving them cold showers"; and expanding nudity from a few hard cases at Guantánamo and Bagram until "nudity of detainees throughout the [Abu Ghraib] Hard Site was common." By October, one training officer from Fort Huachuca, Arizona, observed Army interrogators engaging in numerous nondoctrinal methods, including "sleep deprivation and sleep management," the "use of dogs as an inducement," stripping prisoners naked, and taking photos of "guards being rough with prisoners . . . to scare the prisoners."[10]

Working independently, the International Red Cross completed an investigation of military interrogation at Guantánamo in June 2004 which, along with Fay's report on Abu Ghraib, confirmed that once-covert CIA procedures had now become standard doctrine in U.S. detention centers worldwide. During its periodic inspections of Guantánamo's Camp Delta, the Red Cross found that the psychological methods used on the 550 detainees were, under international law, "tantamount to torture." In particular, the Red Cross objected to the use of health-care personnel, particularly psychiatrists and psychologists on the Behavioral Science Consultation Teams, to advise military interrogators on more effective methods, calling the practice "a flagrant violation of medical ethics." Moreover, medical personnel who treated the detainees conveyed information about their patients to interrogators through the behavioral team, creating an "apparent integration of access to medical care within the system of coercion." Between its first visit to Guantánamo, in January 2002, and one in June 2004, the Red Cross found that the psychological techniques had grown "more refined and repressive," involving "humiliating acts, solitary confinement, temperature extremes, use of forced positions." The organization concluded, in uncharacteristically blunt language: "The construction of such a system, whose stated purpose is production of intelligence, cannot be considered other than an intentional system of cruel, unusual and degrading treatment and a form of torture."[11]

When the *New York Times* first published extracts of the Red Cross report in November 2004, Guantánamo's commander, General Jay W. Hood, insisted that the detainees had "not been tortured in any way"—a statement that seemed to reflect the commonly held, mistaken belief that psychological torture is not torture. In a similar vein, the chair of the Joint Chiefs of Staff, General Richard Myers, dismissed the Red Cross document: "We certainly don't think it's torture." As if to justify whatever it might be, he added: "Let's not forget the kind of people we have down there. These are the people that don't know any moral values." Rumsfeld's spokesman, Lawrence Di Rita, said simply and dismissively that the Red Cross had "their point of view"—one the administration clearly did not share. In effect, this public rejection of a finding by the Red Cross, an impartial international agency, that U.S. psychological methods were "a form of torture," resolved the contradiction, evident since the early 1950s, between Washington's secret propagation of torture and its public embrace of international conventions barring the practice. After half a century of the CIA's covert use of psychological methods, the government now defied the international community by openly defending the techniques and denying that they constituted torture.[12]

Despite the Pentagon's denials, another U.S. agency had compiled detailed reports corroborating the Red Cross complaints. For nearly two years, FBI agents at Guantánamo, in the words of a senior intelligence official, "were outraged" as they observed military guards "slapping prisoners, stripping them, pouring cold water over them and making them stand until they got hypothermia." In December 2004, just three weeks after the release of the Red Cross findings, the *New York Times* published several FBI e-mails from Guantánamo with information that mocked the official denials and confirmed Red Cross claims. Writing the FBI director an "urgent report" dated June 2004, for example, one agent complained that military interrogators were subjecting prisoners to "strangulation, beatings, placement of lit cigarettes into the detainees' ear openings and unauthorized interrogation."[13]

The FBI e-mails provided further confirmation that military intelligence was applying the CIA's trademark techniques of sensory deprivation and self-inflicted pain. In November 2002, an agent observed one detainee "subjected to intense isolation for over three months"; the prisoner was described as "totally isolated (with the exception of occasional interrogations) in a cell that was always flooded with light." This detainee, the agent added, "was evidencing behavior consistent with extreme psychological trauma (talking to non-existent people, reporting hearing voices, crouching in a corner of the cell covered with a sheet for hours on end)." In July 2004, describing other traces of CIA practices, an agent wrote: "I entered interview rooms to find a detainee chained hand and foot in a fetal position to the floor with no chair, food or water. Most times they had urinated or defecated on themselves and had been left there for 18 to 24 hours or more." In some rooms, prisoners were subjected to extremely cold air conditioning that left them shivering, or to extreme, 100-degree heat in unventilated rooms. In one case, an FBI agent observed, "The detainee was almost unconscious on the floor, with a pile of hair next to him. He had apparently been literally pulling his own hair out throughout the night."[14] Yet the bureau reported no signs of the blood or bruises that accompany physical abuse—an indication that the detainees had been reduced to such trauma by the psychological methods alone.

In a revealing, consistent critique, FBI agents reported that this treatment was not producing any intelligence while complicating their own noncoercive approach. From 2002 to 2004, an FBI counterterror team conducted 747 interviews at Guantánamo, using standard bureau methods of building rapport by skillful questioning—making the agents well-placed to assess the military's rough approach. "These tactics," one bureau agent wrote in December 2003, "have produced no intelligence of a threat neutralization nature to date and CITF [Criminal Investigative Task Force, FBI] believes that techniques have destroyed any chance of prosecuting this detainee."[15] Summarizing the feelings of bureau staff at Guantánamo, a senior agent reported that "every time the FBI established a rapport with a detainee, the military would step in and the detainee would stop being cooperative." In some cases, first bureau meetings were promising, but the next time the detainee was interviewed—after an intervening military session of strobe lights, shouting, and loud music—"his level of cooperation was diminished."[16]

The release of the FBI e-mails prompted a high-level Pentagon investigation by Lieutenant General Randall M. Schmidt. In April 2005, he reported that some prisoners had indeed been mistreated in an experimental search for "innovative methods to gain information." In a separate, simultaneous report, a Boston-based group of health professionals, Physicians for Human Rights, concluded, after careful study, that "there is sufficient evidence available now to show a consistent pattern of the use of psychological torture as a key element in the interrogation of detainees by US personnel." Specifically, the group stated that at Guantánamo, "since . . . 2002, the United States has been engaged in systematic psychological torture," using techniques with "devastating health consequences for the individuals subjected to them." A confidential Guantánamo source had told the group of "a system to break people through a combination of humiliating acts, solitary confinement, temperature extremes, and use of forced positions." Detainees released from Guantánamo after such treatment, in the words of the report, "suffer from depression, thoughts of suicide and night-mares, memory loss, emotional problems, and . . . have difficulties maintaining relationships and employment."[17]

In the ongoing media battle, the Bush White House was being whipsawed between internal leaks of documents and assertive jour-nalists determined to restrain the administration's bid for unchecked wartime powers. As the second, post-electoral phase of the debate started in late 2004, these tensions would sharpen into a major politi-cal clash.

With the end of the 2004 presidential campaign and its curious si-lence about Abu Ghraib, the political fight over torture redoubled in intensity. But now, in place of political fumbling and mixed messages, the Bush White House focused on burying the prison scandal. This at-tempt at a cover-up, ironically, served to strengthen resistance by the civil-society coalition, which began to demand an independent in-quiry. Although the battle was clearly unequal, the opposition deliv-ered some unexpected blows, pressuring the White House to repudiate its most extreme claims of executive powers and complicat-ing its efforts to conceal the full extent of torture.

The battle produced yet another set of images, one whose meaning is obvious yet elusive. In the nation's 24/7 news cycle, America's top propagators of torture are seen walking, talking, and dismissing, al-most brazenly, any accountability for what occurred at Abu Ghraib, Afghanistan, and Guantánamo. As if empowered by their capacity to inflict insufferable pain on detainees in dark corners of the globe, the Bush administration's torture advocates strut across television screens and down the corridors of power. In less powerful nations, the process of self-exculpation by those who ordered and practiced torture is called, with a sharply pejorative connotation, "impunity."

Despite photos proving torture and documents identifying those responsible, the White House has denied culpability while protecting, even promoting, almost all the architects of its policy—Alberto Gon-zales, Donald Rumsfeld, William J. Haynes II, Jay Bybee, Stephen Cambone, and Timothy E. Flanigan. The White House counsel who derided the Geneva Conventions as obsolete, Alberto Gonzales, was confirmed as attorney general in February 2005, while avoiding anything akin to an apology at his Senate hearings and defending his earlier statements dismissing the Geneva accords as "absolutely the right decision." The defense secretary who implemented the torture directives, Donald Rumsfeld, survived a cabinet reshuffle and remained for a second term. The Pentagon legal counsel who approved Rumsfeld's expanded interrogation procedures, William Haynes, was nominated for the federal bench, although his appointment was blocked by the threat of a Democratic filibuster. The author of the Justice Department's now notorious August 2002 memo, Jay Bybee, was confirmed as federal judge for the Ninth Circuit in March 2003 with lifetime tenure in the U.S. courts. After Paul Wolfowitz became head of the World Bank in March 2005, Stephen Cambone, the undersecretary of defense for intelligence who had pushed the harsh interrogation policy, was proposed as Rumsfeld's deputy—although the nomination was withdrawn, without explanation, a few weeks later. In July 2005, the administration nominated Timothy Flanigan, who had helped frame torture policies as White House deputy counsel in 2002, for deputy attorney general, the second-ranking post in the Justice Department.[18]

Even those who were not rewarded remain unrepentant. To cite the most prominent example, John Yoo, a former Justice Department lawyer who helped draft the interrogation memos, is back at the law school of the University of California, Berkeley, where he waved away critics of the White House torture policy. "Why is it so hard for people to understand that there is a category of behavior not covered by the legal system?" Professor Yoo asked. "Historically, there were people so bad that they were not given protection of the laws." In his view, the Geneva Conventions' "simple binary classification of civilian or soldier isn't accurate." Arguing that Bush's reelection had ended the discussion, he concluded: "The debate is over. The issue is dying out. The public has had its referendum."[19]

Indeed, as Yoo indicated, during the 2004 presidential elections, the Democratic candidate, the media, and the American public ignored the torture scandal. Despite a precise coincidence between the election campaign and media revelations about Abu Ghraib, none of the Democratic Party challengers, including the ultimate candidate,

John Kerry, mentioned the issue in the hundreds of hours of speeches and debates. As the liberal "soccer mom" vote morphed into the conservative "security mom" constituency in the fearful aftermath of 9/11, there was strong public approval of Bush's hard-line stance against terror. And in this climate of fear, "toughness" seemed a possible code word for tacit acceptance, even admiration, of his use of torture. Faced with the unpleasant political likelihood that a substantial percentage of the American people, although they would never admit it, actually wanted a president who would torture terrorists, the timorous Democrats seemed loath to engage Abu Ghraib.[20]

But once the November elections freed them from the campaign's constraints, the Democrats, together with the loose civil-society coalition, renewed their criticism of the administration's policy. Under constant attack, the White House beat a quiet retreat from its expansive, post-9/11 claims about executive power; just two months after the elections, the administration finally and formally repudiated Bybee's August 2002 memo. On December 30, 2004, just as Gonzales was heading to Capitol Hill for confirmation hearings as attorney general, the Justice Department's Office of Legal Counsel replaced its earlier directive with a document that began: "Torture is abhorrent both to American law and values and to international norms." The earlier decision to skirt international conventions was now deemed "inconsistent with the president's unequivocal directive that United States personnel not engage in torture." And the assertions of August 2002 that the president could defy law and Congress to handle detainees as he wished were now deemed moot. Although rescinding Bybee's extreme equation of "severe" pain with "organ failure," the new document simply returned to a narrow interpretation of the four Reagan-era reservations to the UN antitorture convention and concomitant federal statutes, which affirmed, by implication, the wide ambit for psychological torture the CIA had long enjoyed. There are, moreover, indications that a secret Defense Working Group report dated April 4, 2003, recapitulating "the essence of the torture memorandum" by Bybee, remained in effect, allowing the clandestine continuation of extreme interrogation methods. Significantly, however, the December 30 memo denied any justification for torture done either for "national security" or on the grounds that "the victim might have avoided being tortured by cooperation with the perpetrator"—language that should have raised alarms at CIA headquarters that the agency could well become a casualty of the administration's hasty retreat from its aggressive interrogation policy.[21]

In January 2005, just days after the December 30 memo was released, Gonzales faced a torrent of questions at his confirmation hearing by the Senate Judiciary Committee about Abu Ghraib—producing the first full debate in the United States over the morality of torture. Trying to identify those really responsible, Senator Patrick Leahy (Democrat, Vermont) challenged the Bush administration's view of Abu Ghraib as "a case of a few bad apples." Leahy argued that what had happened at the prison was a part of "incidents at U.S. facilities around the world," resulting from decisions made "in the upper reaches of the executive branch." Gonzales deftly ducked the issue, saying the "photos from Abu Ghraib sickened and outraged me and left a stain on our nation's reputation" and insisting that those responsible "are going to be held accountable."[22]

Calling Abu Ghraib "a shameful chapter in American history," Senator Richard Durbin asked if "the decision of the president to call into question the definition of torture" might have "opened up a permissive environment for conduct." Gonzales, dismissing any idea of a signal from the top, argued that "the sexual abuse, the subject of those pictures" was "limited to the night shift on that cell block." In rebuttal, the senator asserted that the Justice Department memos, particularly Bybee's, went "into the Department of Defense, into Guantánamo, and then migrated somehow to interrogation techniques in Abu Ghraib."[23]

When Senator Edward Kennedy asked about the nominee's role in chairing discussions of CIA techniques such as "threat of live burial and waterboarding," Gonzales justified the measures: "this war on terror is a war about information. If we have information, we can defeat the enemy." Kennedy asked repeatedly if the Bybee memo had been given to the CIA. But Gonzales insisted he could no longer recall, adding that this document had now been "rejected" and replaced by the Justice Department memo dated December 30.[24]

Asked by Senator Herb Kohl (Democrat, Wisconsin) whether he had considered the impact of suspending Geneva on "the hearts and minds of the Arab world," Gonzales insisted that the application of the conventions to Al Qaeda "would limit our ability to solicit information from detainees." In his written replies to the senators, Gonzales went even further, stating that the White House had, since 9/11, exempted the CIA from military restrictions on interrogation, in the belief that "certain terrorists had information that might save American lives" and "there was a desire to explore certain methods of questioning these terrorists." And when asked by Durbin why he had solicited Bybee's August 2002 memo if the military was clearly barred from engaging in torture, Gonzales replied: "In this case, the federal criminal prohibition against torture was one that was not clear, and it appeared appropriate to seek legal advice concerning its meaning." When presented with the list of techniques (simulated drowning, stress positions, and sensory deprivation) and asked to comment, Gonzales admitted that some of the activities "might very well be prohibited, either under the torture statute or under other prohibitions, such as, for example, the standards of conduct contained in the Army Field Manual." But he qualified even this response: "Some [methods] might likewise be permissible in specific circumstances, if appropriately limited, depending on the nature of the precise conduct under consideration." He justified the administration's refusal to publicly disclose the rules of interrogation, those techniques either allowed or disallowed, saying such specifics "would provide al Qaeda with a road map concerning the interrogation that captured terrorists can expect to face and would enable al Qaeda to improve its counter-interrogation training to match it." From his replies, the former Justice Department lawyer Martin Lederman concluded that it was now clear the administration had granted the CIA an exemption from military restraints, allowing it to use methods abroad that would be deemed illegal at home. "It's notable," Lederman explained, "that Gonzales is not willing to tell the senators or anyone else just what techniques the CIA has actually been authorized to use."[25]

Throughout these hearings, the senators persisted in a wide-ranging, relentless critique of Bybee's August 2002 memo, exploring both its flawed legal foundations and its disturbing constitutional implications. In a surprisingly sharp attack, Senator Lindsey Graham (Republican, South Carolina), also a reserve judge advocate in the Air Force, faulted Bybee's opinion for, first, sacrificing "the moral high ground" and, second, putting soldiers at risk of prosecution because "the techniques being espoused in the memo" violated the Uniform Code of Military Justice, which "makes it a crime for a member of our uniform forces to abuse a detainee." Working from Bybee's guidelines, the Defense Department had, Graham said, drawn up thirty-five possible interrogation techniques, prompting strong objections from the Army and Navy judge advocates, who argued that these methods were "totally inconsistent" with the Uniform Code, under which it is "a crime to assault a detainee." Not only had Bybee ignored military law, he had, as Senator Kennedy pointed out, grounded much of his memo's definitions of pain on "federal statutes that define emergency medical conditions for . . . Medicaid," which "is completely unrelated to the whole question [of] torture." And in his expansive interpretation of executive power, Bybee had, as Senator Durbin observed, ignored the landmark *Youngstown* Supreme Court decision that had established, definitively, that the president cannot act in defiance of the law.[26]

In answer to these criticisms, Gonzales could only repeat, over and over, that the Bybee memo "had been withdrawn"; "it has been rejected"; "I categorically reject it"; "it is no longer the position of the executive branch"; and "that analysis has been rejected and I consider it rejected." To this string of denials, Senator Kennedy noted, with withering precision, that "for a two-year period when it was in effect, you didn't object to it." Another lawyer on the committee, Senator Russell Feingold (Democrat, Wisconsin), pointed out that Bybee's assertion that "the president, as commander in chief, may authorize interrogations that violate the criminal laws" had not, in fact, been repudiated in the replacement memo. Beneath his lawyerly circumlocution, Gonzales had, in essence, defended the right to "extreme" interrogation techniques in defiance of the Geneva Conventions and, most important, refused to recuse himself from any future investigation of interrogation abuses, opening the possibility that he would, as attorney general, become a force for impunity. Despite the sharp criticisms and the nominee's many evasions, the Judiciary Committee's Republican majority approved the Gonzales nomination and sent it to the full Senate, which confirmed him by a party-line vote, 60 to 36—the closest margin for any attorney general since 1925.[27]

Then, six months later, the Bush administration nominated Gonzales's former White House deputy counsel, Timothy Flanigan, to join him at Justice in the number-two slot. In his July 2005 confirmation hearings, the Senate Judiciary Committee zeroed in on the nominee's role in framing the executive's torture policy. Asked his opinion of Bybee's August 2002 memo, Flanigan admitted that its assertion of executive power was "sort of sophomoric." He stated that "the president is never above the law," adding that he viewed torture as "abhorrent." Even so, critics were not mollified. The American Civil Liberties Union said that Flanigan's nomination to join Gonzales would mean "the nation's top two law enforcement officials, . . . normally . . . responsible for prosecuting any wrongdoing, will be men who are up to their eyeballs in this scandal—a critique shared by senators whose relentless probing finally forced Flanigan to withdraw."[28]

More broadly within Congress, administration allies fought hard against an independent inquiry into the abuse of detainees and against legislative restrictions on interrogation. In December 2004, the Senate voted 96 to 2 to approve a ban on torture and inhumane treatment of detainees by all intelligence agencies. But the White House forced deletion of this torture ban through "intense, closed door negotiations." The Republican majority, at the behest of the executive branch, further blocked two attempts in the Senate to outlaw cruel CIA interrogation and a third in the House to ban rendition.[29] In March 2005, when the deputy chair of the Senate Intelligence Committee, Senator John D. Rockefeller IV (Democrat, West Virginia), pressed for the "full facts" about the "detention, interrogation and rendition authority," the committee chair, Senator Pat Roberts (Republican, Kansas), blocked any such inquiry.[30] And when the ACLU and retired military officers called for an independent inquiry, Attorney General Gonzales barred the move as "premature" in light of ongoing inquiries inside his department—in effect, using his new office to block an investigation of his earlier actions as White House counsel, a clear conflict of interest.[31]

Adding to the administration's attempt at impunity, in February 2005 Vice Admiral Albert T. Church III delivered the sixth and last of the major military inquiries into Abu Ghraib, minimizing abuse and refusing to blame any senior officers. At Guantánamo, the admiral said, there were "only three cases of closed, substantiated interrogation-related abuse" among 24,000 interrogations. And the "pictured abuses at Abu Ghraib" were not found in any other U.S. facility. "The need for intelligence in the post-9/11 world, and our enemies' ability to resist interrogation," he concluded, "have caused our senior policy makers and military commanders to reevaluate traditional U.S. interrogation methods. . . . [T]his search has always been conducted within the confines of our armed forces' obligation to treat detainees humanely." When the admiral appeared before Congress, Senator James Talent (Republican, Missouri) praised his report and chastised critics for being "unduly sensitive to some of the interrogation techniques" needed to save American lives from bombings in Iraq: "If our guys want to poke somebody in the chest to get the name of a bomb maker so that they can save the lives of Americans, I'm for it. And, if the Department of Defense wants to investigate me for that, and . . . call me inhumane, fine." At about the same time, the Army announced that its internal investigation, done at the direction of the Senate, had exonerated General Barbara G. Fast, the intelligence chief for Iraq from July 2003 to June 2004. Affirming the exoneration, Admiral Church explained, "She really was not particularly engaged in the interrogation techniques." In a sharply worded editorial, the New York Times called the admiral's findings a "whitewash . . . typical of the reports issued by the Bush administration" and seconded the call by the American Bar Association for an independent, bipartisan commission to investigate the nation's interrogation policies.[32]

While General Fast was formally absolved of any responsibility for abuses and murders in Iraq, her low-ranking interrogators were prosecuted within the military justice system. By March 2005, the second anniversary of the occupation of Iraq, 8 ordinary soldiers had been convicted of crimes related to deaths in custody and 13 more were awaiting courts-martial for murder. In addition, after 360 criminal investigations for abusing prisoners in Iraq and Afghanistan, 130 soldiers had been "disciplined."[33] In its first official tally, the Army reported that 27 detainees had been killed in U.S. custody in Afghanistan and Iraq, and that 21 soldiers faced charges in connection with those deaths. Another 17 soldiers, the Army said, would not face trial, for want of evidence. Adding the three detainee deaths investigated by the Navy and four more involving the CIA would bring the official toll for deaths in custody to well over 30. Of this total, there was only one death at Abu Ghraib, showing, in the words of the *New York Times,* "how broadly the most violent abuses extended . . . contradicting early impressions that the wrongdoing was confined to a handful of military police on the prison's night shift."[34]

Despite these disturbing numbers, every senior officer investigated to date, save one, has been exculpated. "The higher up the [courts-martial] go, the more problems they have with people leading to the Pentagon," said Harvey Volzer, lawyer for one of the accused soldiers. "Pappas gives them Sanchez, and they don't want that. Sanchez can give them Rumsfeld, and they don't want that. Rumsfeld can lead to Bush and Gonzales, and they definitely don't want that." Indeed, after interviewing soldiers involved, Scott Horton of the New York City Bar Association concluded that "the highest profile cases in which the severest sanctions are sought consistently involve those soldiers who . . . permitted photographic evidence of the crimes at Abu Ghraib to become public knowledge." In Horton's view, "it wasn't the abuse of prisoners which was being punished, but the fact that the military, and particularly Rumsfeld, has been embarrassed by these matters becoming public."[35]

Completing the process of impunity, in April 2005 the Army's inspector general, Lieutenant General Stanley E. Green, formally exonerated four of the five senior officers present in Iraq during the Abu Ghraib abuse. Ignoring the earlier Schlesinger and Fay findings that General Sanchez had ordered harsh methods, that his deputy General Walter Wodjakowski was complicit, and that his intelligence chief, General Fast, failed to provide proper advice about interrogation, the Army now pronounced them all blameless. Whatever mistakes they may have made were, in Green's view, understandable in the context of an erupting insurgency and overcrowded prisons. Alone among the senior officers, the Army found General Janis Karpinski, the former chief of military police in Iraq, culpable and punished her by removal from command and demotion to colonel, citing an old charge for shoplifting "a cosmetic item" from a Florida PX. With the exception of two mid-level intelligence officers facing a separate inquiry—Colonel Thomas M. Pappas and Lieutenant Colonel Steve Jordan—the formal investigation cleared all twelve officers criticized in earlier reports and effectively closed the Army's books on command responsibility for abuses.[36] In parallel exculpatory moves, the Pentagon promoted many of these same senior officers—elevating General Wodjakowski to command the Army's infantry school at Fort Benning; General Fast to head the Army's intelligence center at Fort Huachuca; and Colonel Marc Warren, formerly the top military lawyer in Baghdad, to brigadier general. Apart from Karpinski, only General Sanchez remained sidelined with a field command in Germany. By the time this elaborate, year-long process of inquiry and indictment was done, the fact remained that nobody above sergeant had gone to jail for prisoner abuse.[37]

The ACLU dismissed General Green's report as "just another effort to paper over the scandal." Similarly, Human Rights Watch denounced the "wall of impunity" surrounding senior officials "responsible for the larger pattern of abuses" and called for a "genuinely independent investigation" into the "coercive methods" the United States "has repeatedly condemned as barbarity and torture when practiced by others." In response to this controversy, the Army announced plans to issue a new field manual for interrogation, the first revision in thirteen years, barring techniques used at Abu Ghraib such as stress positions and the stripping of prisoners. Ironically, the final regulations, including a 200-page classified adjunct, would be approved by General Fast as commander of the intelligence center. "I've been nervous about this whole process," said a Human Rights Watch official. "The existing manual was clear. It was the exceptions that caused the problems."[38]

As the administration struggled to cover up the scandal, the CIA slowly emerged as a possible scapegoat to protect the White House from the growing storm of criticism. In an article on February 16, 2005, headlined "Officials Say Agency Is Fearful of Blame," the *New York Times* cited current and former "intelligence officials" to report that "CIA lawyers . . . were furious about the decision" in June 2004 "to invalidate the opinion" that the administration had issued two years earlier, in August 2002, authorizing brutal interrogation. When senior officials such as Alberto Gonzales publicly sidestepped any responsibility and the White House repudiated its earlier memos, agency insiders became concerned that "the CIA might be left to bear sole responsibility . . . for the use of harsh techniques." The same sources complained about being forced to bear the cost of indefinite detention of three dozen "aging terrorists whose intelligence value is steadily evaporating." One retired CIA employee told *Newsweek*, "Where's the off button? They asked the White House for direction on how to dispose of these detainees . . . The answer was, 'We'll worry about that later.' Now we don't know what to do with these guys. People keep saying, 'We're not going to shoot them.'" CIA sources seemed almost sentimental about the good old days of pump and dump in Vietnam. Writing in the *New York Times*, retired CIA employee Michael Scheuer said, "All Americans owe a debt of gratitude to the men and women of the agency who executed these presidentially . . . approved operations," and he expressed regret that these heroic agents now faced being "abandoned and prosecuted when the policy makers refuse to defend their own decisions."[39]

At this sensitive juncture, the CIA director Porter Goss made an inadvertent admission to Congress that agency bureaucrats scrambled to correct. "At this time," Goss told the Senate in March 2005, "there are no techniques . . . that are being employed that are in any way against the law or would . . . be considered torture." Asked if he could say the same about tactics used right after 9/11, Goss replied: "I am not able to tell you that." Pressed to elaborate, Goss admitted that in the past there had been "some uncertainty" among CIA interrogators about what methods were allowed. When Senator John McCain (Republican, Arizona) asked about "water boarding," the CIA director would say only that it was "an area of what I will call professional interrogation techniques." The *New York Times* splashed his remarks across page one, describing them as the agency's "admission that at least some of its practices might have crossed the legal limits." The CIA's chief publicist was quick to challenge the paper's claim: "All approved interrogation techniques, both past and present, are lawful and do not constitute torture." Pointing out the contradiction in the CIA position, Human Rights Watch charged that Goss could not deny torture and then describe water boarding as "professional interrogation," since that method, which simulates drowning, is "nothing less than torture in violation of United States and international law."[40]

In the midst of the administration's push for closure on Abu Ghraib, civil society offered some sustained resistance. No longer intimidated by the trauma of 9/11, federal judges, in particular, were increasingly assertive, citing the Constitution and international treaties to challenge the White House's endless detention of alleged terrorists.

In the wake of the Supreme Court's June 2004 decision affirming the right of "enemy combatants" to due process under law, federal courts began to overturn the administration's extreme measures in the war on terror. In August, a U.S. district judge determined that the Geneva Conventions apply to Guantánamo, making the special military courts the Pentagon had cooked up to comply with earlier presidential directives and the Supreme Court suddenly illegal. With Guantánamo now firmly under U.S. law, the administration made plans to reduce its prison population. However, a federal judge barred the repatriation of thirteen Yemeni prisoners in March 2005, accepting pleas from defense lawyers that their clients might face torture at home. In February, moreover, a federal judge in South Carolina, Henry Floyd, had ruled that the dirty-bomb suspect Jose Padilla could no longer be held indefinitely under Bush's designation as an "illegal enemy combatant." According to the judge, continued detention on executive orders alone "would totally eviscerate the limits placed on presidential authority to protect the citizenry's individual liberties." Rather than accept the decision and proceed to trial, Attorney General Gonzales appealed the district court ruling, postponing Padilla's release. Nine months later, the conservative Fourth Circuit of the U.S. Court of Appeals overturned this lower court decision, and affirmed the president's right to detain Padilla; but by then federal prosecutors had dropped the "dirty bomb" accusation and were now pressing lesser charges of plotting to blow up residential gas lines in

Chicago. In response, the *New York Times* insisted that there was no legal basis for the White House "to detain innocent people or brutalize even those who are guilty," and called for an independent investigation since "healing the wounds of the prison camps is vital to American values."[41]

In striking contrast to its supine response, before the March 2003 invasion of Iraq, to administration assertions that Baghdad was developing weapons of mass destruction, the national press, led by the *Washington Post* and the *New York Times*, simply refused to let the torture issue die. Both papers pressed ahead with independent investigations and probed for incriminating government documents that, when released, were featured in front-page stories beneath banner headlines. In addition to aggressive reportage, editorial opinion became sharply, even stridently critical of the White House attempt to bury the torture scandal with bland assurances and milquetoast military inquiries. "The atrocities that occurred in prisons like Abu Ghraib were," the *New York Times* editorialized on the second anniversary of the Iraq War, "the product of decisions that began at the very top, when the Bush administration decided that Sept. 11 had wiped out its responsibility to abide by the rules, including the Geneva Conventions and the American Constitution."[42]

Journalists also began investigating the CIA's rendition program, uncovering cases of serious abuse that, in sum, showed the human cost of this clandestine process. In these exposés, the press relied frequently upon foreign sources, courts, and prosecutors, who were determined in their defense of civil liberties. In the first of these articles, the *New York Times* told the story of a Lebanese-born German national, Khaled el-Masri, who had been pulled off a bus at the Macedonia–Serbia border in late 2003. After three weeks of interrogation, handcuffed in a Skopje motel, el-Masri, an ordinary German car salesman on holiday, was bundled onto a CIA aircraft and flown to Kabul on January 25, 2004. There he was confined for four months in a prison called the "salt pit" and, el-Masri said, beaten, shackled, and photographed naked. Upon learning that he had been mistakenly identified, national security adviser Condoleezza Rice personally intervened and he was released, in Albania, on May 29. Confirming his story, *Newsweek* magazine uncovered flight plans for a Boeing 737 aircraft operated by the CIA's "top-secret global charter servicing clandestine interrogation facilities," with movements from Skopje to Kabul that coincided with el-Masri's claims. Moreover, a team of German prosecutors, led by Martin Hofmann in Munich, interviewed el-Masri for two days and concluded that the story of his abduction was credible. When, in April 2005, NBC television news finally revealed Rice's role, el-Masri expressed hope that "America will in the future respect the rights of people."[43]

In a parallel case that began to reveal a pattern, the *New York Times* reported, in February 2005, that an Australian national, Mamdouh Habib, had been taken off a bus in Pakistan right after 9/11 and beaten by local interrogators, with Americans present, before being shipped to Cairo as part of the CIA's rendition program. There, Egyptian interrogators subjected him to a mix of psychological and physical torture, threatening his family and beating him with sticks while suspending him from the ceiling. He made several confessions, which he later claimed were false. After six months in Egypt, he was shipped to Bagram for a week of interrogation with sexual harassment and electric shock. Then he was flown to Guantánamo for more brutal questioning. When the *Washington Post* published an article about his agony, he was quickly released, without charges or explanation, and in January 2005 rejoined his family in Australia after three years of detention.[44]

Similarly, Bob Herbert wrote a series of columns for the *New York Times* describing, in stark detail, how a Canadian engineer, Maher Arar, was transiting through New York's John F. Kennedy airport in September 2002, homeward bound from vacation, when he was shackled, loaded onto a CIA-chartered Gulfstream III jet, and, at 9:36 A.M. on October 8, flown direct to Amman, Jordan. Ten hours later, he was in a Syrian prison, locked in an underground cell, where he remained for a year being beaten and whipped so savagely that he confessed to anything his tormentors suggested. At his release in October 2003, through the efforts of the Canadian government, the Syrian ambassador to Washington stated there was no evidence linking him to terrorism. In this rendition, Washington was aware, in the words of the State Department, that Syrian security's "torture methods include electrical shocks; pulling out fingernails; the forced insertion of objects into the rectum; beatings . . ." Interviewed back home in Ottawa two years after his release, Arar said: "I still have nightmares about being in Syria, being beaten, being in jail. They feel very real. When I wake up, I feel very relieved to find myself in my room." When Arar tried to sue, Washington, in an extraordinary move, blocked the litigation by claiming that a trial would damage the "national security interests of the United States."[45]

Most of these hundred-plus renditions were carried out by local security services, but the CIA conducted several itself with tragicomic results. When Sweden agreed to expel two Egyptian terrorism suspects in December 2001, it asked for U.S. assistance in arranging a charter flight. Instead of a pilot in jacket and tie, the agency sent in a full paramilitary team that arrived "commando-style, in semi-opaque masks," and, said one former CIA official, "went through the standard drill as if they were arresting Khalid Sheik Mohammed," blowing any semblance of secrecy. At Stockholm's airport, half a dozen agents bundled the two Egyptians, Muhammad al-Zery and Ahmed Agiza, into orange jumpsuits, locked them in leg irons, and loaded them on a Gulfstream V jet for the flight to Cairo. There both suspects were "tortured with electrical charges to their genitals." Reported by local Swedish television, this dismal display forced an official, very hostile, government inquiry. A parliamentary investigation found that the Swedish authorities had "secretly invited the CIA to assist" in the rendition, angering many citizens and prompting police to swear off any further cooperation with U.S. intelligence. "In the future we will use Swedish laws, Swedish measures of force and Swedish military aviation when deporting terrorists," said the director of the country's Security Police, Klas Bergenstrand, in March 2005.[46]

Of all these renditions, just one case, that of an Egyptian cleric snatched from the streets of Milan, has come before the courts to provide the press with a revealing window into the process. On February 8, 2003, a team of thirteen CIA paramilitary operatives from the Special Activities Division assembled in Milan, checking into five-star hotels like the Hilton and the Galia, where they racked up credit-card bills of $144,984 for the nine-day operation. Their target was Hassan

Mustafa Osama Nasr, forty-two, a local imam who had been under surveillance by Italian police for possible Al Qaeda ties since his arrival from Albania six years before. In Washington, Nasr had become a target because of his supposed involvement in some suspected "plotting" against the U.S. embassy in Rome. After monitoring his movements, this not-so-secret CIA team surrounded the imam on Milan's Via Guerzoni as he approached the mosque for noon prayers on February 17. They demanded identification, sprayed chemicals in his face, and forced him into a white van which roared off, leaving stunned witnesses to call the police. As the van sped north to the U.S. air base at Aviano, the agents chattered on their cell phones, placing several calls to northern Virginia, including one to CIA headquarters at Langley. Within hours, Nasr was bound for Egypt, first on an Air Force Learjet to Ramstein, Germany, and from there to Cairo on a Gulfstream IV jet under CIA lease from Boston Red Sox owner Philip H. Morse.[47]

Fourteen months later, Nasr emerged from Egyptian prisons hobbling and deaf in one ear from torture that had included beatings and electric shocks. Apparently angered at the unauthorized disruption of their own operations, Italian security cooperated with the Milan courts in an investigation that led to an unprecedented indictment of the thirteen CIA men and a diplomatic uproar over infringement of Italian sovereignty. In their defense, several of the CIA men told the *Washington Post* that their Rome station chief had briefed his counterpart at Sismi, Italy's intelligence service. But one admitted the station chief was eager "to have a notch in his belt," and thus skirted correct protocol which should have been "head of service to the head of service"— Director George Tenet contacting Sismi's General Nicolo Pollari.[48]

Capping this string of disturbing stories, the *New York Times* reported in early March 2005 that the renditions were carried out by the CIA at the behest of President Bush, who had signed a "still-classified Directive" only days after the 9/11 attacks. In an editorial headlined "Torture by Proxy," the *Times* condemned the Bush administration's practice of "putting prisoners in the hands of outlaw regimes for the specific purpose of having someone else torture them." In an investigation of the White House alliance with Uzbekistan's brutal Karimov regime, the paper found that the CIA had sent dozens of detainees to

Tashkent on secret weekly flights for interrogation by local security services that routinely pulled out fingernails, boiled body parts, and administered electroshock to genitalia. So notorious were these practices that the previous July the British ambassador to Tashkent, Craig Murray, had written his Foreign Office, charging the CIA with violations of the UN ban on torture. He recommended that the UK "should cease all cooperation with the Uzbek security services—they are beyond the pale." Under the pressure of the war on terror, however, London ignored the advice, just as Washington took no notice of a formal State Department finding in February 2005 about Uzbekistan that "torture was common in prisons, pretrial facilities, and local police and security service precincts."[49]

In these and similar exposés, much of the media's information was taken from civil liberties groups that had filed lawsuits to extract documents from a reluctant government. In particular, Human Rights Watch added to the torrent of revelations by obtaining copies of the Army's investigation into deaths at the Bagram Collection Point, in Afghanistan.[50] Significantly, these Army documents indicated that Bagram's chief military intelligence officer, Captain Wood, had been evasive, saying that prisoners were chained standing to protect interrogators when, in fact, the method was used "to inflict pain and sleep deprivation." Through its own inquiries, Human Rights Watch found that Afghan detainees "had experienced beatings, prolonged sleep and sensory deprivation, forced nakedness and humiliation." Similarly, in April 2005, the UN human rights commission's expert for Afghanistan, Professor M. Cherif Bassiouni of DePaul University Law School, reported that U.S. prisons in Afghanistan violated the law "by engaging in arbitrary arrests, . . . and committing abusive practices, including torture." Dismissed from his UN post the day after he released this report, Bassiouni was pessimistic about future treatment of detainees. "My guess is that torture will go down at the U.S. facilities," he said, "but what will go up is torture at the Afghan facilities. It's the usual shell game."[51]

The ACLU also filed a succession of lawsuits that, by early 2005, began to bear fruit. In March, this venerable civil liberties group won the release of 1,200 pages of documents relating to prisoner abuse. In one document, dated January 2004, an Army investigation of the 311th Military Intelligence Battalion, at Mosul, Iraq, found evidence that "MI personnel and/or translators engaged in physical torture of detainees." As the ACLU lawyer Amrit Singh explained, these documents show that "torture and abuse of detainees was routine and was considered acceptable practice by U.S. soldiers."[52]

Amid the onslaught of criticism, the White House scrambled for damage control. On March 10, 2005, the administration leaked news of strict military guidelines for interrogation in Iraq, barring the use of muzzled dogs and increasing command responsibility. Responding to press revelations about rendition, President Bush defended this extralegal policy: "We protect our people and our friends from attack" by sending suspects "back to their country of origin with the promise that they won't be tortured." He added, "this country does not believe in torture," but then qualified that remark: "We do believe in protecting ourselves." The president's Commission on Intelligence Capabilities, formed to investigate intelligence failure over Iraq's weapons of mass destruction, echoed the contradictory mix of aggression and assurance: "The Attorney General personally approves any interrogation techniques . . . that go beyond openly published U.S. government interrogation practices." And when "special practices are allowed in extraordinary cases of dire emergency," then, the commission suggested, "those procedures should require permission from sufficiently high-level officials to ensure compliance with overall guidelines."[53] Even after Abu Ghraib, the White House seemed to say, the United States, when confronted with serious threats such as a terrorist with a ticking bomb, would use "special practices . . . in extraordinary cases"—in a word, torture.

Academic pundits, although advocating torture with near unanimity after 9/11, have been conflicted since reports of abuse started emerging from the front lines of the war on terror. Just a few weeks before CBS first broadcast the Abu Ghraib photos, in April 2004, Harvard's Michael Ignatieff, writing in the *New York Times Magazine*, advocated "permissible duress" as a justification for torture, echoing his colleague Alan Dershowitz. Arguing, in effect, for legalization of CIA psychological torture, Ignatieff called for legislation to permit "forms of sleep deprivation that do not result in lasting harm to mental or physical health, together with disinformation and disorientation (like keeping prisoners in hoods) that would produce stress."[54] But just weeks after the prison photos were leaked, he reversed his position, in sharply critical words that seem almost self-referential: "Enthralled by narcissism and deluded by servility, American lawyers forgot their own constitution and its peremptory prohibition of cruel and unusual punishment." At Abu Ghraib, Ignatieff continued, "America paid the price for American exceptionalism, the idea that America is too noble, too special, too great to actually obey international treaties like the Torture Convention."[55]

By contrast, Dershowitz remained resolute in his public campaign for court-ordered torture. Even after the broadcast of the Abu Ghraib photos, Dershowitz published an essay that dismissed his many critics and redoubled his advocacy of formal "torture warrants" to end what he called torture "being done below the radar screen, without political accountability, and indeed with plausible deniability." If the current trend persists, the United States will, he says, move to "a smug, self-satisfied willingness to condemn torture openly, while at the same time encouraging its secret use in extreme cases."[56]

Though his position might seem extreme, even idiosyncratic, there was surprisingly widespread advocacy of state-sanctioned torture among American academics. In June 2004, just weeks after the Abu Ghraib scandal broke, the Harvard Law School faculty, including Dershowitz, circulated a petition signed by 481 prominent professors of law and political science at 110 top universities nationwide, condemning "abuses practiced on detainees under American control." But even in this cry of conscience, these professor-petitioners called for serious consideration of "a coercive interrogation policy . . . made within the strict confines of a democratic process." In effect, America's leading academics were asking citizens to set aside two centuries of Enlightenment principles and think seriously about legalizing torture.[57]

Simultaneously, another group of Harvard faculty lobbied Congress to enact legislation with provisions akin to Dershowitz's "torture warrants." With funding from Homeland Security, a joint project by the law school and the Kennedy School of Government drew up a code for coercive interrogation, with rules, oversight, and accountability. The final recommendations, drafted by law professor Philip B. Heymann, went to Congress, where, in early 2005, they attracted support from the ranking Democrat on the House Intelligence Committee, Representative Jane Harman. "If you're serious about trying to get information in advance of an attack," she told a *New York Times* reporter, "interrogation has to be one of the main tools. I'm O.K. with it not being pretty." But furious opposition from human rights groups and civil liberties concerns in Congress killed this attempt at legalizing torture.[58]

Such advocacy notwithstanding, a surprisingly diverse range of voices now rose to challenge the White House's policy on detainees, breaking the public climate of timid compliance. After the embers of anger over Abu Ghraib were ultimately smothered in official paper, conditions at Guantánamo Bay became the spark for a new firestorm— this time focused not on the physical abuse evident in the Abu Ghraib photos, but on psychological techniques, sometimes called "torture lite." In May 2005, *Newsweek* reported that a Guantánamo guard had flushed a Koran down the toilet, setting off fiery demonstrations across the Muslim world that left seventeen dead in Afghanistan. Although the magazine was forced to retract this story, later U.S. military investigations confirmed that guards had, in five instances, treated the Koran disrespectfully. As the violence finally burned itself out, Afghanistan's prime minister, Hamid Kharzai, demanded, during a state visit to Washington, return of all Afghan prisoners from Guantánamo, a request President Bush dismissed as impractical.[59]

Also in May, the head of Amnesty International in London, Irene Khan, prompted a more considered debate when she released the group's annual report, which said that "Guantánamo has become the gulag of our times." In Washington, the director of Amnesty USA, William F. Schulz, called for President Bush "to prove he is not covering up the misdeeds of . . . political cronies who designed and authorized these nefarious interrogation policies." Rumsfeld called Amnesty's comments "reprehensible"; President Bush branded them "absurd"; Vice President Cheney was "offended." The controversy thrust Amnesty into the national spotlight, making Schulz a media presence everywhere, from conservative Fox Television News to centrist National Public Radio.[60] Speaking with host Neal Conan on NPR's *Talk of the Nation*, Schulz brought Amnesty's perspective to the attention of ordinary Americans:

> CONAN: We're discussing the war of words between Amnesty International and the Bush administration. . . . Peter's with us from Phoenix, Arizona.
>
> PETER (CALLER): Yeah. Hi there. I think my main point is that this is a different kind of war than we've fought in the past, and I really do think that the intelligence information gathering has been very useful . . . So I'm not . . . saying they're doing the right thing by torturing prisoners and so forth, but, you know, I think . . . if we didn't have a place . . . to put people like Guantánamo . . . there'd be a lot more casualties in the field.
>
> CONAN: And, William Schulz, the intelligence aspect is one thing that administration supporters come back to, that these people may have information about deeds yet to come.
>
> MR. SCHULZ: Well, Neal, but we know from the Army Field Manual, we know from FBI manuals about interrogation that, in fact, you can get a great deal of information far more productively without abusing or torturing people than you can by doing so.[61]

Despite the fears of ordinary Americans like Peter from Phoenix, critics escalated their attacks on conditions at Guantánamo Bay. "Shut it down. Just shut it down," wrote *New York Times* columnist Thomas L. Friedman with uncommon boldness. "Just shut it down and then plow it under. It has become worse than an embarrassment. I am convinced that more Americans are dying and will die if we keep the Gitmo prison open than if we shut it down." After sampling comments from newspapers worldwide, he concluded: "Guantánamo Bay is becoming the anti-Statue of Liberty." Echoing its columnist's call, a forceful *Times* editorial branded Guantánamo a "national shame" and "a highly effective recruiting tool for Islamic radicals, including future terrorists." As the White House message machine stirred to crush this criticism, Vice President Cheney told Fox News that the 525 remaining Guantánamo detainees are "bad people." Rumsfeld branded them all "determined killers," arguing that "no detention facility in the history of warfare has been more transparent" than Guantánamo. Then, in a dramatic coda, two former presidents added their voices to the calls for Guantánamo's closure. Jimmy Carter lamented that the prison had become a "blow to our reputation as a champion of human rights." And Bill Clinton called Guantánamo "inimical to a free society," saying "it either needs to be closed down or cleaned up."[62]

The controversy moved to Congress where the Senate Judiciary Committee heard evidence from a Navy defense attorney, Lieutenant Commander Charles D. Swift, that Guantánamo's military tribunal was biased. The lawyer recalled the first meeting with his client, Mr. Hamdan, who had "already been in solitary confinement for . . . 45 days . . . in a windowless room" and was showing signs of "extreme mental stress." Even so, the military's chief prosecutor made it clear that Swift could only see his client "if he agreed that we were going to plead guilty to something." Backed by documents from his superiors, Swift showed that due process was being bent to a predetermined outcome, rebutting administration claims of impartial justice. This military lawyer added that any trial, whether military or civil, "says as much about the society that holds the trial as it does about the individual before it," prompting the *New York Times,* in a June 2005 editorial, to call his testimony "courageous." The paper concluded that Guantánamo has "done immense harm to the nation's image and increased the risk to every American in uniform."[63]

Indeed, little more than a month later, the paper published e-mails from two senior Guantánamo prosecutors charging that the military tribunal, as it prepared for its first trials in early 2004, had been "secretly arranged" to assure convictions. In a confidential message of March 15, 2004, one prosecutor, Captain John Carr of the Air Force, complained to his superior that their office was preparing to "prosecute fairly low-level accused in a process that appears to be rigged." Above all, Carr charged that evidence about brutalization of one of the first four defendants had either been lost or withheld. The prosecution team, he said, had stated, falsely, that it held no evidence of the torture of a defendant,

Ali Hamza Ahmed Sulayman al-Bahlul of Yemen, when in fact it had misplaced his statement to the FBI that "he had been tortured and abused." In a similar message, another prosecutor, Major Robert Preston of the Air Force, said that proceeding with the trials would be "a severe threat to the reputation of the military justice system and even a fraud on the American people." But Colonel Frederick L. Borch, superior officer to both prosecutors, branded the complaints "monstrous lies" and, after a pro-forma investigation, the trials had proceeded as planned in August until stopped by federal court order in November.[64]

Parallel inquiries into the compromised role of medical personnel added to the sinking sense of an ethical miasma at Guantánamo Bay. One military interrogator, describing the role of the Behavioral Science Consultation Teams in detainee interrogation, told the *New York Times* that "their purpose was to help us break them." After similar interviews, two Georgetown University lawyers, writing in the prestigious *New England Journal of Medicine,* found that psychiatrists and psychologists "have been part of a strategy that employs extreme stress, combined with behavior-shaping rewards, to extract actionable intelligence from resistant captives." Since August 2002, moreover, the Southern Command had ordered medical personnel to "convey any information . . . obtained from detainees in the course of treatment to non-medical military or other United States personnel," meaning CIA operatives. Indeed, former military interrogators told the *Times* that doctors, either psychologists or psychiatrists, had given them information from prisoner medical files and advised them how to play upon "a detainee's fears and longings to increase distress," including one prisoner's "fear of the dark" and another's "longing for his mother." Following General Miller's original guidelines, the first BSCT psychologist, Major John Leso, had "prepared psychological profiles for use by interrogators . . . sat in on some interrogations, observed others from behind one-way mirrors, and offered feedback to interrogators." Instead of treating patients, these mental-health professionals had joined the guards to become, in the words of the *New England Journal of Medicine,* "part of Guantánamo's surveillance network." As the controversy continued, the assistant secretary of defense for health matters, Dr. William Winkenwerder Jr., claimed that Defense Department rules allowed doctors to assist lawful interrogations and called press criticism of their role "an outrageous distortion." A senior Pentagon spokesman, Bryan Whitman, insisted that doctors advising interrogators were "behavioral scientists" exempt from "ethics strictures."[65]

But many psychiatrists unreservedly rejected the Pentagon's logic. In condemning the practices at Guantánamo as a clear ethical violation, these doctors cited the American Medical Association's advice to "diligently guard against exploiting information furnished by the patient," to "release confidential information only with the authorization of the patient," and, finally, to avoid evaluating "any person charged with criminal acts prior to access to. . . . legal counsel."[66] The AMA's guidelines are, of course, applications of broader ethical principles—from the ancient Hippocratic oath to do no harm, all the way to the World Medical Association's 1975 ban on participation in "torture or other forms of cruel, inhuman or degrading procedures," and the UN's 1982 Principles of Medical Ethics prohibiting any physician contact with prisoners "which is not solely to evaluate, protect or improve their physical and mental health."[67]

By contrast, the American Psychological Association (APA), reflecting its long involvement in military research and CIA behavioral experiments, claimed that its members were not barred from "national security endeavors." In fact, the APA's code of ethics has stricter, more specific standards for the treatment of laboratory animals than for human subjects such as the Guantánamo detainees. In response to this crisis of ethics, the APA formed a special task force, including military psychologists, which ultimately rejected the Pentagon's proposition that Guantánamo practitioners were ethically exempt, and insisted that "psychologists do not engage in, direct, support, facilitate, or offer training in torture or other cruel, inhuman, or degrading treatment." But this APA conclusion, released in June 2005, failed to bar members from military interrogations outright, saying, simply and vaguely, that they should be "mindful of factors unique to these roles . . . that require special ethical consideration." The task force also refused to recommend that members be bound by "international standards of human rights," neglected to specify their obligations to detainees, and even recommended research to "enhance the efficacy . . . of psychological science . . . to national security," including the "effectiveness of information-gathering techniques."[68]

The military itself was equally conflicted over the proper role of medical professionals during interrogation. In a Pentagon survey of detainee medical care, released in July 2005, Major General Lester Martinez-Lopez, who led the review, recommended the Army stop using psychiatrists and physicians to assist in interrogation, faulting the lack of clear guidelines for the BSCT teams. Only senior psychologists should, he said, work with the teams to insure "safe, legal, ethical and effective interrogation and detainee operations." Rejecting these recommmendations, his superior, Lieutenant General Kevin C. Kiley, the Army's surgeon general, said they found "no evidence of systemic problems in detainee medical care," praised the military's worldwide treatment for detainees, and deferred assessment of the BSCT teams to "more studies." In defense of his position that the role of these behavioral teams is "safe, legal and ethical," Kiley cited the APA task force report, noting that it reminded members to maintain "an ethical view of their duties. But it doesn't prohibit them from assisting in interrogations."[69]

Just as the Pentagon was considering the role of medical professionals, Lieutenant General Randall M. Schmidt appeared before the Senate Armed Services Committee, testifying about his investigation into methods used at Guantánamo—particularly the elusive problem of their interpretation. The treatment of the general prison population was, the general insisted, "safe, secure and humane." The case of the camp's star prisoner, Mohamed al-Kahtani, "the twentieth hijacker," was, however, more complex. Faced with the subjectivity of assessing psychological pain, Schmidt, like Lord Parker, found the "lines were hard to define" in distinguishing the degrees of abuse. The standards for physical "torture" were, he said, clear, but "anything else beyond that was fairly vague"—adding that "something might be degrading but not necessarily torture. And . . . it may be humiliating, but it may not be torture." On balance, the general "felt that the cumulative effect of simultaneous applications of numerous authorized techniques had an abusive and degrading impact on the detainee." But "this treatment did not rise to the level of being inhumane treatment," and certainly "no torture occurred." Even so, the task force recommended that camp commander General Geoffrey Miller be "admonished" for the treatment of al-Kahtani because the general "failed to monitor the interrogation and exercise commander discretion by placing limits on the application of . . . authorized techniques." Moreover, Miller seemed guilty of what might be politely styled inconsistency, telling the task force he had been "unaware of the creative approaches . . . in the interrogation," when in fact he had earlier advised Southern Command that he had personally "approved the interrogation plan" and was enforcing its application "relentlessly." But the investigators' recommendation for Miller's reprimand was overruled by the Southern Command chief, General Bantz J. Craddock, who had once been Rumsfeld's military aide.[70]

In response to the rising tide of revelation, the Republican majority of the Senate Armed Services Committee defended military treatment of detainees and denied that the psychological techniques were anything akin to torture. Dismissing these hearings into alleged abuse as a waste of time, Senator James M. Inhofe (Republican, Oklahoma) insisted "we have nothing to be ashamed of," and rued the damage we are "doing to our war effort by parading these relatively minor infractions before the press and the world again and again and again." Similarly, Senator Pat Roberts remarked that we do not "need to concentrate on three misdemeanors out of 24,000 investigations." After attacking Senator Edward M. Kennedy (Democrat, Massachusetts) for criticizing U.S. treatment of detainees, Senator Jeff Sessions (Republican, Alabama) asked rhetorically if any Guantánamo prisoner "suffered a broken bone or serious permanent injury."[71]

After weeks of intense, often partisan debate over Guantánamo, a half-dozen Republican senators broke ranks with the Bush administration to introduce motions barring any inhumane treatment of military prisoners. Dissatisfied with the Pentagon's refusal to punish responsible senior officers, leading Republicans on the Senate Armed Services Committee—Lindsey Graham (South Carolina), John McCain (Arizona), and John Warner (Virginia)—began lobbying colleagues for legislation to limit executive authority over detainee interrogation. As the White House launched an aggressive effort to quash this initiative, Vice President Cheney met the dissidents for a confrontational thirty minutes, arguing they would weaken the president's ability to defend America against terrorists. Nonetheless, speaking to the Senate on July 25, 2005, McCain, himself a victim of torture for five years as a POW in Hanoi, moved amendments to the massive $442 billion defense appropriation that would require registration of all foreign prisoners with the International Red Cross "to eliminate the problem of 'ghost detainees' we faced in Abu Ghraib prison"; "establish the Army Field Manual as the uniform standard for interrogation" of all prisoners, except those held by the CIA; and bar any cruel or unusual punishment. Warning "we must never simply fight evil with evil," the senator insisted that "we hold ourselves to humane standards of treatment of people no matter how evil or terrible they may be." And, McCain concluded, the costs of our deviation from this principle have been high: "I would argue the pictures, terrible pictures from Abu Ghraib, harmed us not only in the Arab world, . . . but . . . also harmed us dramatically amongst friendly nations, the Europeans, many of our allies." During the floor debate, Senator Sessions, a fellow Republican, opposed the motion, calling the detainees "terrorists," not prisoners of war. But McCain insisted that the issue "is not about who *they* are. It's about who *we* are."[72]

In a strong statement of support for McCain, eleven retired military leaders, including the former chief of the U.S. Central Command, General Joseph Hoar, urged passage of the legislation. "The abuse of prisoners," they wrote, "hurts America's cause in the war on terror, endangers U.S. service members who might be captured by the enemy, and is anathema to the values Americans have held dear for generations." With at least four of his fellow Republicans in open revolt, Senate majority leader Bill Frist lacked the votes to pass the defense appropriation and was forced to postpone its consideration until after the August recess. When the Senate reconvened, McCain delivered an impassioned plea for passage of the amendments, invoking his experience as a POW in Vietnam: "Many of my comrades were subjected to very cruel . . . treatment, a few of them even unto death. But everyone of us—every single one of us— . . . took strength from the belief that we were different from our enemies." Despite a threatened White House veto and a "fierce debate," the Senate voted 90 to 9, including

46 Republicans, to ban "cruel, inhuman or degrading treatment" of anyone in U.S. custody—a stunning repudiation of Bush's interrogation policy. Countering with a bid to legalize torture, the vice president and CIA director then met McCain to urge an exemption for the agency in "clandestine counterterrorism operations conducted abroad." But the senator refused, leaving battle lines clearly drawn.[73]

Throughout these months of heated discussion, the American public, its government, and its media, even as they immersed themselves in Guantánamo's sordid details, persistently failed to examine these psychological interrogation tactics closely and critically to realize that they are, in fact, torture. Indeed, the CIA's psychological techniques have become so standardized within the intelligence community that even military interrogators no longer seem aware that many of their basic methods violate the Geneva and UN conventions.[74] Also overlooked was the fact that Guantánamo's integration of psychologists into routine interrogation perfected the CIA's paradigm, moving beyong a broad-spectrum attack on human senses, sight and sound, to a customized assault on individual phobias or cultural norms, sexual and religious.

Driving this impassioned debate over Guantánamo were very different views about the fundamental nature of torture. Some conservatives argued, forcefully, that torture is an effective and thus necessary means to extract the information that America needs to track down Al Qaeda's top terrorists. Indeed, more than a year after the Abu Ghraib scandal broke, many interrogation practices that U.S. military lawyers had branded "repugnant" persisted. Moreover, the Bush White House was battling the courts to preserve its extreme vision of executive prerogatives—the right to detain foreign combatants endlessly and to prosecute them "without judicial oversight, under ever-changing rules."[75]

Liberals countered, much more reticently, that torture is not only illegal but also damaging to America's moral leadership in this troubled world. Unwittingly, liberal and moderate critics weakened their case by failing to challenge the conservative argument on its own terms, leaving its central contention about torture's extraordinary efficacy both unexamined and unanswered.

6

THE QUESTION OF TORTURE

AS THE WAR on terror approached its fifth year, the question of torture moved from the margins of American consciousness to become, in many ways, the dominant political issue of the day—no longer a mere scandal but a moral touchstone for divergent visions of the Republic. Those willing to tolerate torture as a necessary excess in defense of democracy argued, at least by implication, that it is an efficient, accurate means for extracting information vital to national security. Critics of White House policy have generally tried to shift the discussion from the narrowly construed belief in efficacy to broader questions of legality and morality. What has yet to be explored, closely and carefully, is whether torture is, in fact, an effective and thus necessary weapon for national security.

There is no longer any need, well into the war on terror, to ask whether the United States has engaged in the systematic torture of suspected terrorists. Both the International Red Cross and the FBI have found, from firsthand observations, that U.S. forces have regularly used methods "tantamount to torture" at both Abu Ghraib and Guantánamo Bay. Even the Army, although denying that the practice is systematic, has found dozens of soldiers, from private to general, either culpable or criminal. But the Bush administration, by blaming those few, lowly bad apples and protecting higher-ups, has created a climate in which coercive interrogation will be allowed to continue into the future. Undeterred by the shame of Abu Ghraib, this White House has, moreover, fought doggedly in the courts and Congress to establish limitless detention and unrestrained interrogation as permanent executive powers in any case of national security.

Americans need, therefore, to begin by disabusing themselves of the notion that the harsh techniques seen at Abu Ghraib are part of the past. Many may take President Bush at his word, thinking that his repeated repudiation of those methods, combined with the unprecedented stream of investigations and trials, means that Washington has rejected torture as a weapon in the war on terror. Although the Bush administration has indeed cultivated such an impression, it seems unsupported by the facts at hand. Let us assay the evidence.

In the months following the release of the Abu Ghraib photos, psychological torture continued, according to eyewitness accounts by the International Red Cross at Guantánamo Bay. And despite the multiple military investigations, one key agency has remained exempt from review and reform—the CIA. While the Army has investigated almost every unit and individual implicated at Abu Ghraib, it has avoided comparable probes of Bagram and Guantánamo Bay, where its soldiers worked closely with the CIA in the torture-interrogation of suspected terrorists. The agency has restricted its own review to an internal investigation and a single criminal prosecution that, more than a year after the scandal, are still in process. While the Army has very publicly rewritten its field manual to bar any repetition of Abu Ghraib, the CIA has announced no changes to its procedures. Administration statements rescinding authorization for extreme measures have avoided mention of a secret Defense Department report of April 4, 2003, which allowed CIA abuse to go on. It thus seems likely that some detainees somewhere in the CIA's global gulag—Afghanistan, Diego Garcia, Guantánamo, or Iraq—are being subjected to interrogation that could only be called torture. And it is equally probable that other detainees continue to be tortured, after rendition by the CIA's charter airlines, in nations notorious for medieval methods—whether Morocco, Egypt, Syria, or Uzbekistan. The question of torture thus remains, for all Americans, an immediate concern, political and moral.

With torture incorporated into America's clandestine arsenal for over fifty years and now chosen as the primary weapon in the war on terror, the time has come to interrogate the logic of its use through a succession of hard questions. Is the selective, surgical approach now used by Washington effective? If not, should the United States employ systematic, mass torture, akin to the Vietnam-era Phoenix program, to defeat the Iraqi insurgency? And if it turns out that torture produces limited gains at high political cost, how can any rational American leader condone and continue this practice?

Is Torture of the Few Effective?

To begin this searching self-examination, we must confront the key question underlying the debate: Is torture justified, in these dangerous times, to assure American security? Those who answer yes often harbor the fears that Alan Dershowitz of Harvard Law School conveys so cleverly in his fable of the captured terrorist who knows the precise location of a ticking bomb in, say, Times Square.[1] And they may well secretly share the same moral response to those same fears that Detective Andy Sipowicz of television's *NYPD Blue* portrays so grippingly in his imaginary Manhattan police station.

By confronting the moral choices entailed in unmasking evildoers, Detective Sipowicz, the Everyman hero of ABC-Television's long-running series *NYPD Blue*, became a fixture in popular culture, resolving the ambiguities of interrogation for ordinary Americans. Almost every week, for 261 episodes over twelve seasons, Sipowicz went "face to face with pure evil," a murderer, a rapist, or a kidnapper, in his station house "interrogation room." Ignoring the regular admonitions against abuse from the assistant district attorneys who move in and out of the plot, Sipowicz often put his badge and his pension on the line by deciding to "tune-up" this week's suspect with threatened or actual beatings. Though representatives of the courts regularly told the detectives that intimidation and violence are morally and legally wrong, Sipowicz's approach was always vindicated. In the show's carefully constructed reality, the situation was always urgent, the information sought was always specific, the suspect always had it, and its revelation was usually timely, saving a human life from imminent danger. Looking at and learning from Andy Sipowicz, Americans, or at least the twenty million who watched weekly, know that the "tune-up" is as necessary for effective interrogation as it is wrong. But the war on terror is not a television series.[2]

Living like Detective Sipowicz in a seemingly scripted universe, Professor Dershowitz plays on real-world problems to construct a similarly fictionalized rationale for torture. During his lectures about torture in Israel and America for the past twenty years, audiences, whether civil libertarians or law-and-order advocates, usually come to the same hard question: "But what about the 'ticking-bomb' case?" Indeed, the professor intones, this question is a venerable one, confronted "by many philosophers including Michael Walzer, Jean-Paul Sartre, and Jeremy Bentham." In its current variation, the ticking-bomb scenario, Dershowitz says, usually "involves a captured terrorist who refuses to divulge information about the imminent use of weapons of mass destruction, such as a nuclear, chemical or biological device, that are capable of killing and injuring thousands of civilians." Speaking to Americans, he always asks: "How many of you think that nonlethal torture *would* be used if we were ever confronted with a ticking bomb terrorist case?" Hands always shoot up in near unanimity, although "there is widespread disagreement whether it *should* be used."

From this hypothetical, Dershowitz segues, without skipping a beat, to the realm of reality: "If torture is, in fact, being used and/or would, in fact, be used in an actual ticking bomb terrorist case, would it be *normatively* better or worse to have such torture regulated by some kind of warrant?" Answering his own carefully cooked question, Dershowitz warns, from this land of make-believe to which his logic has now led us, that "if we do nothing, and a preventable act of nuclear terrorism occurs, then the public will demand that we constrain liberty even more." After this sleight-of-hand shift from the fictional to the real, Dershowitz concludes that his putative torture warrants "would reduce the incidence of abuses," since high officials, operating on the record, would never authorize "methods of the kind shown in the Abu Ghraib photographs."[3]

Certainly we could all agree, as would the eminent Judge Richard A. Posner and the resolute Detective Sipowicz, that we must torture this one terrorist, this one monster, to save millions of lives from that ticking atomic bomb.[4] And once we agree to torture in this circumstance, can't we admit that there might be other situations in which torture could save lives, American lives? Clearly we must examine the logic and the likelihood of this nightmare scenario that embodies our deepest fears and makes most of us quietly, unwittingly complicit in the Bush administration's recourse to torture. The ticking-bomb scenario requires no less than a rigorous analysis of its unspoken assumptions.

In the real world, the probability that one terrorist would be captured, in possession of the key information about a nuclear bomb in Times Square, is so slender that the scenario seems an improbable foundation for law, diplomacy, and national security. Yes, there were terrorists who flew airplanes into the World Trade Center. And, yes, the future may well bring us more terrorists, with more bombs. But the precise mix of terrorist, bomb, and perfect prior information will never, in all likelihood, occur in this exact array to make the Times Square threat anything close to reasonable grounds for action.

The fundamental flaw in this fanciful scenario is its pretzel-like, ex post facto logic. It assumes an improbable, even impossible, cluster of variables that runs something like this. First, the FBI or CIA captures a terrorist. Second, the capture takes place at the precise moment between plot's launch and bomb's burst. Third, the interrogators somehow have sufficiently detailed knowledge of the plot to know they must interrogate this very person and do it now, right now. Fourth, these same officers who have sufficient intelligence to know all about this specific terrorist and his ticking bomb are, for some unexplained reason, missing just a few critical details that only torture can divulge. Put simply, this constellation of circumstances is so far-fetched that the logic of Dershowitz's argument is sophistic if not spurious.

Such an extraordinary string of coincidences probably never has and never will occur. Visiting Israel, which lives with the constant threat of terror bombings, to test this torture-stops-ticking-bomb thesis, *New York Times* reporter Joseph Lelyveld was "repeatedly told that coercive interrogation had effectively thwarted . . . would-be suicide bombers." One highly placed source in Israeli security claimed that "hundreds of terror attacks . . . intended to cause the deaths of an inestimable number of innocent civilians" had been stopped time and again by torture. But nobody would cite a single "specific case." Instead of hundreds, Israeli sources finally named just one, a Hamas organizer who was broken under torture, coincidentally "the same one that the Israeli Justice Ministry cited in a letter to Human Rights Watch a couple of months earlier."[5]

With reality so uncooperative, torture advocates spin two sorts of scenarios, the fictional and the fabulous. Usually they stick to that fictional Times Square bomber. But sometimes they twist the truth into a fable, a facsimile of this implausible scenario, by showing, for example, how the timely torture of Abdul Hakim Murad in Manila in 1995 halted a plot to blow up eleven trans-Pacific aircraft and kill four thousand innocent passengers. Except, of course, for the simple fact that, as we have seen, Murad's torture did nothing of the sort.

In another real-world case, without such fictions or fables, an alleged member of the Al Qaeda hijacking crew, Zacarias Moussaoui, sat in a Minneapolis cell for nearly a month before 9/11 under desultory investigation as a possible "suicide hijacker," because the FBI, lacking omniscience, did not have precise foreknowledge of Al Qaeda's plot or Moussaoui's possible role. In pressing for a search warrant before 9/11, the bureau's Minneapolis field supervisor even warned that he was "trying to keep someone from taking a plane and crashing into the World Trade Center." But the reply from FBI headquarters in Washington—that there was no evidence Moussaoui was a terrorist— provides us with yet another reminder of how difficult it is to grasp the significance of even such stunningly accurate insight or intelligence in the absence of foreknowledge. Then, when two jets hit the Twin Towers, everybody, even the FBI, discovers this forgotten flight school dropout in Minnesota. With hindsight and three thousand dead, everybody knows what could have, should have been done: If only we had interrogated him. If only we had gotten a warrant to open his laptop computer. Then just maybe, then just possibly, 9/11 would never have happened. "A maximum U.S. effort to investigate Moussaoui conceivably could have unearthed his connections to [Ramzi] Binalshibh," wrote the 9/11 commission, in a flight beyond the hypothetical into the counterfactual. "Those connections might have brought investigators to the core of the 9/11 plot . . . , though it was not an easy trail to find."[6] But just as FBI and CIA headquarters, in the weeks before the Twin Towers attack, failed to realize Moussaoui's significance, so future FBI or CIA agents, still lacking omniscience, will hold tomorrow's terrorists in ignorance of their intentions. "The CIA and NSA may be sleek and omniscient in the movies," reads the report of the president's Commission on Intelligence Capabilities, "but in real life they and other intelligence agencies are vast government bureaucracies." And as the scholar Elaine Scarry notes in her rebuttal of Dershowitz's ticking-bomb thesis, these are bureaucracies with a record that falls far short of anything akin to omniscience. In the thirty months after 9/11, authorities relied on intelligence to arrest 5,000 terror suspects, found evidence to charge just three, and won only one conviction—an apt measure of the American state's omniscience.[7]

Let us push this twisted logic to its inevitable limits. If the government nabbed only one certain terrorist in 5,000 arbitrary arrests, should we not expect the same security apparatus to perform similarly with warrants for legalized torture—that is, 4,999 innocent victims tortured for every true terrorist interrogated? And what do we do with the hundreds, hypothetically thousands of innocents subjected to life-destroying trauma? Do we tie up the courts for decades in litigation and spend billions of dollars compensating them? Or do we somehow dispose of these victims, via rendition, to other nations or through another, more final solution?

To return to the example of Moussaoui, even had he been tortured, he might have confessed in rambling, half-crazed rhetoric to a nonexistent plot, as he actually did at his trial four years after his arrest: "I am guilty of a broad conspiracy to use a weapon of mass destruction to destroy the White House." Had he actually spoken in this megalomaniacal manner when arrested in August 2001, would his FBI questioners have been able to sort information from disinformation, attributing some significance to these ravings? Testing has found that professional interrogators perform within the 45 to 60 percent range in distinguishing truth from lies—little better than flipping a coin. Even skilled polygraph examiners have only an 85 percent accuracy rate. Thus as intelligence data move through three basic stages—acquisition/ interrogation, analysis, and action—the possibility of human error is infinite and, without the divine gift of foresight, the chances that good intelligence will be ignored are high. "After the event," Roberta Wohlstetter wrote in her classic study of that other great U.S. intelligence failure, Pearl Harbor, "a signal is always crystal clear; we can now see what disaster it was signaling since the disaster has occurred. But before the event it is obscure and pregnant with conflicting meanings."[8]

In the real world, the impossibility of perfect prescience makes the plea to torture the few an opening to torture the many. Once we agree to torture that nonexistent terrorist with the hypothetical ticking bomb, then we admit a possibility, even an imperative, for torturing hundreds who might have ticking bombs or thousands who just might have some knowledge about those bombs. "You can't know whether a person knows where the bomb is," explained Georgetown University law professor David Cole, "or even if they're telling the truth. Because of this, you end up going down a slippery slope and sanctioning torture in general."[9] Those who think this improbable should recall how the United States got to Abu Ghraib. Orders from President Bush and Secretary Rumsfeld for the CIA to torture just a few "high-value" Al Qaeda targets quickly proliferated into the abuse of dozens at Bagram, hundreds at Guantánamo, and thousands at Abu Ghraib and other Iraqi prisons.

As we slide down that slippery slope to torture in general, we should realize that there is a chasm at the bottom called extrajudicial execution. With the agency's gulag full of dozens of detainees of dwindling utility, CIA agents, active and retired, have been vocal in their complaints about the costs and inconvenience of limitless, even lifetime, incarceration for these tortured terrorists. Illegal rendition or legal deportation is a possibility for some low-ranking suspects at Guantánamo—but not for the hundred or so top Al Qaeda prisoners who are too dangerous for release, too tainted for trial. The ideal solution to this conundrum, from a CIA perspective, is extrajudicial execution. Indeed, the systematic French torture of thousands from the Casbah of Algiers in 1957 also entailed over three thousand "summary executions" as "an inseparable part" of this campaign, largely, as one French general put it, to insure that "the machine of justice" not be "clogged with cases" and free terror suspects to launch other attacks. For similar reasons, the CIA's Phoenix program of torture-interrogation in Vietnam during the late 1960s produced over twenty thousand extrajudicial killings.[10] In effect, the logical corollary to state-sanctioned torture is state-sponsored murder.

Can Torture Work against Terror?

After fifty years of fighting enemies, Communist and terrorist, with torture, we now have sufficient evidence to entertain a second question: Is torture an effective weapon in the war on terror? French and American experience, hard won since the 1950s, leads to two clear conclusions. Torture of the few yields little useful information. Torture of the many can produce results, but at a prohibitively high political cost.

As the ancient Roman jurist Ulpian once noted, when tortured the strong will resist and the weak will say anything to end the pain. Most of those rounded up by military sweeps in Iraq and Afghanistan for imprisonment at Abu Ghraib and Guantánamo were indeed the weak. Some 90 percent of Iraqi detainees were, according to U.S. military estimates, innocent civilians. And with up to 750 prisoners at Guantánamo subjected to interrogation "tantamount to torture," presumably with at least a few of the strong among them, there has been surprisingly little useful intelligence. As noted, FBI interrogators found the military's techniques produced little real information and interfered with their own bureau's proven methods of building rapport through long, noncoercive questioning. "The torture of suspects did not lead to any useful intelligence information being extracted," reports James Corum, a professor at the Army Command and General Staff College. "The abusers couldn't even use the old 'ends justify the means' argument, because in the end there was nothing to show but a tremendous propaganda defeat for the United States."[11]

There are further grounds for skepticism about the supposed gains from harsh interrogation. During the first years of the war on terror, intelligence officials were expansive in their claims for torture's yield. In September 2002, Rumsfeld stated that interrogation had extracted "an awful lot of information" to make "life an awful lot more difficult for an awful lot of folks." By December, anonymous "official sources" asserted that four top Al Qaeda leaders had been captured "all partly the result of information gained during interrogations." In March 2003, "federal officials" told *Time* that Khalid Sheikh Mohammed had "given U.S. interrogators the names and descriptions of about a dozen key al-Qaeda operatives believed to be plotting terrorist attacks on America. . . . He has also added crucial details to the descriptions of other suspects and filled in important gaps." But even then, Bill Cowan, a retired Marine lieutenant colonel who served as an interrogator in Vietnam, challenged these claims, saying, "I don't see the proof in the pudding. If you had a top leader like Mohammed talking, someone who could presumably lay out the whole organization for you, I think we'd be seeing sweeping arrests in several different countries at the same time."[12]

Two years later, U.S. intelligence, growing sensitive to a subsequent lack of success, began leaking renewed claims, all unverified, of useful intelligence from Guantánamo and other, unspecified prisons. In interviews with the *New York Times,* anonymous CIA "intelligence officials" were quoted as saying, again and again, that interrogation of Al Qaeda's personnel chief, Abu Zubaydah, and others had provided "useful intelligence."[13] In his March 2005 congressional testimony, CIA director Porter Goss claimed that his agency's tough interrogation of Al Qaeda suspects had led to "documented successes"—and then, in the usual catch-22 logic that surrounds such CIA claims, refused to document those successes. After four years of torture, the agency, in statements on the record and off, could not boast of anything akin to stopping a ticking bomb. And there is good reason for this failure: very few individuals have enough information to make torture worthwhile, and those who do are the least likely, for obvious reasons, to fall into the interrogator's net, or to talk when they do. "We recognize that espionage is always chancy at best," the president's Commission on Intelligence Capabilities reminds us. "50 years of pounding away at the Soviet Union resulted in only a handful of truly important human sources."[14]

Looking back on the past few years of the war on terror, veteran FBI counter-intelligence officer Jack Cloonan felt that Washington had replicated this dismal Cold War result. "Have we gotten enough information out of [Guantánamo Bay] or anywhere else to justify the negative?" he said. "I think the answer from the authorities will be, 'We've gotten great information.' I'm less and less inclined to believe that. There's a certain naiveté in thinking that any shmuck taken off the battlefield on any given day—or taken off a street somewhere and flown half way around the world and being held incommunicado with no rights and no charges—will know where bin Laden is or what's going to be planned in Iraq or Afghanistan."[15]

Nonetheless, torture of the many—tens of thousands in Vietnam and hundreds of thousands in Algeria—can produce results, albeit with long-term political consequences that subvert the effort's larger aims. In 1957, the French Army destroyed the urban underground in Algiers with the systematic abuse of thousands of revolutionary suspects. During the yearlong battle, French soldiers arrested 30 to 40 percent of all males in the city's Casbah and subjected most of them to brutality, using, in the words of one senior officer, "beatings, electric shocks, and, in particular, water torture, which was always the most dangerous technique for the prisoner." Although many resisted to the point of death, mass torture gained sufficient intelligence to break the rebel underground. The CIA's Phoenix program no doubt damaged the Vietcong's Communist infrastructure by the vicious questioning of countless South Vietnamese civilians and twenty thousand extrajudicial executions. So the choices are clear. Major success from limited, surgical torture is a fable, a fiction. But mass torture of thousands of suspects, some guilty, most innocent, can produce some useful intelligence.[16]

What about Mass Torture?

If indiscriminate torture can, in fact, yield useful information, then should the United States deploy systematic, mass arrests, akin to the

Vietnam War's Phoenix program, in Iraq, Afghanistan, or other covert battlegrounds in the war on terror? Would we pay a price, perhaps an unacceptably high one, if we use more extensive torture?

During a tour of the Phoenix program's Provincial Interrogation Centers near Saigon in 1969, a CIA regional chief, Orrin DeForest, was "disgusted" to find them "irretrievable, just a horrible mess . . . commonly considered the sites of the worst tortures—in particular the water treatment, where they forced water down prisoners' throats until their stomachs swelled up, or the torture in which they applied electric shock to the genitals and nipples."[17] Assigned to this particular region as CIA chief for Gia Dinh Province in 1968, Ralph W. McGehee found himself in "the middle of an insane war" that defied rationality and mocked the statistical indices of progress amassed by the vast counterinsurgency program. "The killings by the CIA's assassination teams—the Provincial Reconnaissance Units—and the absurd intelligence-collection activities progressed as in a Greek tragedy," he recalled. "No one seemed to understand what was going on. Yet people died, reports flowed, meetings convened, and the gods frowned."[18] As he left Saigon in 1970, the Phoenix program's founder, Robert Komer, described it as "a small, poorly managed, and largely ineffective effort." Indeed, one Pentagon contract-study of Phoenix's operations found that, in 1970–71, only 3 percent of the Vietcong "killed, captured, or rallied were full or probationary Party members above the district level." Over half the supposed Vietcong captured or killed "were not even party members."[19] CIA veteran McGehee was even blunter: "The truth is that never in the history of our work in Vietnam did we get one clear-cut, high-ranking Vietcong agent."[20] Not surprisingly, a pacification effort based on this problematic program failed either to crush the Vietcong or win the support of Vietnamese villagers, contributing to the ultimate defeat in Vietnam.[21]

Similarly, the French Army won the battle of Algiers but soon lost the war for Algeria, in large part because its systematic torture delegitimated the wider war effort in the eyes of most Algerians and many French. "You might say that the battle of Algiers was won through the use of torture," observed the British historian Sir Alistair Horne, "but that the war, the Algerian war was lost." Even General Jacques Massu, the aging paratroop commander whose name was once synonymous with torture in Algiers, later had his doubts. "Torture," he recently told *Le Monde,* "isn't indispensable in times of war, and one can very well do without it. When I look back on Algeria, it saddens me . . . One could have done things differently."[22] His intelligence chief, Colonel Roger Trinquier, the epitome of the French centurion, shared these doubts, albeit from a strikingly different perspective. "When mounting an insurrection, you must do so fully aware that torture will be used," Trinquier told British television in 1970. "It's not about being for or against it. You must realize every prisoner who is arrested will talk. Unless he makes the sacrifice of suicide, we'll always get his confession. An insurgency must be based on this awareness, so that a prisoner who talks won't bring down the organization."[23] In this desperate game, the state's torture gambit is thus checked by the terrorist's axiomatic countermeasures, minimizing any intelligence yield for the state and maximizing political gains for the terrorists.

Even the comparatively limited torture at Abu Ghraib has done incalculable damage to America's international prestige. "Look," said acting Assistant Secretary of State Michael G. Kozak in February 2005, "the events of Abu Ghraib were a stain on the honor of the U.S.; there's no two ways about it."[24] Army interrogator Chris Mackey saw the face of the enemy at close quarters in Afghanistan. He felt that Abu Ghraib's "images of depravity will inflame anti-American sentiment in the Muslim world for a generation, driving who knows how many would-be jihadists into the ranks of Al Qaeda and other terrorist organizations."[25]

Whether the more limited, individual tortures in the war on terror or the mass, systematic torture in Algeria and Vietnam, the intelligence gains are soon overwhelmed by political costs, as friends and enemies recoil in revulsion at such calculated savagery. Indeed, even the Army's current field manual, *FM: Intelligence Interrogation 34–52,* contains an implicit warning about the high political costs: "Revelation of use of torture by US personnel will bring discredit upon the US and its armed forces while undermining domestic and international support for the war effort."[26]

For the United States and its war on terror, there is a contradiction between stopping terror plots in motion versus stopping terrorism. By pursuing the chimera of halting conspiracies in progress, Washington has used extreme methods, contributing to a larger political climate that fosters terrorism. In effect, the use of torture to stop terrorism has, paradoxically, created more terrorists. "The U.S. is doing what the British did in the 1970s, detaining people and violating their civil liberties," said Tom Parker, a former MI5 agent, of the fight against the IRA. "It did nothing but exacerbate the situation. Most of those interned went back to terrorism. You'll end up radicalizing the entire population."[27] Indeed, the thousands of ordinary Iraqis processed through harsh military prisons since March 2003 emerge bitter about their treatment. "Many of them are innocent civilians swept up," said Bruce Hoffman, a Rand Corporation consultant in Iraq. "Prisons are the main incubators for terrorists and insurgents." In November 2003, reporter Mark Danner asked a young Iraqi man from Falluja about the reasons for the rising resistance to the U.S. presence and was stunned by the intensity of his response. "It is a *shame* for the foreigners to put a bag over their heads, to make a man lie on the ground with your shoe on his neck," the Iraqi said, speaking slowly to emphasize certain words. "This is a great *shame*, you understand? This is a great *shame* for the whole tribe. It is the *duty* of that man, and of that tribe, to get revenge on this soldier— to kill that man. Their duty is to attack them, to *wash the shame*. The shame is a *stain*, a dirty thing—they have to *wash* it. No sleep—we cannot sleep until we have revenge. They have to kill soldiers."[28]

Moreover, the power of those iconic images of torture victims from Abu Ghraib justifies terrorist extremes in the discourse on the Arab street. "When the average Egyptian or Palestinian or Saudi thinks about the Americans in Iraq," the *New York Times* editorialized on the war's second anniversary, "the image is not voters' purple-stained fingers but the naked Iraqi prisoner at the other end of Pfc. Lynndie England's leash."[29] And as a number of commentators noted, those Iraqi videotapes of summary executions broadcast over the pan-Arab TV station Al Jazeera in 2004 often showed foreign victims wearing orange jumpsuits similar to Abu Ghraib prison garb—a symbolic bid to legitimize brutal executions by evoking the brutality of U.S. torture. When Egypt's democratic reformers, writers and filmmakers among them, marched down the streets of Cairo in April 2005, they chanted, in a surprising mix of pro-democracy and anti-American slogans, "Down Down with Mubarak! Guantánamo! Enough! Abu Ghraib! Enough!" Across the Muslim world, from Morocco to Indonesia, Abu Ghraib and Guantánamo Bay have become the fodder for daily media discussion, most of it sharply critical of the United States.[30] Thus, the pervasiveness of those images from the military prisons, indelibly imprinted in Arab consciousness, has subtly subverted American rhetoric about democracy and has damaged the nation's moral leadership in the Middle East.

The war on terror has thus taught some hard lessons that Washington seems determined to ignore. Harsh interrogation, "tantamount to torture," seems to have produced rather little in the way of useful intelligence. While making broad, vague claims of success, the military and the CIA have not leaked any details, quite possibly because the specifics might not support those claims. The CIA does cite significant operational yield from top Al Qaeda captives like Khalid Sheik Mohammed and Nurjaman Riduan Isamuddin (aka "Hambali"), but even these assertions have not been subjected to independent verification.[31] To date, the intelligence yield from the arbitrary detention and parallel torture-interrogation of some ten thousand terrorist suspects worldwide has been a handful of useful sources with information that has proved less than devastating against a disorganized organization like Al Qaeda. If we weigh the tactical value of that paucity of intelligence against the enormity of the damage to U.S. international prestige, the cost clearly outweighs the benefit.[32] It is possible that the massive, systematic torture used in Algeria and Vietnam might have generated greater intelligence against Al Qaeda—but, again, at a proportionally higher political cost. Advocates of torture, by contrast, are arguing for defiance of the Constitution's ban on "cruel and unusual punishment," for the violation of federal statutes, and for the abrogation of UN conventions—all for the sake of limited intelligence gains and the prevention of some hypothetical eventuality.

There are, in fact, well-established American alternatives to torture. During World War II, the legendary Marine interrogator, Major Sherwood F. Moran, used empathy to establish "intellectual and spiritual" rapport with Japanese prisoners. Rejecting the idea of the enemy as fanatics who required tough tactics, Moran, who was fluent in Japanese from his years as a missionary, approached each prisoner "talking as a human being to a human being." His manual of these methods persuaded the Navy and Marines to train their interrogators in Japanese language and culture, producing graduates who "were among the most effective interrogators in the Pacific Island campaigns of 1944 and 1945," supplying complete Japanese order-of-battle intelligence on Saipan and Tinian "within forty-eight hours of landing."[33]

Throughout the war on terror, the FBI has used similar procedures in its tested, by-the-book techniques that can withstand critical examination in open court. In the years before 9/11, the FBI worked on the 1998 Kenya and Tanzania embassy bombing cases, using careful investigation and noncoercive interrogation to build rapport with suspects that yielded, by May 2001, accurate intelligence about Al Qaeda and the conviction of four terrorists, who, in fact, pleaded guilty. One of the bureau agents involved, Dan Coleman, was appalled by the coercive methods Bush administration lawyers authorized for the CIA after 9/11. "Have any of these guys ever tried to talk to anyone who's been deprived of his clothes?" Coleman asked. "He's going to be ashamed and humiliated and cold. He'll tell you anything you want to hear to get his clothes back. There's no value in it." By contrast, FBI reliance on due process has proved effective in terror cases by gaining detainees' trust during interrogation and offering plea bargains to win cooperation. "Brutalization doesn't work," Coleman concluded from his years in FBI counterterrorism. "We know that. Besides, you lose your soul."[34]

Can Torture of Any Kind Work?

After two thousand years of Western judicial torture, from imperial Rome to America's imperium, we should have ample experience to answer a fourth fundamental question: Does any torture work? Does it produce accurate information?

The past two millennia are rich with examples that confirm, time and again, Ulpian's dictum from the third century A.D.: the strong can resist torture and the weak will say anything to end their pain.

Indeed, history is replete with examples of the strong who resisted even the most savage treatment. Court records of 625 persons tortured in France from 1510 to 1750 show that, depending on period and province, over 90 percent refused to confess even after abuse that included drowning, drawing bodies, and crushing joints. A full six months after the July 20, 1944, bomb plot against Hitler, the Gestapo "still had nothing like precise knowledge of the resistance movement" even though its interrogators "employed every means to extract confessions." After four weeks of torture by metal spikes and beatings so severe he suffered a heart attack, Fabian von Schlabrendorff, with a stoicism typical of these conspirators, broke his silence to give the Gestapo a few scraps of vague information—and only because he feared involuntarily blurting out serious intelligence. Similarly, during the Vietnam War, U.S. prisoners held in Hanoi resisted years of brutal Vietnamese tortures. Though 80 percent of those POWs made "statements," they did so with "a deadpan expression, a listless monotone, a glazed or robotic look" that subverted any possible propaganda value. Summarizing these and other cases, the Yale legal historian John Langbein said succinctly: "History's most important lesson is that it has not been possible to make coercion compatible with truth."[35] Let me add a few of my own observations to echo the wisdom of these words.

During a decade's research into military torture in the Philippines under the Marcos dictatorship, I met dedicated Communist cadres whose resistance to savage state violence almost defies comprehension. A visit to Manila in 1986 brought an extraordinary meeting with Julieta Sison, a leading revolutionary and the wife of Communist Party founder Joema Sison, both just released after ten years in a military prison. While shuffling papers at her modest inner-city apartment one evening, Julieta recounted how, afraid she might give up names under torture, she sat alone in her prison cell for days, systematically wiping the names of intimate friends and close comrades from memory, leaving no trace. Could anyone actually do that? Yes, she said. Even now when she meets these same friends, she cannot recall their names. A year later, I visited a midlevel party member in her dark, dank cell inside Manila's city jail, after she had been subjected to days of beatings to her genitalia by burly police. Asked how she was coping with the stress of such an experience, she replied matter-of-factly, "It hurts when I piss." I looked surprised. We expect it, she said, we can handle it.[36] And the famed journalist-turned-Communist-turned-congressman Satur Ocampo resisted weeks of kicking, beating, and stress-shackling, defeating the notorious Colonel Rodolfo Aguinaldo in a duel of wills between the country's top torturer and its leading revolutionary.[37] These three were all highly educated, dedicated revolutionaries who accepted the emotional scars of torture with the same stoicism combat soldiers show when wounded. For ideologues like them, no torture, not even by the toughest CIA-trained interrogator, could make them give up useful information.

And one should not underestimate the impact of torture on the weak. In my Philippine travels I have found the fate of innocent civilians picked up for torture without this psychological toughening strikingly, sadly different. One day during mid-semester break in 1989, the solitude of my university office in Sydney, where I was then teaching, was disturbed by a persistent knocking. Annoyed, I opened the door to find a thirty-something Filipina standing, looking at me expectantly. I stared at her blankly.

"You wrote about me," she said.

Don't know you, I replied.

"I am Maria Elena Ang."

Oh, I said, ushering her, very apologetically, into my office.

Indeed, in August 1976, Maria Ang, then a twenty-three-year-old research assistant at the University of the Philippines, had been picked up on the street and brutally interrogated by one of Marcos's elite military units. Amnesty International made hers a featured case, and there were demonstrations half a world away, in Madison, Wisconsin, when her torturer spoke at the student union in October 1986. As Maria sat there that day in my Sydney office, she was still severely scarred by her experience, seeking me out five thousand miles away from her home because I had mentioned her torture in a Manila magazine. A full thirteen years after her torture, she seemed still wounded, still deeply damaged, suffering a lifelong psychological trauma that can never heal—blocking her, already in her mid-thirties when we met, from career, marriage, children, or friendship, all the meaningful things of this life. For ordinary people like Maria Ang, who are snatched off a street and savaged, torture is not something you walk away from. Some, like Maria, seek solace; some, like former detainees from Abu Ghraib and Guantánamo, may seek vengeance.[38]

Why Do U.S. Leaders Ignore Torture's Cost?

These dismal conclusions lead to a last, uncomfortable question: If torture produces limited gains at such high political cost, why does any rational American leader condone practices "tantamount to torture"? How can one explain why the Bush administration, from the president to Donald Rumsfeld, all the way down to the assistant secretary level, has been so determined to use tactics that have inflicted serious damage to their strategic aims of winning the war on terror and building democracy in the Middle East? How, in short, can we explain such irrationality? One of Professor Dershowitz's loyal defenders, Judge Posner, briefly entertained the idea that "torture, though resorted to frequently," might be "a completely inefficacious method of obtaining true information." But then, wedded to an apparent belief that responsible authorities are necessarily rational, the judge summarily dismissed this possibility as "very unlikely; the practice is too common."[39] If, however, we consider less rational psychological forces to explain torture's commonality, then the answer to the question seems to lie with that prescient CIA observation about Soviet leaders in times of stress. "When feelings of insecurity develop within those holding power," reads the agency's analysis of Kremlin leadership applicable to the post-9/11 White House, "they become increasingly suspicious and put great pressures upon the secret police to obtain arrests and confessions. At such times police officials are inclined to condone anything which produces a speedy 'confession,' and brutality may become widespread." Similarly, a more recent study of interrogation's role in a thousand British criminal cases found that the actual "pay-off is as a rule slight," but questioning of suspects dominates investigations because it "fulfills certain psychological needs" of police for a process that "is immediate, familiar, predictable, and under police control."[40] In sum, the powerful often turn to torture in times of crisis, not because it works but because it salves their fears and insecurities with the psychic balm of empowerment.

Those who consider these analogies inappropriate should compare George Bush's face in those seven minutes of videotape at a Florida school on the morning of 9/11, stunned into fear and indecision, with his stern, strident manner that same evening as he declared war on terror in the knowledge that he would, just a few minutes later, give orders for torture.[41] And these skeptics should compare those seven minutes of fear on Bush's face with his self-confident smile a year later when, standing before Congress, he delivered his belligerent State of the Union address, calling suspected terrorists "no longer a problem for the United States."[42] Even though torture is not, on balance, effective or rational, it persists through its deep psychological appeal, to the powerful and the powerless alike, in times of crisis. In this context, a plea to torture one terrorist with a ticking bomb becomes the rationale for insecure leaders to win the right to torture someone, anyone, to assuage the uncertainties of rule and empower themselves for dominion.

For those Americans and Europeans who place a premium on security, there are legal, long-term alternatives to torture—notably, strict port surveillance, upgraded safety measures at chemical and nuclear facilities, and increased efficiency within the intelligence community. And when real terrorists are captured, FBI counterterrorism agents can, as they have done for decades, question them with legal, noncoercive methods, generating both accurate intelligence and credible evidence that will stand in a court of law—something the CIA's coercive methods have failed to do. While the Army, Navy, and CIA are now mired in painful internal inquiries over torture, the FBI has emerged from four years of the war on terror with no charges of human rights abuse, even after several thousand interrogations alongside the CIA and military intelligence.[43]

Torture will not and cannot serve as a bargain-price shortcut to security. It is a deal with the devil that will leave Satan holding a balloon mortgage on the American birthright of liberty. The time may have come for the United States to heed the hard lessons that Israel has learned from the torture of Palestinian suspects in its own desperate battle against terror. In 1987, the Landau Commission of Inquiry into interrogation by the General Security Service (GSS) had found that "effective interrogation of terrorist suspects is impossible without the use of means of pressure," recommending that such methods should "principally take the form of non-violent psychological pressure" and allowing, should these tactics fail, "a moderate measure of physical pressure." After the Israeli government accepted the commission's recommendations, GSS generally used techniques such as the "shabak" approach, which combined sensory disorientation by hooding and playing loud music with self-inflicted pain through contorted stress positions. Consequently, between 1987 and 1994, Israel's GSS interrogated 23,000 Palestinians and subjected 94 percent to physical abuse or psychological torture, producing an official inquiry, litigation, and a public consensus that it was time to move beyond these methods. "This is the destiny of democracy," wrote Israeli judge Aharon Barak in a 1999 decision banning any further abuse of Palestinian prisoners, "as not all means are acceptable to it, and not all practices employed by its enemies are open before it. Although a democracy must often fight with one hand tied behind its back, it nonetheless has the upper hand."[44]

The Abu Ghraib controversy is not, of course, the first American debate over torture even in recent memory. From 1970 to 1988, Congress tried repeatedly, without success, to expose elements of the CIA torture paradigm, in four major investigations. But on each occasion the public showed little concern, and the practice persisted inside the intelligence bureaucracy. Like postauthoritarian societies in Asia and Latin America, the United States seems to suffer from a culture of impunity over this sensitive topic that has barred both self-examination and serious reform since the Cold War's end in 1989.

But now, through the photographs from Abu Ghraib, ordinary Americans have seen, up close, the interrogation techniques that the intelligence community has propagated for nearly half a century. The public can join the international community in repudiating a practice that, more than any other, represents the denial of democracy. Or, in its desperate search for security, the United States can continue its clandestine torture of terror suspects in the hope of gaining useful information without negative publicity.

In the likely event that Washington adopts the latter strategy, it will be a decision posited on two false assumptions: that torturers can be controlled, and that news of their work can be contained. Once torture begins, it seems to spread uncontrollably, particularly during times of crisis, in a downward spiral of fear and self-empowerment. With the proliferation of visual imaging—on cell phones, personal computers, and microcameras—we can anticipate, in five or ten years, more chilling images and more devastating blows to America's international standing.

The next time, however, the public's moral concern and Washington's apologies will ring hollow, producing even greater damage to the country's prestige. And maybe then we will begin to discover the truth my mother learned as a girl back in 1933, descending into the dungeons of Nuremberg and being beaten on the streets of Berlin: "Torture is evil, pure and simple."

NOTES

Chapter 1: Two Thousand Years of Torture

1. *New York Times,* May 1, 2004; Seymour M. Hersh, "Torture at Abu Ghraib," *The New Yorker,* May 10, 2004, 42–47.

2. *New York Times,* May 8, May 12, 2004.

3. *New York Times,* May 6, May 7, May 9, 2004. Inside a simulated prison on the Stanford University campus, the psychologist Philip Zimbardo conducted an experiment by randomly assigning twenty-one "average, healthy American college males" roles as guards and prisoners. While the guards were given uniforms and clubs, the prisoners had to wear dress-like gowns that symbolized their otherness, their "emasculation." After only six days, Zimbardo was forced to abort his planned two-week experiment because the guards' brutality was escalating dangerously out of control. Significantly, the experiment found that, under conditions of arbitrary authority, power had a transactional quality. The guards' "sense of mastery and control" was matched by the prisoners' feelings of "depression and hopelessness." All eleven guards "behaved sadistically" at least once, but a minority "delighted in the new-found power" and demonstrated "great . . . cruelty in the forms of degradation they invented for the prisoners." All subjects were capable of cruelty, but, Zimbardo concluded, some were more capable than others. See Philip G. Zimbardo, "On the Ethics of Intervention in Human Psychological Research: With Special Reference to the Stanford Prison Experiment," *Cognition* 2, no. 2 (1973), 243–44; Philip G. Zimbardo et al., "A Pirandellian Prison: The Mind Is a Formidable Jailer," *New York Times Magazine,* April 8, 1973, 38, 60.

4. Senate, Judiciary Committee, Confirmation Hearing, Transcript, January 6, 2005, 18–19, 22, 48, http://www.nytimes.com/2005/01/06/politics/06 TEXT -GONZALES.html?ei+5070&3n+5f; accessed March 14, 2005; *Washington*

Post, May 13, 2004; Seymour M. Hersh, "The Gray Zone: How a Secret Pentagon Program Came to Abu Ghraib," *The New Yorker,* May 24, 2004, 41.

5. Hans-Peter Gasser, "An Appeal for Ratification by the United States," *American Journal of International Law* 81, no. 4 (1987), 912–45; David P. Forsythe, "The United States, the United Nations, and Human Rights," in Margaret P. Karns and Karen A. Mingst, eds., *The United States and Multilateral Institutions: Patterns of Changing Instrumentality and Influence* (Boston: Unwin Hyman, 1990), 261–84; Kenneth Roth, "The Charade of US Ratification of International Human Rights Treaties," *Chicago Journal of International Law* (Fall 2000), 347–53.

6. Christopher Simpson, *Science of Coercion: Communication Research and Psychological Warfare, 1945–1960* (New York: Oxford University Press, 1994), 9.

7. *New York Times,* May 7, 2004. Medical research into torture supports this idea of the cumulative effect of multiple psychological techniques. For example, in his discussion of the common symptoms of mental torture such as sleep disturbance, impaired memory, and depression, Ole Vedel Rasmussen noted, "These symptoms were not caused by one specific torture type. They are rather a total accumulated effect of all the different 'stressors.'" See Ole Vedel Rasmussen, "Medical Aspects of Torture," *Danish Medical Bulletin* 37, no. 1 (1990), 41.

8. Peter Watson, *War on the Mind: The Military Uses and Abuses of Psychology* (New York: Basic Books, 1978), 266–67.

9. After interviews with two hundred victims, most of whom had been tortured years before, a team of Danish doctors found fifty-seven of the seventy-six who had been subjected to isolation for up to fourteen days (75 percent) were still suffering serious "mental symptoms." Of the 101 who had been blindfolded and denied visual stimuli, seventy-three (or 72 percent) had mental symptoms. (See Rasmussen, "Medical Aspects of Torture," 30–31.)

10. Otto Doerr-Zegers, Lawrence Hartmann, Elizabeth Lira, and Eugenia Weinstein, "Torture: Psychiatric Sequelae and Phenomenology," *Psychiatry* 55, no. 2 (May 1992), 178–79; Lawrence Hartmann et al., "Psychopathology of Torture Victims," *Torture* 3, no. 2 (1993), 36–38.

11. Doerr-Zegers, "Torture," 179–83. Similarly, a group of six Argentine psychotherapists found, from treating survivors, that "torture targets the individual's identity," which they defined as "a complex of representations of self . . . that produces the feeling of oneness and allows one to maintain internal coherence in time." See Diana Kordon, Lucila Edelman, et al., "Torture in Argentina," in Metin Basoglu, ed., *Torture and Its Consequences: Current Treatment Approaches* (Cambridge: Cambridge University Press, 1992), 433–51.

12. José A. Saporta Jr. and Bessel A. van der Kolk, "Psychobiological Consequences of Severe Trauma," in Basoglu, *Torture,* 151–57.

13. *Outlawing an Ancient Evil: Torture. Convention against Torture and Other Cruel, Inhuman or Degrading Treatment or Punishment* (New York: United Nations, Department of Public Information, 1985); Ahcene Boulesbaa, *The U.N. Convention on Torture and the Prospects for Enforcement* (The Hague: Martinus Nijhoff, 1999), 1–2.

14. Lawrence E. Hinkle Jr. and Harold G. Wolff, "Communist Interrogation and Indoctrination of 'Enemies of the States': Analysis of Methods Used by the Communist State Police (a Special Report)," *Archives of Neurology and Psychiatry* 76 (1956), 135.

15. David P. Forsythe, "Human Rights in U.S. Foreign Policy: Retrospect and Prospect," *Political Science Quarterly* 105, no. 3 (1990), 435–54.

16. *Human Rights: A Compilation of International Instruments of the United Nations* (New York: United Nations, 1973), 1–3.

17. Adam Roberts and Richard Guelff, eds., *Documents on the Laws of War* (New York: Oxford University Press, 2000), 243–44, 250, 278–79, 361, 368. For example, legal commentary published by the International Red Cross makes it clear that, under Article 87 of Convention III, "the lighting must be sufficient to enable them [prisoners] to read and write without difficulty." See Jean de Preaux, *The Geneva Conventions of 12 August 1949: Commentary. Geneva Convention III Relative to the Treatment of Prisoners of War* (Geneva: International Committee of the Red Cross, 1960), 431–32.

18. Roberts and Guelff, *Documents,* 312. In the view of International Red Cross lawyers, Article 31 represented a marked expansion of Article 44 of the 1907 Hague Regulations and now covered "all protected persons, thus including even civilian aliens on the territory of a party to the conflict." See Oscar M. Uhler et al., *The Geneva Conventions of 12 August 1949: Commentary. Geneva Convention IV Relative to the Protection of Civilian Persons in Time of War* (Geneva: International Committee of the Red Cross, 1958), 431–32.

19. David P. Forsythe, "The United Nations and Human Rights, 1945–1985," *Political Science Quarterly* 100, no. 2 (Summer 1985), 249–52.

20. Edward Peters, *Torture* (Philadelphia: University of Pennsylvania Press, 1996), 1, 14–18, 25–33, 35; Malise Ruthven, *Torture: The Grand Conspiracy* (London: Weidenfeld and Nicolson, 1978), 25, 30–31; Michael Gargarin, "The Torture of Slaves in Athenian Law," *Classical Philology* 91, no. 1 (1996), 1–18; P. A. Brunt, "Evidence Given under Torture in the Principate," *Zeischrift der Savigny-Stiftung für Rechtsgeschichte* 97 (1980), 256–65; Peter Garnsey, *Social Status and Legal Privilege in the Roman Empire* (Oxford: Clarendon Press, 1970), 213–16; Denise Grodzynski, "Tortures mortelles et catégories sociales: Les *Summa suplica* dans le Droit Romain aux IIIe et IVe Siècles," in *Du châtiment dans la cité: Supplice corporels et peine de mort dans le monde antique* (Rome: L'École Française de Rome, 1984), 361–403.

21. Ruthven, *Torture,* 43–48.

22. John H. Langbein, *Torture and the Law of Proof: Europe and England in the Ancien Regime* (Chicago: University of Chicago Press, 1977), 7; Peters, *Torture,* 40–62.

23. Peters, *Torture,* 62–67; Ruthven, *Torture,* 57–59.

24. Mitchell B. Merback, *The Thief, the Cross and the Wheel: Pain and the Spectacle of Punishment in Medieval and Renaissance Europe* (Chicago: University of Chicago Press, 1999), 69–70, 129–57, 199–217; James Carroll, "The Bush Crusade," *The Nation,* September 20, 2004, 17.

25. Alec Mellor, *La torture: Son histoire, son abolition, sa réapparition au XXe siècle* (Paris: Horizons Littéraires, 1949), 105–15; Merback, *The Thief, the Cross and the Wheel,* 158–70.

26. Langbein, *Torture and the Law of Proof,* 10–12, 60–69; Ruthven, *Torture,* 12–15; John H. Langbein, "The Legal History of Torture," in Sanford Levinson, ed., *Torture: A Collection* (New York: Oxford University Press, 2004), 93–100; Peter Gay, *Voltaire's Politics: The Poet as Realist* (New York: Vintage, 1965), 275; Marcello Maestro, *Voltaire and Beccaria as Reformers of Criminal Law* (New York: Columbia University Press, 1942), 86–88.

27. Ruthven, *Torture,* 218–78; Peters, *Torture,* 102–40; Eyal Press, "In Torture We Trust?" *The Nation,* March 31, 2003, 11–15.

28. Peters, *Torture,* 103, 121–25, 138–39; Ernst Winkler, *Four Years of Nazi Torture* (New York: Appleton-Century, 1943), 1, 42–43, 57–59, 71, 75–77, 124–26; John Marks, *The Search for the "Manchurian Candidate": The CIA and Mind Control* (New York: Times Books, 1979), 8–10. The quotation about torture's revival as "an engine of the state, not of law" is borrowed from famed eighteenth-century English jurist William Blackstone who originally used the phrase to describe trends in his own period. (Peters, *Torture,* 8, 108.)

29. George J. Annas and Michael A. Grodin, eds., *The Nazi Doctors and the Nuremberg Code: Human Rights in Human Experimentation* (New York: Oxford University Press, 1992), 2, 102–7.

30. Peters, *Torture,* 139; Adam Shatz, "The Torture of Algiers," *New York Review of Books,* November 21, 2002, 53–57.

31. Peters, *Torture,* 138–40; Shatz, "The Torture of Algiers," 53–57; Henri Alleg, *The Question* (New York: Braziller, 1958), 54–67; interview with Saada Yacef, FLN military commander for the Casbah, 1956–57, in *The Battle of Algiers: Remembering History* (produced by Kim Hendrickson, Criterion Collection, 2004); Paul Aussaresses, *The Battle of the Casbah: Terrorism and Counter-Terrorism in Algeria, 1955–1957* (New York: Enigma, 2002), 120–21, 126–27, 162–63.

32. Alleg, *The Question,* 61; interview with Henri Alleg, *The Battle of Algiers;* Shatz, "The Torture of Algiers," 57.

33. Peters, *Torture,* 138–40; interview with Benjamin Stora, *The Battle of Algiers.*

34. William Colby and Peter Forbath, *Honorable Men: My Life in the CIA* (New York: Simon & Schuster, 1978), 271.

Chapter 2: Mind Control

1. Seymour Fisher, *The Use of Hypnosis in Intelligence and Related Military Situations* (Washington: Study SR 177-D, Contract AF18 [600] 1977, Technical Report No. 4, Bureau of Social Science Research, December 1958), 3; Stephen L. Chorover, "The Pacification of the Brain," *Psychology Today* (May 1974), 59–69.

2. Alexander Cockburn and Jeffrey St. Clair, *Whiteout: The CIA, Drugs and the Press* (New York: Verso, 1998), 145–54.

3. Irving L. Janis, *Are the Cominform Countries Using Hypnotic Techniques to Elicit Confessions in Public Trials?* (Santa Monica: Rand Corporation, Air Force Project Rand Research Memorandum, RM-161, April 25, 1949), 1, 3, 6–7,

16–20; Walter Bowart, *Operation Mind Control* (New York: Dell, 1978), 67–71, 109–10.

4. Janis, *Are the Cominform Countries Using Hypnotic Techniques to Elicit Confessions in Public Trials?* 19–20.

5. Senate, 94th Congress, 2nd sess., *Foreign and Military Intelligence, Book I: Final Report of the Select Committee to Study Governmental Operations with Respect to Intelligence Activities* (Washington: Government Printing Office, April 1976), 393; John Ranelagh, *The Agency: The Rise and Decline of the CIA* (New York: Simon and Schuster, 1986), 202–4; John Marks, *The Search for the "Manchurian Candidate": The CIA and Mind Control* (New York: Times Books, 1979), 125–26, 223; CIA, "Defense against Soviet Mental Interrogation and Espionage Technique," February 10, 1951, File: Drugs-Artichoke (1), Box 6, CIA Behavior Control Experiments Collection, National Security Archive, Washington (also quoted in Bowart, *Operation Mind Control*, 108–9).

6. CIA, Summary of Remarks by Mr. Allen W. Dulles at the National Alumni Conference of the Graduate Council of Princeton University, Hot Springs, VA, April 10, 1953, File: Artichoke Docs. 362–388, Box 5, CIA Behavior Control Experiments Collection, National Security Archive, Washington; Alan Scheflin, "Freedom of the Mind as an International Human Rights Issue," *Human Rights Journal* 3, no. 1 (1982), 49.

7. G. H. Estabrooks, with Leslie Lieber, "Hypnosis: Its Tremendous Potential as a War Weapon Is Revealed Here for the First Time," *Argosy*, February 1950, 26–29, 90–92; George H. Estabrooks, *Hypnotism* (New York: Dutton, 1957).

8. Edward Hunter, *Brain-Washing in Red China: The Calculated Destruction of Men's Minds* (New York: Vanguard Press, 1951), 4, 10–12, 301–2; Robert Jay Lifton, *Thought Reform and the Psychology of Totalism: A Study of Brainwashing in China* (London: Victor Gollancz, 1961), 3; Scheflin, "Freedom of the Mind as an International Human Rights Issue," 33; R. Harris Smith, *OSS: The Secret History of America's First Central Intelligence Agency* (Berkeley: University of California Press, 1972), 366–67.

9. Lifton, *Thought Reform and the Psychology of Totalism*, 3–4.

10. Christopher Simpson, *Science of Coercion: Communication Research and Psychological Warfare, 1945–1960* (New York: Oxford University Press, 1994), 8–9.

11. Senate, *Foreign and Military Intelligence, Book I*, 9; Loch K. Johnson, "On Drawing a Bright Line for Covert Operations," *American Journal of International Law* 86, no. 2 (April 1992), 293–94; *New York Times*, June 10, 2004.

12. James L. Sundquist, *The Decline and Resurgence of Congress* (Washington: The Brookings Institution, 1981), 107; Loch K. Johnson, *A Season of Inquiry: The Senate Intelligence Investigation* (Lexington: University Press of Kentucky, 1985), 7. Although the Office of Naval Intelligence and the Military Intelligence Division were established in the 1880s, they focused on the collection and analysis of information rather than on covert operations. Until the start of World War II, the only federal agency with a secret operational capacity was the Bureau of Narcotics, which did small, narrowly focused undercover investigations for drug seizures. See John C. McWilliams and Alan A. Block, "On the Origins of American Counterintelligence: Building a Clandestine Network," *Journal of Policy History*

1, no. 4 (1989), 353–72; Alan A. Block, "A Modern Marriage of Convenience: A Collaboration between Organized Crime and U.S. Intelligence," in Robert J. Kelly, ed., *Organized Crime: A Global Perspective* (Totowa: Rowman & Littlefield, 1986), 58–78.

13. Ranelagh, *The Agency,* 110–11; *New York Times,* June 10, 2004.

14. Simpson, *Science of Coercion,* 38–39.

15. Apart from those cited in this chapter, books that deal with CIA drug experiments include, for example, Jay Stevens, *Storming Heaven: LSD and the American Dream* (New York: Grove Press, 1987), 78–87; Peter Watson, *War on the Mind: The Military Uses and Abuses of Psychology* (New York: Basic Books, 1978), 265–79; Jim Keith, *Mind Control, World Control* (Kempton: Adventures Unlimited Press, 1998), 73–105.

16. Marks, *The Search for the "Manchurian Candidate,"* 22–23; Cockburn and St. Clair, *Whiteout,* 153–61.

17. Senate, *Foreign and Military Intelligence, Book I,* 387–88; Harvey M. Weinstein, *Psychiatry and the CIA: Victims of Mind Control* (Washington: American Psychiatric Press, 1990), 128–29.

18. Marks, *The Search for the "Manchurian Candidate,"* 62–64; Ranelagh, *The Agency,* 204–8, 575–76, 778.

19. CIA, Memorandum For: Director of Central Intelligence, Subject: Successful Application of Narco-Hypnotic Interrogation (ARTICHOKE), July 14, 1952, File: Artichoke Docs. 156–199, Box 5, CIA Behavior Control Experiments Collection, National Security Archive, Washington (also quoted in Bowart, *Operation Mind Control,* 102–3).

20. CIA, Memorandum for the Record, SUBJECT: Project ARTICHOKE, January 31, 1975, CIA Behavior Control Experiments Collection, National Security Archive, Washington, http://gwu.edu/nsarchive/NSAEBB/NSAEBB54/st02.pdf; accessed June 3, 2005.

21. Senate, *Foreign and Military Intelligence, Book I,* 387–88.

22. Marks, *The Search for the "Manchurian Candidate,"* 30, 34–43; Senate, 95th Congress, 1st sess., *Project MKUltra: The CIA's Program of Research in Behavioral Modification. Joint Hearing before the Select Committee on Intelligence and the Subcommittee on Health and Scientific Research of the Committee on Human Resources* (Washington: Government Printing Office, 1977), 90–102. During World War II when military psychologists joined the services in large numbers, the Navy integrated them and their research more fully than the Army. For example, 47 percent of Navy psychologists had PhDs and 95 percent were officers, versus only 26 percent of Army psychologists with doctorates and 63 percent with commissions. See Steuart Henderson Britt and Jane D. Morgan, "Military Psychologists in World War II," *The American Psychologist* 1, no. 10 (1946), 437.

23. CIA, Memorandum For: The Record, Subject: Discussion with . . . Chief . . . Division, and . . . , Chief of . . . on utilization of . . . Assets, August 9, 1960, [Sgd.] Sidney Gottlieb, Deputy Chief, TSD/Research Branch, File: Subproject 121 MKUltra, Box 4, CIA Behavior Control Experiments Collection, National Security Archive, Washington; Ranelagh, *The Agency,* 204–8, 575–76, 778; Weinstein, *Psychiatry and the CIA,* 129–30.

24. Senate, *Foreign and Military Intelligence, Book I,* 404–5.

25. Ibid., 406–7.

26. Ibid., 390–91.

27. Ibid., 422.

28. Marks, *The Search for the "Manchurian Candidate,"* 58–61.

29. Weinstein, *Psychiatry and the CIA,* 130, 179–80.

30. Marks, *The Search for the "Manchurian Candidate,"* 31, 131.

31. Ibid., 31–32, 88–95; Cockburn and St. Clair, *Whiteout,* 189–208; Senate, *Project MKUltra,* 7, 12, 21, 57, 91–92.

32. Senate, *Foreign and Military Intelligence, Book I,* 392–93.

33. Ted Gup, "The Coldest Warrior," *Washington Post Magazine,* December 16, 2001, W-9.

34. Michael Horowitz, "Interview: Albert Hofmann," *High Times* 11 (July 1976), 25–28, 31, 81; Bowart, *Operation Mind Control,* 76–78.

35. Ranelagh, *The Agency,* 208–10; *New York Times,* July 22, July 23, 1975; Gup, "The Coldest Warrior"; Weinstein, *Psychiatry and the CIA,* 130; Marks, *The Search for the "Manchurian Candidate,"* 84–85; Michael Ignatieff, "What Did the C.I.A. Do to His Father?" *New York Times Magazine,* April 1, 2001, 56–61; Commission on CIA Activities within the United States, *Report to the President* (Washington: Government Printing Office, 1975), 226–28.

36. Fisher, *The Use of Hypnosis in Intelligence and Related Military Situations,* ii, 22; Marks, *The Search for the "Manchurian Candidate,"* 196, 203.

37. In his study of the military's use of psychology, the journalist Peter Watson, who reported on the British army's psychological interrogation in Ulster for the *Times* of London, concluded that the CIA drug experiments "came to naught" and "failed as science." They are, he said, "significant mainly for the publicity they have attracted as a kind of public bogey. But in the longer term they tell us less about the ways to change (or 'control') behaviour than other sections in this book" dealing with topics such as psychological interrogation. (See Watson, *War on the Mind,* 13–14, 278–79.)

38. CIA, Project NM 001 056.0, May 1, 1952, File: Naval Research, Box 8, CIA Behavior Control Experiments Collection, National Security Archive, Washington; H. E. Page, "The Role of Psychology in ONR," *The American Psychologist* 9, no. 10 (1954), 621–22.

39. Simpson, *Science of Coercion,* 4, 9, 60–61, 72, 81–82, 134, 156–57.

40. Jack W. Dunlap, "Psychologists and the Cold War," *The American Psychologist* 10, no. 3 (1955), 107–9; Britt and Morgan, "Military Psychologists in World War II," 423–37; American Psychological Association, "Program of the Sixty-First Annual Meeting of the American Psychological Association, September 4–9, 1953, Cleveland, Ohio," *The American Psychologist* 8, no. 7 (1953), 271, 295. Even a decade after the end of World War II, the Division of Military Psychology, through its funding ties to the military services, remained a strong presence within a greatly expanded American Psychological Association. See American Psychological Association, "Program of the Sixty-Second Annual Meeting of the American Psychological Association, September 3–8, 1954, New York, New York," *The American Psychologist* 9, no. 7 (1954), 296–305; American

Psychological Association, "Symposia and Other Meetings," *The American Psychologist* 9, no. 8 (1954), 507–8. In response to an e-mail query about psychologists taking the Hippocratic oath, Stephen Behnke, JD, PhD, director of the Ethics Office, American Psychological Association, replied: "As far as I am aware, most psychologists do not take the Hippocratic Oath (although there is nothing that would preclude them from doing so)." (E-mail message to author from Stephen Behnke, July 13, 2005.)

41. CIA, Office Memorandum, To: Chief, Technical Branch, From: [Blacked-out], Subject: National Meetings of the American Psychological Association, September 30, 1954, File: APA Subproject 107, Box 6; CIA, n.d., File: APA-Subproject 107, Box 6; Memorandum for: The Record, Subject: MKUltra, Subproject 107, January 22, 1960, File: APA-Subproject 107, Box 6, CIA Behavior Control Experiments Collection, National Security Archive, Washington.

42. Steven J. Haggbloom, "The 100 Most Eminent Psychologists of the 20th Century," *Review of General Psychology* 6, no. 2 (2002), 146–47.

43. Simpson, *Science of Coercion,* 72, 134, 156–57; Albert D. Biderman and Herbert Zimmer, eds., *The Manipulation of Human Behavior* (New York: Wiley, 1961), 29; CIA, *Kubark Counterintelligence Interrogation* (July 1963), File: Kubark, Box 1: CIA Training Manuals, National Security Archive, Washington, 110.

44. James Meek, "Nobody Is Talking," *Guardian,* February 18, 2005. Tizard Diary, May to June 1951, Friday, June 1, 1951; letter to Sir Henry Tizard from Chairman, Defense Research Board, May 29, 1951, HTT 479; letter to Sir Henry Tizard from Kenrick Gunn, Chairman, Local Committee, Canadian Association of Physicists, June 7, 1951, HTT 479; Sir Henry T. Tizard Papers, Imperial War Museum, London. CIA, Minutes of Meeting, June 6, 1951, File: Artichoke Docs. 59–155, Box 5; CIA, Memorandum For: Assistant Director, SI, Subject: Progress on BLUE-BIRD, July 9, 1951, File: Artichoke Docs. 59–155, Box 5, CIA Behavior Control Experiments Collection, National Security Archive, Washington. Indicating the secrecy of Tizard's June 1 meeting in Montreal, his official biographer offers only the most oblique references to this 1951 journey, and no discussion of his continuing interest in what Tizard called "applied psychology"—in contrast to the detailed descriptions of his other Canadian visits in 1940, 1947, and 1954. See Ronald W. Clark, *Tizard* (London: Methuen, 1965), 393, 395, 400, 413–14; Confidential—Notes on Visit to Canada, September 1954, HTT 482, Sir Henry T. Tizard Papers, Imperial War Museum, London.

45. David Zimmerman, *Top Secret Exchange: The Tizard Mission and the Scientific War* (Montreal: McGill–Queen's University Press, 1996), 3–5, 7, 19–20, 29, 49–50, 96–129, 147–48, 154–66, 190–204; Clark, *Tizard,* 386–402; R. V. Jones, "Tizard's Task in the 'War Years' 1935–1952," *Biographical Memoirs of the Fellows of the Royal Society,* vol. 7 (London: Royal Society, 1961), 338–41.

46. Marks, *The Search for the "Manchurian Candidate,"* 29–31; Zimmerman, *Top Secret Exchange,* 19. CIA, Minutes of Meeting, June 6, 1951; CIA, Memorandum For: Assistant Director, SI, Subject: Progress on BLUEBIRD, July 9, 1951.

In an article published in a useful but sometimes erratic investigative magazine, *Lobster,* one writer using the pen name Armen Victorian cites a document stamped "from the collection of the manuscript division, Library of Congress," which describes this Montreal meeting's agenda as: "Research into the general phenomena indicated by such terms as 'confessions,' 'mentacide,' 'intervention in the individual's mind' together with methods concerned in psychological coercion, change of opinions and attitudes, etc. etc." Citing a similarly marked document, this same author quotes from Dr. Ormond Solandt's reply, dated January 25, 1954, to an unnamed Canadian cabinet minister about the funding for Dr. Hebb's McGill experiment. It "originated from a discussion among Sir Henry Tizard, representatives of the US Central Intelligence Agency, Dr. Hebb . . . and myself in June 1951" (Armen Victorian, "Following in Uncle Sam's Dirty Footsteps: Chemical and Biological Warfare Testing in the UK," *Lobster* 36 [Winter 1998–99], 25–28).

Though the information in these articles is interesting, their provenance and the author's background preclude uncritical use in the main text. According to a web-log posting by "Glenn Campbell," this author's name, Armen Victorian, is a pseudonym for Henry Azadehdel who "is an active contributor to a Canadian orchid mailing list," http://www.ufomind.com/misc/1997/sep/d27-002.shtml; accessed July 13, 2005. Following this lead, it seems that Henry Azadehdel has had a controversial involvement in the worlds of UFO sightings, crop circles, and orchid smuggling. Aspects of Henry Azadehdel's career are treated in a variety of reliable sources, including a documentary film, *The Mythologist* by John Lundberg, which was broadcast by BBC 4 on March 25, 2004 (broadcast confirmed in an e-mail from the BBC Four Website Team, www.bbc.co.uk/bbcfour, July 27, 2005); and in an essay by one of the principals in the film, Robert Irving ("The Henry X File," available online at the film's website, http://www.mythologist.co .uk/reading/html; accessed July 26, 2005).

Several books and newspaper features on the orchid obsession discuss Azadehdel's landmark conviction for opium smuggling. Susan Orlean's *The Orchid Thief* (New York: Random House, 1998) states, on pages 187–88, that Azadehdel "pleaded guilty in 1989 to four counts of 'smuggling, harboring, and selling endangered orchids,'" admitting to the court that he had made over $400,000 "dealing in black-market orchids." Since his conviction, Azadehdel "has adopted several pseudonyms, including Dr. Armen Victorian," and "is promoting a UFO conspiracy theory involving an alien spacecraft landing in South Africa."

47. Weinstein, *Psychiatry and the CIA,* 274; Meek, "Nobody Is Talking"; Marks, *The Search for the "Manchurian Candidate,"* 32–33; Ignatieff, "What Did the C.I.A. Do to His Father?" 60.

48. Watson, *War on the Mind,* 497–98; Weinstein, *Psychiatry and the CIA,* 99–100, 117–20, 135; Meek, "Nobody Is Talking"; Jack A. Vernon, *Inside the Black Room* (New York: Clarkson N. Potter, 1963), xvi–xvii; D. O. Hebb et al., "Experimental Deafness," *Canadian Journal of Psychology* 8, no. 3 (1954), 152–56.

49. W. H. Bexton, W. Heron, and T. H. Scott, "Effects of Decreased Variation in the Sensory Environment," *Canadian Journal of Psychology* 8, no. 2 (1954), 70–76; Meek, "Nobody Is Talking"; D. O. Hebb, "Drives and the C.N.S.

(Conceptual Nervous System)," *The Psychological Review* 62, no. 4 (1955), 243–54. In his first report of this research at the American Psychological Association in 1953, Hebb stated that his results were of "considerable practical significance for certain occupations, both military and civilian (e.g., watching a radar screen)." See W. Heron, W. H. Bexton, and D. O. Hebb, "Cognitive Effects of a Decreased Variation in the Sensory Environment," *The American Psychologist* 8, no. 8 (1953), 366.

50. Woodburn Heron, "The Pathology of Boredom," *Scientific American* 196 (January 1957), 52–56.

51. CIA, Office Memorandum, To: Chief, Technical Branch, From: [Blacked-out], Subject: National Meetings of the American Psychological Association, September 30, 1954, File: Artichoke Docs. 59–155, Box 5, CIA Behavior Control Experiments Collection, National Security Archive, Washington; Fillmore N. Sanford, "Summary Report of the 1954 Annual Meeting," *The American Psychologist* 9, no. 11 (1954), 708. At the symposium on "Effects of Drugs on Behavior" on September 6, the participants included G. R. Wendt ("The Effects of Drugs on Social and Emotional Behavior"), Daniel Wilner ("Some Social Factors in Drug Use"), and Conan Kornetsky ("The Effects of Drugs on Personality"). The presidential address for the "Division of Experimental Psychology," also on September 6, was by D. O. Hebb ("Drives and the C.N.S."). See American Psychological Association, "Program of the Sixty-Second Annual Meeting of the American Psychological Association," 295, 500, 501. This presidential address, evidently somewhat revised, was published a year later as D. O. Hebb, "Drives and the C.N.S."

52. Weinstein, *Psychiatry and the CIA,* 135, 139–40; Philip Solomon et al., eds., *Sensory Deprivation: A Symposium Held at Harvard Medical School* (Cambridge: Harvard University Press, 1961), 239–57; Stephen E. Glickman, "Hebb, Donald Olding," in Alan E. Kazdin, ed., *Encyclopedia of Psychology* (New York: Oxford University Press, 2000), 105–6.

Although Hebb later admitted, with some sense of remorse, the clandestine source of his funding, he still incorporated findings from the sensory deprivation experiments, without any apparent regrets, into the theoretical reflections that contributed to his rising scholarly reputation. In his *Essay on Mind*, published in 1980 after all the revelations about CIA funding and Dr. Ewen Cameron's abusive research, Hebb wrote that his "so-called sensory-deprivation experiment" demonstrated "that the integrity of the mind at maturity continues to depend on . . . the sensory stimulation of the normal complex environment." These tests, Hebb concluded, "supported the prediction that . . . such conditions would have a disorganizing effect on thought" and contributed to his conviction that "cell-assemblies exist, but the isolation experiment . . . shows that there is much we do not understand about how they function." (D. O. Hebb, *Essay on Mind* [Hillsdale: Lawrence Erlbaum Associates, 1980], 96–97.)

53. CIA, Memorandum for the Record, SUBJECT: Project ARTICHOKE, January 31, 1975.

54. Marks, *The Search for the "Manchurian Candidate,"* 23–25, 32–33, 106, 137–38, 201–2.

001/001

55. *Kubark Counterintelligence Interrogation* (July 1963), 88–89; John C. Lilly, "Mental Effects of Reduction of Ordinary Levels of Physical Stimuli on Intact, Healthy Persons," *Psychiatric Research Reports* 5, no. 1 (1956), 1–9; Marks, *The Search for the "Manchurian Candidate,"* 142–44.

After his resignation from NIMH, Lilly continued to explore the frontiers of human consciousness. Taking LSD while immersed naked in a watery isolation tank, he described this "expanded state of pleasure" as dangerously "seductive" since "one can become quite lazy and return to this state at every opportunity." He set up an elaborate laboratory in the Virgin Islands to explore dolphin consciousness, concluding that their brains were acoustically so far advanced beyond humans' that "the problem is not for us to learn how they speak, but for them to learn how we speak." After teaching one dolphin to count to ten, he found that this student had taught the dolphin in the adjacent tank the same skill through "systematic coaching." In the Hollywood film *Day of the Dolphin* which dramatized these experiments, actor George C. Scott played Lilly (Maya Pines, *The Brain Changers: Scientists and the New Mind Control* [New York: Harcourt Brace Jovanovich, 1973], 16–17, 94–96).

56. Donald Wexler, Jack Mendelson, Herbert Leiderman, and Philip Solomon, "Sensory Deprivation: A Technique for Studying Psychiatric Aspects of Stress," *A.M.A. Archives of Neurology and Psychiatry* 79, no. 1 (1958), 225–33; *Kubark Counterintelligence Interrogation* (July 1963), 89.

57. "Bruner, Jerome S.," *Encyclopaedia Britannica.* http://www.search.eb.com/eb/article?tocId=9016778; accessed, June 29, 2005; "Wiener, Norbert," *Encyclopaedia Britannica,* http://www.search.eb.com/eb/article?tocId=9076934; accessed June 29, 2005; D. O. Hebb, *The Organization of Behavior: A Neuropsychological Theory* (New York: Wiley, 1949); Woodburn Heron and D. O. Hebb, "Cognitive and Physiological Effects of Perceptual Isolation," in Philip Solomon et al., eds., *Sensory Deprivation: A Symposium Held at Harvard Medical School* (Cambridge: Harvard University Press, 1961), v–xvi, 1–2, 6–33; Solomon, *Sensory Deprivation,* v–xvi, 1–2, 239–57. On one of the CIA contract researchers attending, Dr. Louis J. West, see Alan W. Scheflin and Edward M. Opton, Jr., *The Mind Manipulators: A Non-Fiction Account* (New York: Paddington Press, 1978), 75–77, 149–50, 316–20; Senate, 93d Congress, 2d sess., Subcommittee on Constitutional Rights, Committee on the Judiciary, *Individual Rights and the Federal Role in Behavioral Modification* (Washington: Government Printing Office, 1974), 354–55, 357; Peter Schrag, *Mind Control* (New York: Pantheon Books, 1978), 1–9; Keith, *Mind Control,* 103–4.

58. George E. Ruff, Edwin Z. Levy, and Victor H. Thaler, "Factors Influencing Reactions to Reduced Sensory Input," in Solomon, *Sensory Deprivation,* 72–76, 80, 90; Weinstein, *Psychiatry and the CIA,* 118.

59. Vernon, *Inside the Black Room,* xi–xvii, 3–10, 25–34, 156–57, 197–203.

60. Lawrence E. Hinkle Jr., "A Consideration of the Circumstances under Which Men May Be Interrogated, and the Effects That These May Have upon the Function of the Brain," 1, 5, 6, 11–14, 18, File: Hinkle, Box 7, CIA Behavior Control Experiments Collection, National Security Archive, Washington.

61. Weinstein, *Psychiatry and the CIA,* 135, 139–40; Gordon Thomas, *Journey into Madness: Medical Torture and the Mind Controllers* (London: Bantam Press, 1988), 380.

62. Weinstein, *Psychiatry and the CIA,* 136–37; American Psychiatric Association, "Cameron, Donald Ewen," *Biographical Directory of the Fellows and Members of the American Psychiatric Association* (New York: Bowker, 1963), 76; Thomas, *Journey into Madness,* 168; D. Ewen Cameron, "Psychic Driving," *The American Journal of Psychiatry* 112, no. 7 (1956), 502–9.

63. Elizabeth Nickson, "My Mother, the CIA and LSD," *The Observer* (London), October 16, 1994, 48–52; Weinstein, *Psychiatry and the CIA,* 110–20, 140–41; Thomas, *Journey into Madness,* 114, 166–70, 176–77; Marks, *The Search for the "Manchurian Candidate,"* 132–41; D. Ewen Cameron et al., "The Depatterning Treatment of Schizophrenia," *Comprehensive Psychiatry* 3, no. 3 (1962), 65–76.

64. Thomas, *Journey into Madness,* 149–50, 262–72.

65. Nickson, "My Mother, the CIA and LSD," 48–52; *Mrs. David Orlikow, et al. v. United States of America,* 682 F. Supp. 77, U.S. District Court, District of Columbia, January 18, 1988; Weinstein, *Psychiatry and the CIA,* 142, 158–59, 166–67, 250, 268–71, 278–79.

66. Marks, *The Search for the "Manchurian Candidate,"* 147–63; Weinstein, *Psychiatry and the CIA,* 133–35; Thomas, *Journey into Madness,* 168.

67. Weinstein, *Psychiatry and the CIA,* 32–34; Marks, *The Search for the "Manchurian Candidate,"* 127–30, 147–63; Lawrence E. Hinkle Jr. and Harold G. Wolff, "Communist Interrogation and Indoctrination of 'Enemies of the States': Analysis of Methods Used by the Communist State Police (a Special Report)," *Archives of Neurology and Psychiatry* 76 (1956), 116–17, 128–30, 134–35.

68. Weinstein, *Psychiatry and the CIA,* 130, 179–80.

69. Irving L. Janis, "Excerpt from *Victims of Groupthink,*" Swans Commentary, http://www.swans.com/library/art9/xxx099.html; accessed June 8, 2005. As noted in the text, the Physiological Psychology branch of the Office of Naval Research funded a major conference on sensory deprivation at Harvard Medical School attended by several CIA contract researchers. See Solomon, *Sensory Deprivation,* v–xv. During the 1950s and early 1960s, moreover, the ONR had a number of contracts with the agency to funnel CIA funds to other federal agencies. See, for example, CIA, Memorandum For: Chief of Naval Research, Subject: Transfer of Funds for Continuation of a Research Project at the Addiction Research Center, U.S. Public Health Service Hospital, Lexington, Kentucky, August 16, 1957, File: Naval Research, Box 8, CIA Behavior Control Experiments Collection, National Security Archive, Washington. (This file also contained updated, verbatim copies of this memorandum for July 18, 1958, September 15, 1959, October 4, 1960, and November 7, 1960.)

70. Thomas Blass, *The Man Who Shocked the World: The Life and Legacy of Stanley Milgram* (New York: Basic Books, 2004), 65–72, 235–42.

71. Stanley Milgram, *Obedience to Authority: An Experimental View* (New York: Harper & Row, 1974), 1–43; Blass, *The Man Who Shocked the World,* 76,

115–16; Stanley Milgram, "Group Pressure and Action against a Person," *Journal of Abnormal and Social Psychology* 9, no. 2 (1964), 137–43; Arthur G. Miller, *The Obedience Experiments: A Case Study of Controversy in Social Science* (New York: Praeger, 1986); Christopher R. Browning, *Ordinary Men: Reserve Police Battalion 101 and the Final Solution in Poland* (New York: HarperCollins, 1992), 171–77.

72. Blass, *The Man Who Shocked the World,* 76, 112–13, 115–18, 123–30, 152–54, 157–59, 164–65, 298–99; Diana Baumrind, "Some Thoughts on Ethics of Research: After Reading Milgram's 'Behavioral Study of Obedience,'" in Arthur G. Miller, ed., *The Social Psychology of Psychological Research* (New York: Free Press, 1972), 106–11; Judy Green and Jeanna LaDuke, "Mina Spiegel Rees (1902–1997)," *Notices of the AMS* 45, no. 7 (August 1998), 867.

73. Milgram, *Obedience to Authority,* xv.

74. Senate, *Project MKUltra,* 51–52, 62.

75. Senate, *Foreign and Military Intelligence, Book I,* 390–91.

76. Ibid., *Book I,* 400–3.

77. Cockburn and St. Clair, *Whiteout,* 208–9.

78. *Kubark Counterintelligence Interrogation* (July 1963), 1–2, 41, 76–78.

79. Ibid., 77, 85.

80. Ibid., 88, 90, 94.

81. Ibid., 1–2, 41, 45, 76–77, 84–85, 88, 90–91, 93–94, 98–99, 111–12.

82. Mark Bowden, "The Dark Art of Interrogation: A Survey of the Landscape of Persuasion," *The Atlantic Monthly,* October 2003, 72.

83. Lord Parker of Waddington, *Report of the Committee of Privy Counsellors Appointed to Consider Authorised Procedures for the Interrogation of Persons Suspected of Terrorism* (London: Stationery Office, Cmnd. 4901, 1972), 3, 12, 17; S. Smith and W. Lewty, "Perceptual Isolation in a Silent Room," *Lancet* 2 (September 12, 1959), 342–45; Meek, "Nobody Is Talking"; "Lancaster Moor Hospital," http://www.institutions.org.uk/asylums/england/LAN/lancaster_moor_asylum.htm; accessed June 23, 2005.

84. Sir Edmund Compton, *Report of the Enquiry into Allegations against the Security Forces of Physical Brutality in Northern Ireland Arising out of Events on the 9th August, 1971* (London: Stationery Office, Cmnd. 4823, November 1971), para. 46; Parker of Waddington, *Report of the Committee of Privy Counsellors Appointed to Consider Authorised Procedures for the Interrogation of Persons Suspected of Terrorism,* 1–3, 23–24.

85. Parker of Waddington, *Report of the Committee of Privy Counsellors Appointed to Consider Authorised Procedures for the Interrogation of Persons Suspected of Terrorism,* 1, 12; Roderic Bowen, *Report by Mr. Roderic Bowen, Q.C., on Procedures for the Arrest, Interrogation and Detention of Terrorists in Aden* (London: Stationery Office, Cmnd. 3165, December 1966), 3–7, 16–24.

86. European Court of Human Rights, *Ireland v. The United Kingdom,* No. 5310/17, January 18, 1978, para. 32, 34, 39, 81, 96–97, http://www.worldlii.org/eu/cases/ECHR/1978/1.html; accessed June 6, 2004.

87. Ibid., para. 96.

88. Compton, *Report of the Enquiry into Allegations against the Security Forces of Physical Brutality in Northern Ireland,* para. 1; *Times* (London), October 17, October 19, October 20, 1971.

89. Compton, *Report of the Enquiry into Allegations against the Security Forces of Physical Brutality in Northern Ireland,* para. 46–52, 64, 92, 98; *Times,* November 17, November 18, 1971, July 9, 1973.

90. *Times,* November 9, November 11, March 13, 1972; Amnesty International, *Report of an Enquiry into Allegations of Ill-Treatment in Northern Ireland* (London: Amnesty International, March 1972), 36–38.

91. *Times,* March 3, 1972; Parker of Waddington, *Report of the Committee of Privy Counsellors Appointed to Consider Authorised Procedures for the Interrogation of Persons Suspected of Terrorism,* Majority Report, 2, 4–5, 16–17.

92. *Times,* May 14, August 27, September 3, 1976; *Ireland v. The United Kingdom,* para. 102, 147, 166–67, 246; Meek, "Nobody Is Talking."

93. *Ireland v. The United Kingdom,* Separate Opinion of Judge Evrigenis.

94. Watson, *War on the Mind,* 274–75.

95. Aldo Migliorini, *Tortura Inquisizione Pena di Morte: Brevi Considerazioni sui Principali Strumenti Commentati in Merito ai Tre Argomenti dal Medioevo all'Epoca Industriale* (Poggibonsi: Lalli Editore, 1997), 118; Susan Sontag, "Regarding the Torture of Others," *New York Times Magazine,* May 23, 2004, 25–26; *New York Times,* March 9, 2003, May 5, May 13, 2004.

96. Migliorini, *Tortura Inquisizione Pena di Morte,* 56; Mellor, *La torture,* 77–80; *New York Times,* March 9, 2003, May 5, May 13, 2004.

Chapter 3: Propagating Torture

1. *New York Times,* February 16, 1986.

2. Michael T. Klare, *War without End: American Planning for the Next Vietnams* (New York: Knopf, 1972), 241, 245, 247, 250; Thomas David Lobe, "U.S. Police Assistance for the Third World" (doctoral dissertation, University of Michigan, 1975), 82.

3. Lobe, "U.S. Police Assistance for the Third World," 42–44.

4. Ibid., 46.

5. Robert Komer, memorandum to McGeorge Bundy and General Taylor, "Should Police Programs Be Transferred to the DOD?" Secret (declassified), April 18, 1962.

6. A. J. Langguth, *Hidden Terrors* (New York: Pantheon, 1978), 47–52, 124–26, 300.

7. Lobe, "U.S. Police Assistance for the Third World," 56–57, 60–61, 72.

8. Klare, *War without End,* 241, 245, 247, 250, 260–65.

9. General Accounting Office, *Stopping U.S. Assistance to Foreign Police and Prisons* (Washington: General Accounting Office, 1976), 14.

10. Klare, *War without End,* 382–83; Amnesty International, *Report on Torture* (London: Duckworth, 1975), 114–239; R. Matthew Gildner, "Torture and U.S. Foreign Policy" (honor's thesis, Department of History, University of Wisconsin–Madison, 2001), 2.

11. Senate, 93rd Congress, 2nd Session, *Congressional Record* (Washington: Government Printing Office), vol. 120, pt. 25, October 2, 1974, 33474.

12. Ibid.

13. Ibid., 33475.

14. Langguth, *Hidden Terrors,* 125–28, 138–40, 251–52.

15. Klare, *War without End,* 261–64; Douglas Valentine, *The Phoenix Program* (New York: William Morrow, 1990), 59–60.

16. Valentine, *The Phoenix Program,* 63, 77–85. On page 84, Valentine identifies the CIA officers who trained the Vietnamese Special Branch as "experts from the CIA's Support Services Branch." In other accounts, this unit is identified as the Technical Services Division (Langguth, *Hidden Terrors,* 138–40).

17. Victor Marchetti and John D. Marks, *The CIA and the Cult of Intelligence* (New York: Knopf, 1974), 245–46.

18. Andrew F. Krepinevich Jr., *The Army and Vietnam* (Baltimore: Johns Hopkins University Press, 1986), 227–28.

19. Ian McNeill, *The Team: Australian Army Advisers in Vietnam 1962–1972* (St. Lucia: University of Queensland Press, 1984), 385–411.

20. *New York Times,* February 18, 1970.

21. Lloyd H. Cotter, M.D., "Operant Conditioning in a Vietnamese Mental Hospital," *American Journal of Psychiatry* 124, no. 1 (1967), 23–28; Gordon Thomas, *Journey into Madness: Medical Torture and the Mind Controllers* (London: Bantam Press, 1988), 281–82.

22. Thomas, *Journey into Madness,* 286–87; Alexander Cockburn and Jeffrey St. Clair, *Whiteout: The CIA, Drugs and the Press* (New York: Verso, 1998), 210.

23. *New York Times,* August 6, August 7, August 9, August 12, August 14, August 15, August 16, August 17, August 20, August 29, September 26, September 27, September 28, September 30, October 1, November 8, 1969; James Olson, ed., *Dictionary of the Vietnam War* (New York: Bedrick Books, 1987), 389–90.

24. *New York Times,* February 18, 1970.

25. Ibid., April 7, 1971.

26. Ibid., July 16, 1971.

27. *New York Times,* July 20, August 2, 1971; Marchetti and Marks, *The CIA and the Cult of Intelligence,* 246.

28. *New York Times,* July 20, August 2, 1971; House of Representatives, 92nd Congress, 1st sess., Subcommittee of the Committee on Government Operations, Hearings on August 2, 1971, *U.S. Assistance Programs in Vietnam* (Washington: Government Printing Office, 1971), 349.

29. House of Representatives, *U.S. Assistance Programs in Vietnam,* 319–21, 327, 349; Senate, 93rd Congress, 1st sess., Committee on Armed Services, Hearings on July 2, 20, 25, 1973, *Nomination of William E. Colby to Be Head of Central Intelligence* (Washington: Government Printing Office, 1973), 101–17; Dale Andradé, "Pacification," in Stanley Kutler, ed., *Encyclopedia of the Vietnam War* (New York: Scribner's, 1996), 423.

30. In its report, the Army Intelligence Command faulted K. Barton Osborn for refusing "to identify specific persons . . . on two occasions"—an understandable discretion when dealing with a CIA assassination program. In a personal

comment that casts doubts upon his own credibility, William Colby added in a statement to Congress about Osborn: "The Phoenix program was essentially instituted during the summer of 1968 and began to work during the fall. . . . Mr. Osborn served in Vietnam from September 1967, to December 1968. In other words, his service essentially was before the Phoenix program really got rolling in any degree." If we examine Colby's comment objectively, Osborn's Vietnam service overlapped with Phoenix from June to December 1968, a period of at least six months and fully half of the standard military tour of duty in Vietnam—in short, a substantial period of service. Senate, 93d Congress, 1st sess., Armed Services Committee, *Nomination of William E. Colby*, 116–17.

31. Mark Moyar, *Phoenix and the Birds of Prey: The CIA's Secret Campaign to Destroy the Viet Cong* (Annapolis: Naval Institute Press, 1997), 89–99; Senate, Armed Services Committee, *Nomination of William E. Colby*, 116–17.

32. John Ranelagh, *The Agency: The Rise and Decline of the CIA* (New York: Simon and Schuster, 1986), 571–77, 585, 589.

33. Ibid., 571–76, 584–99.

34. Cockburn and St. Clair, *Whiteout*, 210–11.

35. *New York Times,* June 11, 1979.

36. Frank Snepp, *Decent Interval: The American Debacle in Vietnam and the Fall of Saigon* (London: Allen Lane, 1980), 42–49.

37. *New York Times,* November 18, November 19, November 20, November 23, December 4, December 20, 1977.

38. Department of Defense, Office of the Assistant Secretary of Defense Command, Control, Communications and Intelligence, Memorandum for the Record, Subject: USSOUTHCOM CI Training–Supplemental Information (U), July 31, 1991, File: Project X, Consortium News, Arlington, Virginia; Department of Defense, Assistant to the Secretary of Defense, Memorandum for Secretary of Defense, Subject: Interim Report on Improper Material in USSOUTHCOM Training Manuals (U)–Information Memorandum, [Sgd.] Werner E. Michel, October 4, 1991, File: Project X, Consortium News, Arlington, Virginia.

39. Department of the Army, Office of the Deputy Chief of Staff for Intelligence, Robert W. Singleton, Memorandum Thru the General Counsel, ATTN: PWC, Subject: History of Project X, November 4, 1991, File: Project X, Consortium News, Arlington, Virginia; Robert Parry, *Lost History: Contras, Cocaine and Other Crimes* (Arlington: Media Consortium 1997), 48–49.

40. Department of Defense, Office of the Assistant Secretary of Defense Command, Control, Communications and Intelligence, Point Paper Concerning USSOUTHCOM Proposed Counterintelligence (CI) Training to Foreign Governments, July 30, 1991, File: Project X, Consortium News, Arlington, Virginia.

41. *New York Times,* August 1, 1970.

42. Ibid., August 11, 1970.

43. Ibid., August 16, 1970; Langguth, *Hidden Terrors,* 252–54, 285–88.

44. *New York Times,* August 5, 1978; Manuel Hevia Cosculluela, *Pasaporte 11333: Ocho Años con la CIA* (Havana: Editorial de Ciencias Sociales, 1978), 121–24, 279–87.

45. Senate, 92nd Congress, 1st sess., Committee on Foreign Relations, Sub-committee on Western Hemisphere Affairs, *United States Policies and Programs in Brazil* (Washington: Government Printing Office, 1971), 17–20, 39–40.

46. Langguth, *Hidden Terrors,* 299–301.

47. Ibid., 301; Senate, 93rd Congress, 2nd sess., Committee on Foreign Relations, *Foreign Assistance Act of 1974: Report of the Committee on Foreign Relations United States Senate on S. 3394 to Amend the Foreign Assistance Act of 1961, and for Other Purposes* (Washington: Government Printing Office, 1974), 42.

48. Lobe, "U.S. Police Assistance for the Third World," 415, 421.

49. Darius M. Rejali, *Torture and Modernity: Self, Society, and State in Modern Iran* (Boulder: Westview Press, 1994), 77–79.

50. CIA, Special Group (CI), Memorandum for the Record, Subject: Minutes for Meeting of Special Group (CI), 2 p.m., Thursday, August 9, 1962, Collection: Iran Revolution, National Security Archive, Washington.

51. John D. Jernegan, "Memorandum from the Acting Assistant Secretary of State for Near Eastern and South Asian Affairs (Jernegan) to the Special Group (Counterinsurgency), Washington, March 2, 1964," in Nina D. Howland, ed., *Foreign Relations of the United States, 1964–68,* vol. XXII, Iran (Washington: Government Printing Office, 1999), 15.

52. *New York Times,* June 11, 1979.

53. Ranelagh, *The Agency,* 649–50.

54. Amnesty International, *Amnesty International Briefing: Iran* (London: Amnesty International, 1976), 9.

55. *New York Times,* June 11, 1979.

56. Reza Baraheni, "The Savak Documents," *The Nation,* February 23, 1980, 198–202.

57. *New York Times,* June 18, 1979.

58. For a fuller description of the impact of torture on the Armed Forces of the Philippines, see Alfred W. McCoy, *Closer Than Brothers: Manhood at the Philippine Military Academy* (New Haven: Yale University Press, 1999), chapter 6.

59. Patricia Weiss Fagen, "Repression and State Security," in Juan E. Corradi, Patricia Weiss Fagen, and Manuel Antonio Garreton, eds., *Fear at the Edge: State Terror and Resistance in Latin America* (Berkeley: University of California Press, 1992), 49–55, 58–60; Neil J. Kritz, ed., *Transitional Justice: How Emerging Democracies Reckon with Former Regimes.* Vol. III, *Laws, Rulings, and Reports* (Washington: U.S. Institute for Peace, 1995), 146–47; Joan Dassin, ed., *Torture in Brazil: a Report* (New York: Vintage Books, 1986), 204–5, 235–38; *New York Times,* November 10, 1986. In addition to the 125 "disappeared," there are loose estimates of another 175 extrajudicial killings under Brazil's military dictatorship. See Kritz, *Transitional Justice.* Vol. II, *Country Studies,* 431. A journalist gives figures of 125 disappeared and 144 murdered in Brazil. See Lawrence Weschler, *A Miracle, a Universe: Settling Accounts with Torturers* (New York: Pantheon, 1990), 53.

60. Richard J. Kessler, *Rebellion and Repression in the Philippines* (New Haven: Yale University Press, 1989), 137. Kessler's partial statistics on the number of extrajudicial killings, or salvagings, in 1984 are supplemented by data from the Reverend La Verne D. Mercade and Sister Mariani Dimaranan, *Philippines:*

Testimonies on Human Rights Violations (Geneva: World Council of Churches, 1986), 89, 136.

61. The precise origins of the neologism *salvaging* are murky. In a lead editorial on the "summary killings and disappearances" of the Marcos era, the *Philippine Daily Inquirer* (June 29, 1996) commented, "we call this 'salvaging,' demonstrating our talent to reinvent the English language." During the Marcos dictatorship, the military apparently coined the term to describe its torture operations in the mid-1970s and it was soon taken up by the country's human rights groups. A 1978 report noted in a discussion of "the elimination of detainees after torture instead of placing them in official detention centers" that "the military refers to this kind of elimination as 'salvaging.'" See Task Force on Detainees, *Political Detainees of the Philippines*, Book 3 (Manila: Association of Major Orders of Religious Superiors, March 1978), 41–43.

62. Harold W. Maynard, "A Comparison of Military Elite Role Perceptions in Indonesia and the Philippines" (doctoral dissertation, American University, 1976), 461–62; McCoy, *Closer Than Brothers*, chapters 7–8; Alistair Horne, *A Savage War of Peace: Algeria 1954–1962* (London: Macmillan, 1977), 206–7, 232–34, 428–30, 436–60, 526–28, 541–44; Weschler, *A Miracle, a Universe,* 65–68.

63. "Torturer in US for Training," *Tanod* (Manila) 1, no. 3 (1978), 3; Task Force on Detainees, Association of Major Religious Superiors in the Philippines, *Pumipiglas: Political Detention and Military Atrocities in the Philippines* (Manila: TFDP, 1980), 106–7.

64. Army Intelligence Center and School, Fort Huachuca, Arizona, United States Army, Foreign Intelligence Assistance Program, Project X, Annual List of Instructional Material, August 1977, File: Project X, Consortium News, Arlington, Virginia.

65. Department of Defense, Assistant to the Secretary of Defense, Report of Investigation: Improper Material in Spanish-Language Intelligence Training Manuals, March 10, 1992, File: Project X, Consortium News, Arlington, Virginia.

66. Alfred W. McCoy, *Priests on Trial* (New York: Penguin Books, 1984), 212–15.

67. On February 16, 1990, Colonel Hernani F. Figueroa filed a libel suit against the author for a series titled "RAM Boys" published a month earlier (January 1–8) in Manila's largest newspaper, the *Philippine Daily Inquirer*. Five days after that series appeared, the press secretary to President Corazon Aquino, Tomas Gomez III, faxed a formal request, on January 13, for the author's permission to translate the series into Filipino languages and publish it as both "printed pamphlets" and in "comic book form" for mass distribution. Several weeks later, the PDI reprinted the articles in a pamphlet that sold 50,000 copies in three days.

During the wide circulation of these articles, Figueroa filed a "complaint-affidavit" with Manila's office of the city fiscal prosecutor, naming the author and the paper's editors and publisher as respondents. He stated that he was a graduate of the Philippine Military Academy (1966) and an active-duty officer who had "been awarded numerous spot promotions and decorations for exemplary behavior and gallantry as a Filipino soldier." After reproducing several long passages from the *Inquirer* articles, including the extracts quoted from Father Kangleon's memoir, the colonel stated that "the article pretends to enumerate various wrongdoings, crimes, violations of human rights, corruptions, cruelty, and other atrocities allegedly committed by the herein complainant." For what he called these "malicious and vicious actuations" which, he said, "have caused undue and irreparable injury to me as a professional soldier, and to the Armed Forces of Philippines of which I proudly belong," the colonel demanded "moral, actual, and exemplary" damages of P20 million. In response to a long-distance telephone call from the paper's editor-in-chief, Federico Pascual, the author sent him, on April 5, a copy of Father Kangleon's original handwritten letter, an affidavit from another priest similarly tortured, and other supporting documents. Some months later, Pascual called to say that Figueroa's attorney had not appeared to answer the paper's response to the colonel's original complaint and the suit had therefore been dismissed.

Looking back on this incident fifteen years later, this lawsuit seems best understood in the political context of an ongoing quest for power, via coup d'état, by the RAM military faction that Colonel Figueroa had once headed. In 1988, a prominent Manila newsmagazine, *National Midweek,* had published the author's "RAM Boys" series (September 21, 28, and October 12, 1988) with the same passages about Colonel Figueroa that later appeared in the *Inquirer* series of January 1990. In a period of relative quiet in 1988 with few coups, none of the RAM officers mentioned in the *National Midweek* series made any complaints or filed lawsuits. Then in December 1989, just weeks before my articles appeared in the *Daily Inquirer,* RAM launched an abortive weeklong coup that was ultimately blocked from taking Malacanang Palace when President George H. W. Bush scrambled two U.S. Air Force jets from Clark Field, just north of Manila, for a low flyover across the city, warning the RAM rebel forces of the possibility of U.S. intervention in defense of the Aquino government. After the failure of that coup, RAM's leaders retreated into a rebel underground for five more years of coup plotting against the Philippine state. Hence, it was in this hyper-heated atmosphere, with the future of the Philippines hanging in the balance, that the *Daily Inquirer* decided to republish my "RAM Boys" articles. President Aquino's press secretary was interested in reprinting the same material as a part of a government information campaign to create a climate unsympathetic to future coups. In this context, the RAM group had an apparent political motivation in filing suit to challenge my work and one officer, Colonel Figueroa, came forward to file the complaint. Nine years later, when my monograph, *Closer Than Brothers,* was published by Yale University Press in 1999, including the same material about Father Kangleon's interrogation, there were no complaints. In 2000, when the monograph was reprinted in the Philippines, verbatim, the Manila publisher, Anvil Press, made no changes to the text, which includes the passages quoted above, and has received no complaints after marketing that book through the country's largest commercial bookstore, National Books, for the past five years. In sum, the author has published this material about Father Kangleon's interrogation on three occasions in the Philippines—1988, 1990, and 2000—and it was only during the period of intense coup and counter-coup activity in 1990 that any of the officers mentioned complained about the text.

68. Father Edgardo Kangleon, "A Moment of Uncertainty" (ms, December 8, 1982), enclosed in letter To: Dear Papa/Mama/Rey, September 30, 1983 (copy furnished by Father Niall O'Brien, St. Columban's Mission Society, Bacolod City). An excerpt of this letter was published in *That We May Remember* (Quezon City: Promotion of Church People's Rights, May 1989), 168–73.

69. Kangleon, "A Moment of Uncertainty," 13–16.

70. Church People's Rights, *That We May Remember,* 172–73.

71. Sheila S. Coronel, "RAM: From Reform to Revolution," in *Kudeta: The Challenge to Philippine Democracy* (Manila: Philippine Center for Investigative Journalism, 1990), 65. In one of the early reports about Lieutenant Batac's involvement in torture, the human rights group Task Force on Detainees stated: "Other officers of the 5th CSU who have been implicated in torture accounts of political detainees and against whom no public investigation has been made: Capt. (now Major) Cecilio Penilla, Capt. Virgilio Saldajeno, Lt. Rodolfo Aguinaldo, Lt. Victor Batac, Lt. Robert Delfin, Lt. Cesar Alvarez." See Task Force on Detainees, *Political Detainees of the Philippines,* Book 3 (Manila: Association of Major Orders of Religious Superiors, March 1978), 5. For details on Lieutenant Batac's treatment of prisoners see interviews with Jose Ma. Sison, Alan Jazmines, and "Gene," University of the Philippines, Interdisciplinary Forum on Political Detainees, April 16, 1986.

72. Danilo P. Vizmanos, Proof of Claim Form for Torture Victims (May 5, 1993), *In Re. Estate of Ferdinand E. Marcos Human Rights Litigation,* 910 F Supp. 1460, 1462–63, Case No. 94–16739, MDL No. 840, U.S. Ninth Circuit Court of Appeals; *Honolulu Star-Bulletin,* September 11, 1992; *Bulletin Today,* August 15, 1976.

73. Task Force on Detainees, *Political Detainees in the Philippines,* Book 2 (Manila: Association of Major Orders of Religious Superiors, March 31, 1977), 8–9; *The Daily Cardinal* (Madison, Wisconsin), October 16, 1986, 9. The International Commission of Jurists report, as quoted in this account in the *Daily Cardinal,* reads: "Maria Elena Ang was arrested on August 5, 1976, by a combined force of 5 MIG (ISAFP-NISA) agents led by Maj. Esguerra; kept incommunicado for fifteen days at the ISAFP headquarters in Bago Bantay, Quezon City, and in a safe house; subjected to electric shock, water cure, sleep deprivation, sexual indignities, pistol whipping, and threats to relatives. Named Maj. Esguerra and Maj. Riola of ISAFP, Atty. Castillo of NISA, and *Lt. Batac of 5CSU as her torturers*" (emphasis added).

74. *Daily Cardinal,* October 17, 1986; *Capital Times* (Madison, Wisconsin), October 17, 1986.

75. Interview with Maria Elena Ang, Sydney, Australia, May 9, 1989.

76. Danilo P. Vizmanos, *Through the Eye of the Storm: Random Notes of Danilo P. Vizmanos* (Quezon City: Ken Inc., 2000), 68, 127; interview with Captain Danilo P. Vizmanos (ret.), Makati, November 6, 1998.

77. Department of Defense, Subject: USSOUTHCOM CI Training–Supplemental Information (U), July 31, 1991; Department of the Army, Army

Intelligence Center and Fort Huachuca, Memorandum for Deputy Chief of Staff for Intelligence, Subject: History of Project X, [Sgd.] William J. Teeter, September 12, 1991, File: Project X, Consortium News, Arlington, Virginia.

78. Department of Defense, Assistant to the Secretary of Defense, Report of Investigation: Improper Material in Spanish-Language Intelligence Training Manuals, March 10, 1992.

79. Army Intelligence Center and School, Study Manual: Handling of Sources—1989 (Secret. Not Releasable to Foreign Nationals, Declassified by Authority of the Secretary of the Army, September 19, 1996), Box 2: Intelligence Training Course Manuals, Folder: Handling of Sources, National Security Archive, Washington, 5–6, 24–25, 42–44, 65–66, 110–12, 116–33.

80. Department of Defense, Point Paper Concerning USSOUTHCOM Proposed Counterintelligence (CI) Training to Foreign Governments, July 30, 1991; Department of Defense, Subject: USSOUTHCOM CI Training–Supplemental Information, July 31, 1991; Department of Defense, Subject: Interim Report on Improper Material in USSOUTHCOM Training Manuals (U)–Information Memorandum, October 4, 1991.

81. Department of Defense, Subject: Interim Report on Improper Material in USSOUTHCOM Training Manuals (U)–Information Memorandum, October 4, 1991.

82. Army Intelligence Center and School, Project X, Annual List of Instructional Material, August 1977.

83. Senate, Select Committee on Intelligence, "Transcript of Proceedings before the Select Committee on Intelligence: Honduran Interrogation Manual Hearing," 14–15.

84. CIA, Human Resource Exploitation Training Manual—1983, June 8, 1988 (Box 1 CIA Training Manuals, Folder: Resources Exploitation Training Manual, National Security Archive, Washington), I–D.

85. Ibid., K–1.B.
86. Ibid., I–22.
87. Ibid., K–1.F–G.
88. Ibid., F–1.A.
89. Ibid., F–5.E, F–14.F, F–15.H.
90. Ibid., K–5.D.
91. Ibid., L–17.
92. Ibid., L–1, L–2.
93. Ibid., L–3.
94. Ibid., L–3, L–4.
95. Ibid., L–11.D.
96. Ibid., L–12.
97. Ibid., L–12–E.
98. Ibid., I–26.III.

99. Baltimore Sun, January 27, 1997; Washington Post, January 28, 1997; New York Times, January 29, 1997.

100. James LeMoyne, "Testifying to Torture," New York Times Magazine, June 5, 1988, 47, 62.

101. Ibid., 45–47, 62–65.

102. Senate, Select Committee on Intelligence, "Transcript of Proceedings before the Select Committee on Intelligence: Honduran Interrogation Manual Hearing," 3–5.

103. Ibid., 14.

104. Ibid., 5, 15, 21–22.

105. Ibid., 23–24.

106. Ibid., 24, 30.

107. Ibid., 25–27.

108. Ibid., 28–29.

109. Ibid., 33–35.

110. Congressional Fact Sheet, June 8, 1988, introduction to Central Intelligence Agency, *Human Resource Exploitation Training Manual—1983*, Box 1, CIA Training Manuals, National Security Archive, Washington.

111. *New York Times,* July 9, 1996; Ole Vedel Rasmussen, "Medical Aspects of Torture," *Danish Medical Bulletin* 37, no. 1 (1990), 3, 30–31; William Rees-Mogg, "The Torture Industry," in Rehabilitation and Research Centre for Torture Victims, *Annual Report 1995* (Copenhagen: Rehabilitation and Research Centre for Torture Victims, 1996), 5–6; Inge Genefke, "Some Steps towards a World with Less Torture," in Rehabilitation and Research Centre, *Annual Report 1995,* 15–16; Rehabilitation and Research Centre, *Annual Report 1995,* 21–23, 32–34; Keith Carmichael et al., "The Need for REDRESS," *Torture* 6, no. 1 (1996), 7; Helena Cook, "The Role of Amnesty International in the Fight against Torture," in Antonio Cassese, ed., *The International Fight against Torture* (Baden-Baden: Nomos Verlagsgesellschaft, 1991), 172–86.

112. Erik Holst, "International Efforts on the Rehabilitation of Torture Victims," in June C. Pagaduan Lopez and Elizabeth Protacio Marcelino, eds., *Torture Survivors and Caregivers: Proceedings of the International Workshop on Therapy and Research Issues* (Quezon City: University of the Philippines Press, 1995), 8–14, 190–91, 291–316, 356–57.

113. Senate, 100th Congress, 2d sess., Treaty Doc. 100–20, *Message from the President of the United States Transmitting the Convention against Torture and Other Cruel, Inhuman or Degrading Treatment or Punishment* (Washington: Government Printing Office, 1988), iii–iv; Ahcene Boulesbaa, *The U.N. Convention on Torture and the Prospects for Enforcement* (The Hague: Martinus Nijhoff, 1999), 19.

114. Boulesbaa, *The U.N. Convention on Torture,* 19; Senate, 101st Congress, 2d sess., Committee on Foreign Relations, *Convention against Torture: Hearing before the Committee on Foreign Relations* (Washington: Government Printing Office, 1990), 1, 12–18, 34, 35, 40–43, 66–69, 70–71.

115. Senate, 102d Congress, 1st sess., Report 102–249, Committee on the Judiciary, *The Torture Victims Protection Act* (Senate, Calendar No. 382, 26 November 1991), 6–7; United States, *Congressional Record. Proceedings and Debates of the 102d Congress. First Session. Volume 137–Part 23* (Washington: Government Printing Office, 1991), November 25, 1991, 34785; United States, *Congressional Record. Proceedings and Debates of the 102d Congress.*

Second Session. Volume 138–Part 3 (Washington: Government Printing Office, 1992), March 3, 1992, 4176–78.

116. *New York Times,* June 13, 1993.

117. United States, *Congressional Record. Proceedings and Debates of the 103d Congress. Second Session. Volume 140—Part 1* (Washington: Government Printing Office, 1994), February 2, 1994, 827; *Foreign Relations Authorization Act,* PL 103–236, Title V, Sec. 506, 108 Stat. 463 (1994), 18 USC§ 2340–2340A.

118. United States, *Weekly Compilation of Presidential Documents* 32, no. 34 (Washington: Government Printing Office, 1996), 1482; House of Representatives, 104th Congress, 2nd sess., *Congressional Record* (Washington: 142, pt. 14, 1996), 19562–63.

119. Department of the Army, Headquarters, *FM 34–52: Intelligence Interrogation* (Washington: Department of the Army, September 28, 1992), iv–v, 1–7, 1–8.

120. Ibid., 1–8.

121. Ibid., 3–1, 3–2, 3–9, 3–10 to 3–23; CIA, *Human Resource Exploitation Training Manual—1983,* F-1.

122. Department of the Army, *FM 34–52,* 1–8, 3–17 to 3–20.

123. Klare, *War without End,* 300–304; *New York Times,* June 24, 2001.

124. James Hodge and Linda Cooper, *Disturbing the Peace: The Story of Father Roy Bourgeois and the Movement to Close the School of the Americas* (Maryknoll: Orbis Books, 2004), 1–4, 148–208.

125. Ibid., 157–66.

126. Werner E. Michel, Assistant to the Secretary of Defense (Intelligence Oversight), Subject: Improper Material in Spanish-Language Intelligence Training Manuals, March 10, 1992, Box 2, Intelligence Training Source Manuals, Folder: Untitled, National Security Archive, Washington.

127. *Baltimore Sun,* January 27, 1997; *Washington Post,* January 28, 1997; *New York Times,* January 29, 1997.

Chapter 4: War on Terror

1. Ron Baer, *See No Evil: The True Story of a Ground Soldier in the CIA's War on Terrorism* (New York: Three Rivers Press, 2002), 268–69.

2. *The 9/11 Commission Report: Final Report of the National Commission on Terrorist Attacks upon the United States* (New York: Norton, 2004), 90–93.

3. *New York Times,* March 6, 2005; Jane Mayer, "Outsourcing Torture: Annals of Justice," *The New Yorker,* February 14, 2005, 108–9.

4. Marites Dañguilan Vitug and Glenda M. Gloria, *Under the Crescent Moon: Rebellion in Mindanao* (Quezon City: Ateneo Center for Social Policy and Public Affairs, 2000), 222–23, 224, 227.

5. *Washington Post,* October 21, 2001; Gordon Thomas, *Journey into Madness: Medical Torture and the Mind Controllers* (London: Bantam Press, 1988), 348.

6. *Los Angeles Times,* October 28, 2001.

7. *Wall Street Journal,* October 23, 2001.

8. Jonathan Alter, "Time to Think about Torture," *Newsweek*, November 5, 2001, 45.

9. Steve Randall, "Pro-Pain Pundits," *Extra!* (January–February 2002), http://fair.org/extra/0201/pro-pain.html; accessed December 22, 2002.

10. *60 Minutes* (co-host, Mike Wallace; executive producer, Don Hewitt), January 20, 2002; *Los Angeles Times*, November 8, 2001; Alan M. Dershowitz, *Why Terrorism Works: Understanding the Threat, Responding to the Challenge* (New Haven: Yale University Press, 2002), 136–39.

11. Richard A. Posner, "The Best Offense," *The New Republic*, September 2, 2002, 28–31.

12. *Boston Globe*, February 16, 2002.

13. Vitug and Gloria, *Under the Crescent Moon*, 222–24, 229–30, 232.

14. Richard A. Clarke, *Against All Enemies: Inside America's War on Terror* (New York: Free Press, 2004), 24.

15. George W. Bush, "Notice: Detention, Treatment, and Trial of Certain Non-Citizens in the War against Terrorism," White House, November 13, 2001, 66 *Federal Register* (FR) 57833, http://www.law.uchicago.edu/tribunals/docs/exec_orders.pdf; accessed June 14, 2004; Memo 2: Executive Orders. Federal Register: November 16, 2001, Military Order of November 13, 2001, in Karen J. Greenberg and Joshua L. Dratel, eds., *The Torture Papers: The Road to Abu Ghraib* (New York: Cambridge University Press, 2005), 25–28; *New York Times*, March 6, March 27, November 2, 2005; Mayer, "Outsourcing Torture," 112–14; *Washington Post*, November 2, 2005.

16. John Barry et al., "The Roots of Torture," *Newsweek*, May 24, 2004, 29–30; Mayer, "Outsourcing Torture," 112–14; Department of Justice, Office of Legal Counsel, Memorandum for William J. Haynes II, General Counsel, Department of Defense, From: John Yoo, Deputy Assistant Attorney General, and Robert J. Delabunty, Special Counsel, January 9, 2002, in Greenberg and Dratel, *The Torture Papers*, 38–39, 43–44, 47, 57, 79.

17. Human Rights Watch, *The Road to Abu Ghraib* (June 2004), 5, http://www.hrw.org/reports/2004/usa0604.pdf; accessed October 12, 2005; *Chicago Tribune*, December 28, 2001.

18. Department of Justice, Office of Legal Counsel, Memorandum for William J. Haynes II, General Counsel, Department of Defense, December 28, 2001, From: Patrick F. Philbin, Deputy Assistant Attorney General, and John C. Yoo, Deputy Assistant Attorney General, in Greenberg and Dratel, *The Torture Papers*, 29, 37.

19. Alberto R. Gonzales, Memorandum for the President, Subject: Decision Re. Application of the Geneva Convention on Prisoners of War to the Conflict with Al Qaeda and the Taliban, January 25, 2002, DRAFT 1/25/2002—3:30 pm, http://www.msn.com/id/4999148/site/newsweek/; accessed May 24, 2004.

20. Secretary of Defense, Memorandum for Chairman of the Joint Chiefs of Staff, Subject: Status of Taliban and Al Qaeda, January 19, 2002, in Greenberg and Dratel, *The Torture Papers*, 80.

21. Jay S. Bybee, Assistant Attorney General, Office of Legal Counsel, Department of Justice, Memorandum for Alberto R. Gonzales, Counsel to the President, and William J. Haynes II, General Counsel of the Department of Defense,

January 22, 2002, 37, http://www.washingtonpost.com/wp-srv/nation/documents/012202 bybee.pdf; accessed June 28, 2004; Barry et al., "The Roots of Torture," 31; *New York Times,* June 8, 2004, November 9, 2005.

22. Gonzales, Memorandum for the President, January 25, 2002, 2.

23. Colin L. Powell, Memorandum, To: Counsel to the President, Subject: Draft Decision Memorandum for the President on the Applicability of the Geneva Convention to the Conflict in Afghanistan, n.d., http://msnbc.com/modules/newsweek/pdf.powell_memo.pdf; accessed June 20, 2004; George Bush, "Memorandum for the Vice President," Subject: Humane Treatment of al Qaeda and Taliban Detainees, February 7, 2002, http://www.washingtonpost.com/wp-srv/nation/documents/0207026bush.pdf; accessed June 28, 2004; Barry, "The Roots of Torture," 31; *New York Times,* June 8, 2004; *Washington Post,* February 8, 2002; The White House, Press Briefing by Ari Fleischer, February 7, 2002, http://www.whitehouse.gov/news/releases/2002/02print/20020207-6.html; accessed June 8, 2005; *American Forces Information Service News Articles,* February 8, 2002, http://www.defenselink.mil/news/Feb2002;t02082002_t0208sd.html; accessed July 1, 2004.

24. *New York Times,* November 23, 2002, March 9, 2003; Seymour M. Hersh, *Chain of Command: The Road from 9/11 to Abu Ghraib* (New York: HarperCollins, 2004), 16–17, 47–50, 64; Seymour M. Hersh, "The Gray Zone: How a Secret Pentagon Program Came to Abu Ghraib," *The New Yorker,* May 24, 2004, 38–39.

25. *Washington Post,* December 26, 2002, December 17, 2004, November 2, 2005; *New York Times,* November 23, 2002, March 9, 2003, June 17, June 18, 2004; Barry et al., "The Roots of Torture," 31–33; Mayer, "Outsourcing Torture," 106–8.

26. *The Observer,* June 13, 2004; *New York Times,* March 4, 2003, January 9, March 6, March 8, March 30, May 31, 2005; Barry, "The Roots of Torture," 31–32; Mayer, "Outsourcing Torture," 106–7; *Washington Post,* December 26, 2002; Mark Bowden, "The Dark Art of Interrogation: A Survey of the Landscape of Persuasion," *The Atlantic Monthly,* October 2003, 54; Department of State, Bureau of Democracy, Human Rights, and Labor, *Country Reports on Human Rights Practices—2004* (February 28, 2005), http://www.state.gov/g/drl/rls/hrrpt/2004/41584.htm; accessed March 29, 2005.

27. Mayer, "Outsourcing Torture," 112, 114–16; *Newsweek,* June 21, 2004, 50; Jason Vest, "Pray and Tell," *The American Prospect* 16, no. 7 (July 2005), 49–50.

28. Mayer, "Outsourcing Torture," 112, 114–16; *Newsweek,* June 21, 2004, 50, July 5, 2004, 6; House and Senate Intelligence Committees, "Hearings on Pre-9/11 Intelligence Failures," September 26, 2002, http://web.lexis-nexis.com/congcomp/printdoc; accessed March 29, 2005.

29. Hersh, *Chain of Command,* 270.

30. Mayer, "Outsourcing Torture," 110.

31. *New York Times,* February 6, March 5, April 8, 2004, March 22, 2005.

32. Mayer, "Outsourcing Torture," 110.

33. *New York Times,* March 3, March 4, March 7, March 9, 2003, June 27, June 28, 2004, July 27, 2005; *Washington Post,* January 5, 2005.

34. *Washington Post,* January 5, 2005.

35. Jay S. Bybee, Memorandum for Alberto R. Gonzales, August 1, 2002, 1–2, 8, 16–22, http://www.washingtonpost.com/wp-srv/nation/documents/dojinter rogationmemo20020801.pdf; accessed June 20, 2004; *New York Times,* June 27, June 28, 2004, November 2, 2005; Mayer, "Outsourcing Torture," 112–14.

36. *New York Times,* June 25, 2004.

37. Ibid., March 19, 2005; Mayer, "Outsourcing Torture," 114.

38. Senate Judiciary Committee, Confirmation Hearing, Transcript, January 6, 2005, 81, http://www.nytimes.com/2005/01/06/politics/06 TEXT-GONZALES .html?ei+5070&3n+5f; accessed March 14, 2005.

39. *Youngstown Sheet & Tube Co. et al. v. Sawyer,* Supreme Court, no. 744, June 2, 1952, *United States Reports,* vol. 343 (Washington: Government Printing Office, 1952), 644; Maeva Marcus, *Truman and the Steel Seizure Case: The Limits of Presidential Power* (New York: Columbia University Press, 1977); Alan I. Bigel, *The Supreme Court on Emergency Powers, Foreign Affairs, and Protection of Civil Liberties, 1935–1975* (Lanham: University Press of America, 1986), 135–50.

40. *New York Times,* March 3, March 7, 2003, May 13, June 27, June 28, 2004.

41. Chris Mackey and Greg Miller, *The Interrogators: Inside the Secret War against Al Qaeda* (New York: Little, Brown, 2004), 471–72.

42. *New York Times,* March 2, March 4, March 8, March 16, 2005; Leon Worden, SCV Newsmaker of the Week: Brig. Gen. Janis Karpinski, *Signal Newspaper* (Santa Clarita, California), July 4, 2004.

43. George W. Bush, State of the Union Address of the President to the Joint Session of Congress," January 28, 2003, C-Span.Org, http://www.c-span.org/ executivetranscript.asp?cat+current_event&code+bush_admin&year=2003; accessed March 29, 2005.

44. *Washington Post,* December 26, December 28, 2002; *Toronto Star,* December 28, 2002; *The Economist,* January 11, 2003, 11; Mackey and Miller, *The Interrogators,* 247.

45. *New York Times,* March 4, 2003, September 17, 2004, March 12, May 22, 2005; Human Rights Watch, *The Road to Abu Ghraib,* 21–23.

46. *Washington Post,* October 16, December 26, 2002; *New York Times,* November 23, 2002, March 9, 2003, June 21, June 22, June 23, 2004, January 1, May 30, 2005; M. Gregg Bloche and Jonathan H. Marks, "Doctors and Interrogators at Guantánamo Bay," *New England Journal of Medicine* 353, no. 1 (July 7, 2005), 7; Barry et al., "The Roots of Torture," 31–33; *Boston Globe,* June 24, 2004; *Guardian* (Manchester), May 19, 2004; William J. Haynes II, General Counsel, Department of Defense, For: Secretary of Defense, Subject: Counter-Resistance Techniques, November 27, 2002, http://www.washingtonpost.com/wp-srv/nation/ documents/dodmemos.pdf; accessed June 28, 2004; Department of Defense, Special Defense Department Briefing, July 7, 2005, http://www.defenselink.mil/ transcripts/2005/tr20050707-3301.html; accessed July 11, 2005.

47. Barry et al., "The Roots of Torture," 31–33; William J. Haynes II, General Counsel, Department of Defense, For: Secretary of Defense, Subject: Counter-Resistance Techniques, November 27, 2002.

48. *New York Times,* June 21, 2005; Adam Zagorin and Michael Duffy, "Inside the Interrogation of Detainee 063," *Time* 165, no. 25 (June 20, 2005), 26–33.

49. *Washington Post,* December 26, 2002; *New York Times,* November 23, 2002, March 9, 2003, June 21, June 22, June 23, 2004, January 1, 2005; Michael Hirsh, "A Tortured Debate," *Newsweek,* June 21, 2004, 50; *Boston Globe,* June 24, 2004; Jane Mayer, "The Experiment," *The New Yorker,* July 11 and 18, 2005, 70.

50. *New York Times,* July 28, July 30, 2005; Donald Rumsfeld, Memorandum for the General Counsel of the Department of Defense, Subject: Detainee Interrogations, January 15, 2003, http://www.washingtonpost.com/wp-srv/nation/documents/011503rumsfeld.pdf; accessed June 28, 2004; Working Group Report on Detainee Interrogations in the Global War on Terrorism: Assessment of Legal, Historical, Policy, and Operational Considerations, March 6, 2003, http://www.informationclearinghouse.info/pdf/military-0604.pdf; accessed June 14, 2004; Major General Jack L. Rives, Memorandum for SAF/GC, February 6, 2003, Senate, 109th Congress, 1st sess., *Congressional Record* (Washington: vol. 151, no. 102, July 25, 2005), S8794–95; Major General Jack L. Rives, Memorandum for SAF/GC, February 5, 2003, Senate, *Congressional Record* (July 25, 2005), S8796–97.

51. Rear Admiral Michael F. Lohr, Subj: Working Group Recommendations Relating to Interrogation of Detainees, February 6, 2003, Senate, *Congressional Record* (July 25, 2005), S8795; Major General Thomas J. Romig, Memorandum for General Counsel of the Department of the Air Force, March 3, 2003, Senate, *Congressional Record* (July 25, 2005), S8794.

52. *Washington Post,* December 26, 2002; *New York Times,* November 23, 2002, March 9, 2003, June 22, June 23, 2004, January 1, July 28, July 30, 2005; Barry et al., "The Roots of Torture," 32–33; Hirsh, "A Tortured Debate," 50; *Boston Globe,* June 24, 2004; Mayer, "The Experiment," 70–71; Working Group Report on Detainee Interrogations in the Global War on Terrorism: Assessment of Legal, Historical, Policy, and Operational Considerations, March 6, 2003; Donald Rumsfeld, Memorandum for the Commander, Southern Command, April 16, 2003, http://www.washingtonpost.com/wp-srv/nation/documents/041603 rumsfeld.pdf; accessed June 28, 2004.

53. *New York Times,* July 13, July 14, July 15, 2005; Department of Defense, "Army Regulation 15-6: Final Report: Investigation into FBI Allegation of Detainee Abuse at Guantánamo Bay, Cuba Detention Facility" (April 1, 2005; amended June 9, 2005) 12, 14–21, http://www.defenselink.mil/news/Jul2005/d20050714report.pdf; accessed July 18, 2005; Senate Armed Services Committee, "Hearing on Guantánamo Bay Detainee Treatment" (July 13, 2005), 13–17, http://web.lexis-nexis.com/congcom/printdoc; accessed July 18, 2005; Human Rights Watch, *The Road to Abu Ghraib,* 13; *Chicago Sun–Times,* January 28, 2005; *Washington Post,* February 10, 2005.

54. *New York Times,* June 8, 2004; Hersh, "The Gray Zone," 42; Scott Horton, "Betr: Strafanzeige gegen den US–Verteidigungsminister Donald Rumsfeld, u.a." An den: Herrn Generalbundesanwalt, Beim Bundesgerichtshof, Karlsruhe, January 29, 2005, para. 4, http://www.rav.de/StAR_290105_Horton.htm; accessed April 14, 2005.

55. Hersh, "The Gray Zone," 40–42; Hersh, *Chain of Command,* 57–59;

Worden, "Brig. Gen. Janis Karpinski"; Mark Danner, *Torture and Truth: America, Abu Ghraib, and the War on Terror* (New York: New York Review of Books, 2004), 33.

56. Worden, "Brig. Gen. Janis Karpinski"; Joint Interrogation and Debriefing Center, Abu Ghurayb, Iraq, http://www.publicintegrity.org/docs/AbuGhraib/Tag29.pdf; accessed March 29, 2005; *Washington Post,* May 9, 2004; M. G. Antonio M. Taguba, Article 15–6 Investigation of the 800th Military Police Brigade, February 26, 2004, 37, http://www.cbsnews.com/htdocs/pdf/tagubareport.pdf; accessed May 10, 2004.

57. Hersh, *Chain of Command,* 16–17, 47–50, 59–60.

58. Hersh, "The Gray Zone," 41–42; Hersh, *Chain of Command,* 46–48, 52–53, 61–65; Worden, "Brig. Gen. Janis Karpinski"; *New York Times,* December 4, 2004.

59. Taguba, Article 15–6 Investigation of the 800th Military Police Brigade, 7, 8, 15; *New York Times,* May 24, May 26, June 22, 2004, March 30, May 30, 2005; Human Rights Watch, *The Road to Abu Ghraib,* June 2004, 32–33; Hersh, *Chain of Command,* 30–31; Scott Horton, "Betr: Strafanzeige gegen den US–Verteidigungsminister Donald Rumsfeld, u.a.," para. 16; Mayer, "The Experiment," 63.

60. Worden, "Brig. Gen. Janis Karpinski"; Mayer, "The Experiment," 63; *New York Times,* May 24, May 26, June 22, 2004, March 30, May 30, 2005.

61. James R. Schlesinger et al., "Final Report of the Independent Panel to Review DoD Detention Operations," August 2004, 9, http://news.findlaw.com/cnn/docs/dod/abughraibrpt.pdf; accessed August 26, 2004; ABC News, *Nightline,* "Broken Chain of Command," May 12, 2005.

62. Ricardo S. Sanchez, Memorandum for: C2, Combined Joint Task Force Seven, Baghdad, Iraq 09335, Subject: CJTF–7 Interrogation and Counter-Resistance Policy, September 14, 2003, http://www.aclu.org/SafeandFree/SafeandFree.cfm?ID=17851&c=206; accessed March 30, 2005; Ricardo S. Sanchez, Memorandum for: C2, Combined Joint Task Force Seven, Baghdad, Iraq 09335, Subject: CJTF–7 Interrogation and Counter-Resistance Policy, October 12, 2003, http://www.aclu.org/SafeandFree/SafeandFree.cfm?ID=17851&c=206; accessed March 30, 2005; Translation of Sworn Statement by [name blacked out], 1430/21 JAN 04, in Danner, *Torture and Truth,* 247–48; *New York Times,* September 24, 2005.

63. CIA, *Human Resource Exploitation Training Manual—1983,* June 8, 1988 (Box 1, CIA Training Manuals, Folder: Resources Exploitation Training Manual, National Security Archive, Washington), E–33, I–D, I–5, I–22, L–3, I–12; *Kubark Counterintelligence Interrogation* (July 1963), File: Kubark, Box 1: CIA Training Manuals (National Security Archive, Washington), 47; Sanchez, Memorandum for: C2, Combined Joint Task Force Seven, Baghdad, Iraq 09335, Subject: CJTF–7 Interrogation and Counter-Resistance Policy, September 14, 2003.

64. Taguba, Article 15–6 Investigation of the 800th Military Police Brigade, February 26, 2004, 7, 8, 15; *New York Times,* May 24, May 26, June 22, 2004, March 30, 2005; *Washington Post,* July 27, 2005; Human Rights Watch, *The Road to Abu Ghraib,* 32–33; Worden, "Brig. Gen. Janis Karpinski."

65. Taguba, Article 15–6 Investigation of the 800th Military Police Brigade, 38; Worden, "Brig. Gen. Janis Karpinski"; *New York Times,* May 19, 2004.

66. Taguba, Article 15–6 Investigation of the 800th Military Police Brigade, 16, 18; *New York Times,* May 19, 2004.

67. Taguba, Article 15–6 Investigation of the 800th Military Police Brigade, 18; Hersh, *Chain of Command,* 29–30.

68. M. Gregg Bloche and Jonathan H. Marks, "When Doctors Go to War," *New England Journal of Medicine* 352 (January 6, 2005), 4; Joint Interrogation and Debriefing Center, Abu Ghurayb, Iraq, 16, 23.

69. Joint Interrogation and Debriefing Center, Abu Ghurayb, Iraq, 16, 23, 32–33, 40; *New York Times,* June 4, June 8, June 9, June 14, 2004.

70. Report of the International Committee of the Red Cross (ICRC) on the Treatment by the Coalition Forces of Prisoners of War and Other Protected Persons by the Geneva Conventions in Iraq during Arrest, Internment and Interrogation, February 2004, 3–4, 6, 8, 11, 12, http://www.redress.btinternet.co.uk/icrc_iraq.pdf; accessed May 12, 2004; *Newsday,* May 5, 2004; *USA Today,* May 31, 2004.

71. Report of the International Committee of the Red Cross, February 2004, 13, 15, 17–18.

72. Hersh, "The Gray Zone," 42; *New York Times,* July 3, 2004.

73. Worden, "Brig. Gen. Janis Karpinski."

74. Hersh, "The Gray Zone," 42; Worden, "Brig. Gen. Janis Karpinski." For a complete gallery of the comparatively few photos from Abu Ghraib prison leaked to the press among the hundreds on Darby's original CD, see Danner, *Torture and Truth,* 215–24.

75. Worden, "Brig. Gen. Janis Karpinski"; Taguba, Article 15–6 Investigation of the 800th Military Police Brigade, 44; Hersh, "The Gray Zone," 41.

76. Worden, "Brig. Gen. Janis Karpinski"; Taguba, Article 15–6 Investigation of the 800th Military Police Brigade, 13, 44.

77. Senate, Judiciary Committee, Confirmation Hearing, January 6, 2005, 77–80; *Washington Post,* October 24, 2004; *New York Times,* October 26, 2004.

78. *New York Times,* May 1, 2004; Seymour M. Hersh, "Torture at Abu Ghraib," *The New Yorker,* May 10, 2004, 42–47; Worden, "Brig. Gen. Janis Karpinski"; "Abuse of Iraqi POWs by GIs Probed," CBS NEWS.com, April 28, 2004, http://www.cbsnews.com/stories/2004/04/27/60II/printable614063.shtml; accessed March 29, 2005.

79. In a possible reprise of medieval cultural politics, the administration's interrogation policy was mirrored in the release, just weeks before CBS's Abu Ghraib story, of Mel Gibson's film, *The Passion of the Christ.* Just as grisly medieval icons depicting Christ's suffering normalized that era's gory spectacles of punishment and public execution, so the film's blood-soaked scourging of the Messiah may have prepared the American public for quiet acceptance of the prison photos. Within one month, Gibson's gruesome film broke box-office records across America, grossing $370 million; the next month, Americans reacted blandly to CBS Television's iconic images of grotesque prisoner abuse. For figures on the film's gross see *Killer Movies,* http://www.killermovies.com/p/passion/; accessed March 29, 2005.

80. Supreme Court of the United States, Oral Arguments, *Donald H. Rumsfeld v. Jose Padilla*, No. 03-1027, http://www.supremecourtus.gov/oral_arguments/argument_transcripts/03-1027.pdf; accessed July 5, 2004.

81. *New York Times,* May 31, 2004; Human Rights Watch, *The Road to Abu Ghraib,* 28–29; Hersh, *Chain of Command,* 44–45; *Denver Post,* May 19, May 28, 2004; *Washington Post,* August 3, 2005.

82. *NewsHour with Jim Lehrer,* May 4, 2004, http://www.pbs.org/newshour/bb/military/jan-june04/abuse1_05_04.html; accessed June 14, 2004; *New York Times,* May 11, May 15, May 25, 2004; *Report of the United Nations High Commissioner for Human Rights and Follow Up to the World Conference on Human Rights* (Geneva: Commission on Human Rights, 61st Session, E/CN.4/2005/4, Advance Edited Edition, June 9, 2004), 18; "President Outlines Steps to Help Iraq Achieve Democracy and Freedom," May 24, 2004, http://www.whitehouse.gov/news/release/2004/05/print/20040524-10.html; accessed June 14, 2004; *Washington Post,* May 13, June 22, 2004.

83. *New York Times,* June 30, 2004.

84. Ibid., June 5, 2004; *Report of the United Nations High Commissioner for Human Rights and Follow Up to the World Conference on Human Rights,* 32.

85. *International Herald Tribune,* June 19–20, 2004; *New York Times,* June 18, June 24, 2004.

86. *New York Times,* February 16, 2005.

87. Supreme Court of the United States, Oral Arguments, *Donald H. Rumsfeld v. Jose Padilla,* No. 03-1027; *New York Times,* July 4, 2004.

88. *New York Times,* June 29, July 1, July 4, 2004; Supreme Court of the United States, *Yaser Esam Hamdi, et al. v. Donald Rumsfeld, Secretary of Defense, et al.,* No. 03-6696, http://caselaw.lp.findlaw.com/cgi-bin/getcase.pl?court=US&navby=case&vol=000&invol=03-6696; accessed July 5, 2004.

89. Mayer, "Outsourcing Torture," 123; *New York Times,* November 9, 2004, February 1, March 24, March 27, 2005; *Capital Times* (Madison, Wisconsin), April 9–10, 2005.

90. *New York Times,* May 30, July 15, July 16, 2005.

Chapter 5: Impunity in America

1. Michael Ignatieff, "Mirage in the Desert," *New York Times Magazine,* June 27, 2004, 14.

2. John Conroy, *Unspeakable Acts, Ordinary People: The Dynamics of Torture* (New York: Knopf, 2000), 112–13, 244–47.

3. *New York Times,* July 23, 2004; Department of the Army, Inspector General, *Detainee Operations Inspection* (July 21, 2004), foreword, 13, 22, 31, 38, http://www.washingtonpost.com/wp-srv/world/iraq/abughraib/detaineereport.pdf; accessed July 28, 2004.

4. Deborah Solomon, "Questions for Trent Lott," *New York Times Magazine,* June 20, 2004, 15.

5. *New York Times,* July 24, 2004; *Los Angeles Times,* July 23, 2004; [Major

General] Antonio M. Taguba, Article 15-6 Investigation of the 800th Military Police Brigade, February 26, 2004, 16, http://www.cbsnews.com/htdocs/pdf/tagubareport.pdf; accessed May 10, 2004.

6. *New York Times*, August 25, 2004; James R. Schlesinger et al., "Final Report of the Independent Panel to Review DoD Detention Operations," August 24, 2004, 5, 6, 13, 15, 29, 35, 37, http://news.findlaw.com/cnn/docs/dod/abughraibrpt.pdf; accessed August 26, 2004.

7. [Major General] George R. Fay, "AR 15-6 Investigation of the Abu Ghraib Detention Facility and 205th Military Intelligence Brigade (U)," 7–9, 29, 42, 44, 45, 53, 55, 118, http://news.bbc.co.uk/nol/shared/bsp/hi/pdfs/26_08_04_fayreport.pdf; accessed August 26, 2004.

8. Ibid., 23, 25–26, 29; *Washington Post*, May 26, 2004; Scott Horton, "Betr: Strafanzeige gegen den US–Verteidigungsminister Donald Rumsfeld, u.a." An den: Herrn Generalbundesanwalt, Beim Bundesgerichtshof, Karlsruhe, January 29, 2005, para. 11–15, http://www.rav.de/StAR_290105_Horton.htm; accessed April 14, 2005.

9. Fay, "AR 15-6 Investigation of the Abu Ghraib Detention Facility and 205th Military Intelligence Brigade (U)," 29; *New York Times*, August 25, August 27, 2004.

10. *New York Times*, August 25, August 27, 2004; Fay, "AR 15-16 Investigation of the Abu Ghraib Detention Facility and 205th Military Intelligence Brigade (U)," 8, 10, 17, 19, 23, 40–42, 63–64, 70, 83, 88, 117–19.

11. *New York Times*, November 30, 2004.

12. *New York Times*, November 30, December 1, 2004; *Indianapolis Star*, December 1, 2004.

13. Seymour M. Hersh, *Chain of Command: The Road from 9/11 to Abu Ghraib* (New York: HarperCollins, 2004), 6–7; *New York Times*, December 21, 2004.

14. Letter from T. J. Harrington, Deputy Assistant Director, Counterterrorism Division, Federal Bureau of Investigation, to Major General Donald J. Ryder, Criminal Investigation Command, Department of the Army, July 14, 2004, http://www.aclu.org/torturefoia/released/FBI_4622-2624.pdf; accessed March 8, 2005; *New York Times*, December 21, 2004.

15. *New York Times*, December 21, 2004; Detainee Interviews (Abusive Interrogation Issues), 5/6/04, http://www.aclu.org/torturefoia/released/FBI_4194.pdf; accessed March 8, 2005; To: Bald, Gary, Battle, Frankie, Cummings, Arthur, Subject: Impersonating FBI at GTMO, Date: December 5, 2003, http://www.aclu.org/torturefoia/released/FBI_3977.pdf; accessed January 27, 2005.

16. To: Caproni, Valene E (OGC) (FBI), Subject: FW GTMO, Sent: July 30, 2004, http://www.aclu.org/torturefoia/released/FBI_4737–4738.pdf; accessed March 8, 2005; FBI, To: Inspection, From: CIRG, Title: Counterterrorism Division, GTMO, Inspection Special Inquiry, Date: 7/13/2004, http://www.aclu.org/torturefoia/released/FBI_4499–4501.pdf; accessed March 8, 2005.

17. *New York Times*, May 1, 2005; *Break Them Down: Systematic Use of Psychological Torture by US Forces* (Cambridge: Physicians for Human Rights, 2005), 2, 8, 9, 17, 20.

18. *New York Times,* January 6, 2004, January 7, January 19, January 26, February 4, February 15, March 17, April 1, May 24, July 27, 2005; White House, Presidential Nomination, Jay Scott Bybee, http://www.whitehouse.gov/news/nominations/187.html; accessed March 18, 2005.

19. Jane Mayer, "Outsourcing Torture: Annals of Justice," *The New Yorker,* February 14, 2005, 106; *New York Times,* February 19, 2005.

20. *New York Times,* March 7, 2003, September 19, 2004.

21. *Wall Street Journal,* January 5, 2005; Daniel Levin, acting Assistant Attorney General, "Memorandum for James B. Comey, Deputy Attorney General, Re: Legal Standards Applicable under USC§§ 2340–2340A" (Office of Legal Counsel, Department of Justice), December 30, 2004; Horton, "Betr: Strafanzeige gegen den US-Verteidigungsminister Donald Rumsfeld, u.a.," para. 27.

22. Senate Judiciary Committee, Confirmation Hearing, Transcript, January 6, 2005, 5, 12, 19, http://www.nytimes.com/2005/01/06/politics/06TEXT-GONZALES.html?ei+5070&3n+5f; accessed March 14, 2005.

23. Ibid., 47–50.

24. Ibid., 22–23, 59–60.

25. Ibid., 33–34; *New York Times,* January 19, 2005; Responses of Alberto R. Gonzales, Nominee to Be Attorney General of the United States, to Written Questions of Senator Richard J. Durbin, 1, 3 (e-mail attachment from Martin Lederman, March 18, 2005).

26. Senate Judiciary Committee, Confirmation Hearing, 35–37, 49, 75, 81–82.

27. Ibid., 59, 66–67, 75, 80; *New York Times,* February 4, 2005; Horton, "Betr: Strafanzeige gegen den US–Verteidigungsminister Donald Rumsfeld, u.a.," para. 30–32.

28. *New York Times,* July 27, October 8, 2005.

29. *New York Times,* January 13, 2005; Mayer, "Outsourcing Torture," 114.

30. *New York Times,* March 2, 2005.

31. National Public Radio, *News,* March 21, 2005.

32. *New York Times,* March 10, March 11, March 12, 2005; Executive Summary (U), 14, 21, http://www.defenselink.mil/news/Mar2005/d20050310exe.pdf; accessed March 14, 2005; Senate Armed Services Committee, "Detainee Interrogation," March 10, 2005, Lexis–Nexis Congressional, http://web.lexis-nexis.com/congcomp/printdoc; accessed March 29, 2005.

33. *New York Times,* March 16, April 30, 2005.

34. *Capital Times* (Madison, Wisconsin), March 26–27, 2005; *New York Times,* March 26, June 28, October 23, 2005.

35. *New York Times,* January 17, 2005; Horton, "Betr: Strafanzeige gegen den US-Verteidigungsminister Donald Rumsfeld, u.a.," para. 18.

36. *New York Times,* April 23, May 12, 2005; ABC News, *Nightline,* "Broken Chain of Command," May 12, 2005; *Record* (Bergen County, New Jersey), May 14, 2005.

37. *New York Times,* June 29, 2005.

38. *New York Times,* April 28, May 9, 2005; *Wisconsin State Journal* (Madison), April 24, 2005; Human Rights Watch, *Getting Away with Torture?: Command*

Responsibility for the U.S. Abuse of Detainees 17, no. 1 [G], April 2005, 1–2, http://www.hrw.org/reports/2005/us0405.pdf; accessed April 25, 2005.

39. *New York Times,* February 16, March 2, March 11, 2005; *Newsweek,* February 28, 2005, 32–34.

40. *New York Times,* March 18, March 19, March 21, 2005.

41. Ibid., March 3, March 11, March 13, 2005.

42. Ibid., March 18, 2005.

43. Ibid., January 9, March 6, April 23, 2005; *Newsweek,* February 28, 2005, 32–34.

44. *New York Times,* January 29, February 13, March 6, 2005; Mayer, "Outsourcing Torture," 118.

45. *New York Times,* February 18, February 25, February 28, March 6, March 30, 2005; Mayer, "Outsourcing Torture," 106, 120–21.

46. *Boston Globe,* December 31, 2001; *Washington Post,* March 13, June 30, 2005; Mayer, "Outsourcing Torture," 118.

47. *New York Times,* June 25, July 1, 2005; *Washington Post,* March 13, June 30, 2005.

48. *New York Times,* June 25, June 27, June 29, July 1, July 2, 2005; *Washington Post,* March 13, June 30, 2005.

49. *New York Times,* March 6, March 8, May 1, 2005.

50. Ibid., March 12, 2005.

51. Ibid., March 12, May 22, 2005; Human Rights Watch, *Getting Away with Torture?*; Commission on Human Rights, *Advisory Services and Technical Cooperation in the Field of Human Rights: Report of the Independent Expert on the Situation of Human Rights in Afghanistan, M. Cherif Bassiouni* (New York: United Nations Economic and Social Council, ECN 4/2005/122, 11 March 2005).

52. *Washington Post,* March 26, 2005.

53. *New York Times,* March 10, March 17, 2005; Office of the President of the United States, *The Commission on the Intelligence Capabilities of the United States Regarding Weapons of Mass Destruction* (Washington, March 31, 2005), 373.

54. Michael Ignatieff, "Lesser Evils," *New York Times Magazine,* May 2, 2004, 86.

55. Ignatieff, "Mirage in the Desert," 15.

56. Alan Dershowitz, "Tortured Reasoning," in Sanford Levinson, ed., *Torture: A Collection* (New York: Oxford University Press, 2004), 257, 274.

57. "Harvard Law Professors Urge Congress to Review Interrogation Policy and Hold Executive Branch Accountable," http://www.iraq-letter.com; posted June 14, 2004.

58. *New York Times Magazine,* June 12, 2005, 43.

59. *New York Times,* May 12, May 13, May 16, May 24, May 26, May 27, May 28, May 31, 2005.

60. *New York Times,* May 26, May 31, June 1, June 2, 2005; "Amnesty International Report 2005, Speech by Irene Khan at Foreign Press Association," May 25, 2005, http://www.amnesty.org/library/print/ENGPOL100142005; accessed June 7, 2005; Fox News Channel, *Fox News Sunday* (Host: Chris Wallace), June 5, 2005.

61. National Public Radio, *Talk of the Nation,* June 6, 2005.

62. *New York Times,* May 27, June 5, June 8, June 13, June 15, June 18, 2005; BBC News, June 20, 2005, http://newsvote.bbc.co.uk/mpapps/pagetools/print/ news.bbc.co.uk/2/hi/americas/4110388.stm; accessed June 23, 2005.

63. *New York Times,* June 16, June 18, 2005; Panel II of a Hearing of the Senate Judiciary Committee, Subject: Detainees, Chaired by: Senator Arlen Specter (R-PA), June 15, 2005, http://web.lexis-nexis.com/congcomp/printdoc; accessed June 21, 2005.

64. *New York Times,* August 1, 2005.

65. *New York Times,* June 24, July 6, 2005; M. Gregg Bloche and Jonathan H. Marks, "Doctors and Interrogators at Guantánamo Bay," *New England Journal of Medicine* 353, no. 1 (July 7, 2005), 6–8.

66. *New York Times,* June 24, June 27, July 6, 2005; *The Principles of Medical Ethics: With Annotations Especially Applicable to Psychiatry* (Washington: American Psychiatric Association, 2001), 7–9.

67. Ole Vedel Rasmussen, "Medical Aspects of Torture," *Danish Medical Bulletin* 37, no. 1 (1990), 43, 83, 86.

68. *New York Times,* June 24, June 27, July 6, 2005; American Psychological Association, "Report of the American Psychological Association Presidential Task Force on Psychological Ethics and National Security" (June 2005), 1, 5, 8–9, http://www.apa.org/releases/PENSTaskForceReportFinal.pdf; accessed July 7, 2005. In its "ethical principles," updated in June 2005, the APA suggests that researchers "make reasonable efforts to minimize the discomfort, infection, illness, and pain of animal subjects" but only requires that its members "take reasonable steps to avoid harming their clients/patients" who happen to be human beings. (American Psychological Association, "Ethical Principles of Psychologists and Code of Conduct," http://www.apa.org/ethics/code/2002.pdf; accessed June 29, 2005). In a letter to the *New York Times,* the APA president, Ronald F. Levant, faulted the critical tone of the paper's July 6 coverage of his association's ambiguous stance in this controversy, insisting that "using a phobia to inflict severe psychological distress is clearly prohibited by the task force report." But the task force report, cited in the text above, indicates that the *Times*'s account did indeed capture the unresolved ambiguity of the APA's relationship with national security. (*New York Times,* July 7, 2005.)

69. *Washington Post,* July 8, July 9, 2005; *Capital Times,* July 9–10, 2005; *New York Times,* July 8, 2005; Department of Defense, Special Defense Department Briefing, July 7, 2005, http://www.defenselink.mil/transcripts/2005/ tr20050707-3301.html; accessed July 11, 2005.

70. Department of Defense, "Army Regulation 15-6: Final Report: Investigation into FBI Allegation of Detainee Abuse at Guantánamo Bay, Cuba Detention Facility" (April 1, 2005; amended June 9, 2005), 1, 20, http://www.defenselink.mil/news/ Jul2005/d20050714report.pdf; accessed July 18, 2005; Senate Armed Services Committee, Hearing on Guantánamo Bay Detainee Treatment (July 13, 2005), 19, 20, 35, 55, http://web.lexis-nexis.com/congcom/printdoc; accessed July 18, 2005.

71. *New York Times,* July 13, July 14, July 15, 2005; Senate Armed Services Committee, Hearing on Guantánamo Bay Detainee Treatment (July 13, 2005), 42, 50, 54–56.

72. *New York Times,* July 24, August 1, 2005; *Los Angeles Times,* July 27, 2005; Statement of Senator John McCain, Amendment on Army Field Manual, U.S. Senator John McCain, Arizona, News Center, July 25, 2005, http://mccain .senate.gov/index.cfm?fuseaction=Newscenter4.ViewPressRelease&Content_id= 1595; accessed July 29, 2005; Senate, 109th Congress, 1st Session, *Congressional Record* (Washington: vol. 151, no. 102, July 25, 2005), S8789–90, 8798–99.

73. *New York Times,* July 24, August 1, October 6, October 25, November 2, 2005; U.S. Newswire, Washington, July 24, 2005, http://proquest.umi.com/ pdqweb?index; accessed July 29, 2005; letter to Senator McCain from General Joseph Hoar (Ret. USMC) et al., July 25, 2005, http://www.humanrightsfirst.org/ us_law/etn/pdf/mccain-072205.pdf;_accessed August 2, 2005; *New York Times,* October 6, 2005; *International Herald Tribune,* October 7, 2005.

74. Mark Bowden, "The Dark Art of Interrogation: A Survey of the Landscape of Persuasion," *The Atlantic Monthly,* October 2003, 54, 72–76.

75. *New York Times,* September 10, 2005.

Chapter 6: The Question of Torture

1. A number of legal commentators noted the pervasive influence of the "ticking bomb" argument in public support for torture during the first years of the war on terror. "How do those who speak in our name justify such barbarity?" asked a New York State Supreme Court judge about torture advocates. "By invoking the image of the 'ticking bomb,' they claim the right to torture a man to save innocent lives." (See Gustin L. Reichbach, "Sartre's Torture and Ours," *New York Law Journal,* June 8, 2005.) Similarly, a professor at the University of Virginia Law School commented: "The so-called ticking bomb scenario has proved remarkably effective as a rhetorical tactic for defusing opposition to controversial interrogation techniques. Once you've admitted you would turn to torture in some circumstances, how can you object to merely 'coercive' techniques—such as sleep deprivation—if they might get detainees to cough up something of intelligence value?" (Rosa Brooks, "Ticking Bombs and Slippery Slopes," *Los Angeles Times,* May 28, 2005.)

2. Associated Press, "'NYPD Blue' Signs Off after 12 Seasons," MSNBC .com, March 2, 2005, http://msnbc.msn.com/id/7052431/print/1/displaymode/ 1098/; accessed June 13, 2005; *The Star-Ledger* (Newark, New Jersey), February 27, 2005, http://www.stwing.upenn.edu/~sepingwal/farewell1.html; accessed June 13, 2005; *Clarkson Integrator* (Potsdam, New York), February 28, 2005, http://www.clarksonintegrator.com/global_user_elements/printpage.cfm?storyid= 878822; accessed June 13, 2005; *USA Today,* http://www.usatoday.com/life/ television/reviews/2005-02-28-nypd-blue_x.htm; accessed June 21, 2005.

3. Alan Dershowitz, "Tortured Reasoning," in Sanford Levinson, ed., *Torture: A Collection* (New York: Oxford University Press, 2004), 257–59, 266–67, 274, 276–77.

4. Richard A. Posner, "The Best Offense," *The New Republic,* September 2, 2002, 28–31.

5. *New York Times Magazine,* June 12, 2005, 42–43.

6. *The 9/11 Commission Report: Final Report of the National Commission on Terrorist Attacks upon the United States* (New York: Norton, 2004), 273–76.

7. Elaine Scarry, "Five Errors in the Reasoning of Alan Dershowitz," in Levinson, *Torture*, 284; Office of the President of the United States, *The Commission on the Intelligence Capabilities of the United States Regarding Weapons of Mass Destruction* (Washington, March 31, 2005), 5–6.

8. *New York Times*, April 21, April 23, April 27, 2005; Aldert Vrij, *Detecting Lies and Deceit: The Psychology of Lying and the Implications for Professional Practice* (New York: Wiley, 2000), 74–76, 96–97, 159–60; Gisli H. Gudjonsson, *The Psychology of Interrogations, Confessions, and Testimony* (New York: Wiley, 1996), 183–85; Roberta Wohlstetter, *Pearl Harbor: Warning and Decision* (Stanford: Stanford University Press, 1962), 387.

9. Eyal Press, "In Torture We Trust?" *The Nation*, March 31, 2003, 11–15; Richard H. Weisberg, "Loose Professionalism, or Why Lawyers Take the Lead on Torture," in Levinson, *Torture*, 304.

10. Paul Aussaresses, *The Battle of the Casbah: Terrorism and Counter-Terrorism in Algeria 1955–1957* (New York: Enigma, 2002), 126–28, 162–63; *New York Times*, July 20, August 2, 1971.

11. Stephen Budiansky, "Intelligence: Truth Extraction," *The Atlantic Monthly*, June 2005, 32–35.

12. Mark Bowden, "The Dark Art of Interrogation: A Survey of the Landscape of Persuasion," *The Atlantic Monthly*, October 2003, 55–56; *Washington Post*, December 26, 2002; *Time*, March 24, 2003, http://www.time.com/time/nation/printout/0,8816,436061,00.html; accessed July 7, 2005.

13. *New York Times*, December 18, 2004, January 1, February 16, 2005.

14. *New York Times*, March 18, 2005; Office of the President of the United States, *The Commission on the Intelligence Capabilities of the United States Regarding Weapons of Mass Destruction*, 15–16.

15. Jason Vest, "Pray and Tell," *The American Prospect* 16, no. 7 (July 2005), 50.

16. Seymour M. Hersh, *Chain of Command: The Road from 9/11 to Abu Ghraib* (New York: HarperCollins, 2004), 270; Dale Andradé, "Pacification," in Stanley Kutler, ed., *Encyclopedia of the Vietnam War* (New York: Scribner's, 1996), 421–23; Aussaresses, *The Battle of the Casbah*, 128; Alistair Horne, *A Savage War of Peace: Algeria 1954–1962* (London: Macmillan, 1977), 195–200.

17. Orrin DeForest and David Chanoff, *Slow Burn: The Rise and Bitter Fall of American Intelligence in Vietnam* (New York: Simon & Schuster, 1990), 54–57.

18. Ralph W. McGehee, *Deadly Deceits: My 25 Years in the CIA* (New York: Sheridan Square Publications, 1983), 142–44.

19. Andrew F. Krepinevich Jr., *The Army and Vietnam* (Baltimore: Johns Hopkins University Press, 1986), 228–29.

20. McGehee, *Deadly Deceits*, 156.

21. Douglas Valentine, *The Phoenix Program* (New York: Morrow, 1990), 320–26; Andradé, "Pacification," 417–23.

22. Adam Shatz, "The Torture of Algiers," *New York Review of Books*, November 21, 2002, 53–54; interview with Alistair Horne, *The Battle of Algiers: Remembering*

History (documentary film produced by Kim Hendrickson, Criterion Collection, 2004).

23. Interview with Colonel Roger Trinquier, by Oliver Todd for "La Bataille d'Alger," BBC Panorama, 1970, replayed in *The Battle of Algiers: Remembering History.*

24. *New York Times,* March 1, 2005.

25. Chris Mackey and Greg Miller, *The Interrogators: Inside the Secret War against Al Qaeda* (New York: Little, Brown, 2004), 472.

26. *FM 34–52: Intelligence Interrogation* (Washington: Department of the Army, September 28, 1992), 1–8.

27. Jane Mayer, "Outsourcing Torture: Annals of Justice," *The New Yorker,* February 14, 2005, 116–18.

28. *New York Times,* March 4, 2005; Mark Danner, *Torture and Truth: America, Abu Ghraib, and the War on Terror* (New York: New York Review of Books, 2004), 1.

29. *New York Times,* March 18, 2005.

30. Ibid., October 22, 2004, April 28, May 21, 2005.

31. *Washington Post,* December 17, 2004.

32. To: Bald, Gary, Battle, Frankie, Cummings, Arthur, Subject: Impersonating FBI at GTMO, Date: December 5, 2003, http://www.aclu.org/torturefoia/released/FBI_3977.pdf; accessed January 27, 2005.

33. Budiansky, "Intelligence: Truth Extraction," 32–35.

34. Mayer, "Outsourcing Torture," 110–12.

35. John H. Langbein, "The Legal History of Torture," in Levinson, *Torture,* 101; Peter Hoffmann, *The History of the German Resistance 1933–1945* (Montreal: McGill–Queen's University Press, 1996), 518–23; Lisa Silverman, *Tortured Subjects: Pain, Truth, and the Body in Early Modern France* (Chicago: University of Chicago Press, 2001), 182; Stuart I. Rochester and Frederick Kiley, *Honor Bound: American Prisoners of War in Southeast Asia, 1961–1973* (Annapolis: Naval Institute Press, 1999), 163–87, 344–45.

36. Interview with Julieta Sison, Quezon City, July 18, 1986.

37. For a description of this torture session, see Alfred W. McCoy, *Closer Than Brothers: Manhood at the Philippine Military Academy* (New Haven: Yale University Press, 1999), 213–14; interview with Satur Ocampo, Quezon City, August 27, 1996.

38. Interview with Maria Elena Ang, Sydney, Australia, May 9, 1989; *Daily Cardinal,* October 17, 1986; *Capital Times* (Madison, Wisconsin), October 17, 1986.

39. Richard A. Posner, "Torture, Terrorism, and Interrogation," in Levinson, *Torture,* 294.

40. Lawrence E. Hinkle Jr. and Harold G. Wolff, "Communist Interrogation and Indoctrination of 'Enemies of the States': Analysis of Methods Used by the Communist State Police (a Special Report)," *Archives of Neurology and Psychiatry* 76 (1956), 135; Michael McConville and John Baldwin, "The Role of Interrogation in Crime Discovery and Conviction," *British Journal of Criminology* 22, no. 1 (1982), 165–74.

41. Michael Moore, *Fahrenheit 9/11* (Lions Gate Films, 2004).

42. George W. Bush, "State of the Union Address of the President to the Joint Session of Congress," January 28, 2003, C-Span.Org, http://www.c-span.org/

executivetranscript.asp?cat+current_event&code+bush_admin&year=2003; accessed March 29, 2005.

43. From: (INSD) (FBI), To: Harrington, FJ (CTD) (FBI), Sent: August 17,
2004, http://www.aclu.org/torturefoia/released/FBI_4737-4738.pdf; accessed
March 8, 2005.

44. Jean Maria Arrigo, "A Consequentialist Argument against Torture Interrogation of Terrorists" (Joint Service Conference on Professional Ethics, January
30–31, 2003, Springfield, Virginia), http://atlas.usafa_af.mil/jscope/JSCOPE03/
Arrigo03.html; accessed April 17, 2005; Supreme Court of Israel, "Judgment Con-
cerning the Legality of the General Security Service's Interrogation Methods," in
Levinson, *Torture*, 180–81; *New York Times,* February 15, 2005; Association of
the Bar of the City of New York, Committee on International Human Rights,
Committee on Military Affairs and Justice's Report, Human Rights Standards
Applicable to the United States' Interrogation of Detainees, April 2004, in Karen
J. Greenberg and Joshua L. Dratel, eds., *The Torture Papers: The Road to Abu
Ghraib* (New York: Cambridge University Press, 2005), 603–5.

BIBLIOGRAPHY

Articles

"Abuse of Iraqi POWs by GIs Probed." CBS NEWS.com (April 28, 2004). http://www.cbsnews.com/stories/2004/04/27/60II/printable614063.shtml.

Alter, Jonathan. "Time to Think about Torture." *Newsweek,* November 5, 2001, 45.

American Psychiatric Association. "Cameron, Donald Ewen." *Biographical Directory of the Fellows and Members of the American Psychiatric Association.* New York: R. R. Bowker, 1963, 76.

Andradé, Dale. "Pacification." In Stanley Kutler, ed., *Encyclopedia of the Vietnam War.* New York: Scribner's, 1996, 417–23.

Baraheni, Reza. "The Savak Documents." *The Nation,* February 23, 1980, 198–202.

Barry, John, et al. "The Roots of Torture." *Newsweek,* May 24, 2004, 26–34.

Baumrind, Diana. "Some Thoughts on Ethics of Research: After Reading Milgram's 'Behavioral Study of Obedience.'" In Arthur G. Miller, ed., *The Social Psychology of Psychological Research.* New York: Free Press, 1972, 106–11.

Bexton, W. H., W. Heron, and T. H. Scott. "Effects of Decreased Variation in the Sensory Environment." *Canadian Journal of Psychology* 8, no. 2 (1954), 70–76.

Bloche, M. Gregg, and Jonathan H. Marks. "Doctors and Interrogators at Guantánamo Bay." *New England Journal of Medicine* 353, no. 1 (July 7, 2005), 6–8.

———. "When Doctors Go to War." *New England Journal of Medicine* 352 (January 6, 2005), 3–5.

Block, Alan A. "A Modern Marriage of Convenience: A Collaboration between Organized Crime and U.S. Intelligence." In Robert J. Kelly, ed., *Organized Crime: A Global Perspective.* Totowa: Rowman & Littlefield, 1986, 58–78.

Bowden, Mark. "The Dark Art of Interrogation: A Survey of the Landscape of Persuasion." *The Atlantic Monthly,* October 2003, 51–76.

Brooks, Rosa. "Ticking Bombs and Slippery Slopes." *Los Angeles Times,* May 28, 2005.

Britt, Steuart Henderson, and Jane D. Morgan. "Military Psychologists in World War II." *The American Psychologist* 1, no. 10 (1946), 423–37.

Brunt, P. A. "Evidence Given under Torture in the Principate." *Zeischrift der Savigny-Stiftung für Rechtsgeschichte* 97 (1980), 256–65.

Budiansky, Stephen. "Intelligence: Truth Extraction." *The Atlantic Monthly,* June 2005, 32–35.

Cameron, D. Ewen. "Psychic Driving." *The American Journal of Psychiatry* 112, no. 7 (1956), 502–9.

Cameron, D. Ewen, et al. "The Depatterning Treatment of Schizophrenia." *Comprehensive Psychiatry* 3, no. 3 (1962), 65–76.

Carmichael, Keith, et al. "The Need for REDRESS: Why Seek a Remedy? Reparations as Rehabilitation." *Torture* 6, no. 1 (1996), 7.

Carroll, James. "The Bush Crusade." *The Nation,* September 20, 2004, 14–19.

Chorover, Stephen L. "The Pacification of the Brain." *Psychology Today* (May 1974), 59–69.

Cook, Helena. "The Role of Amnesty International in the Fight against Torture." In Antonio Cassese, ed., *The International Fight against Torture.* Baden-Baden: Nomos Verlagsgesellschaft, 1991, 172–86.

Coronel, Sheila S. "RAM: From Reform to Revolution." In *Kudeta: The Challenge to Philippine Democracy.* Manila: Philippine Center for Investigative Journalism, 1990, 51–85.

Cotter, Lloyd H., M.D. "Operant Conditioning in a Vietnamese Mental Hospital." *American Journal of Psychiatry* 124, no. 1 (1967), 23–28.

Dershowitz, Alan M. "Tortured Reasoning." In Sanford Levinson, ed., *Torture: A Collection.* New York: Oxford University Press, 2004, 257–80.

———. "Is There a Torturous Road to Justice?" *Los Angeles Times,* November 8, 2001, B-19.

Doerr-Zegers, Otto, Lawrence Hartmann, Elizabeth Lira, and Eugenia Weinstein. "Torture: Psychiatric Sequelae and Phenomenology." *Psychiatry* 55, no. 2 (May 1992), 177–84.

Dunlap, Jack W. "Psychologists and the Cold War." *The American Psychologist* 10, no. 3 (1955), 107–9.

Estabrooks, G. H., with Leslie Lieber. "Hypnosis: Its Tremendous Potential as a War Weapon Is Revealed Here for the First Time." *Argosy,* February 1950, 26–29, 90–92.

Fagen, Patricia Weiss. "Repression and State Security." In Juan E. Corradi, Patricia Weiss Fagen, and Manuel Antonio Garreton, eds., *Fear at the Edge: State Terror and Resistance in Latin America.* Berkeley: University of California Press, 1992, 39–71.

Forsythe, David P. "Human Rights in U.S. Foreign Policy: Retrospect and Prospect." *Political Science Quarterly* 105, no. 3 (1990), 435–54.

———. "The United Nations and Human Rights, 1945–1985." *Political Science Quarterly* 100, no. 2 (Summer 1985), 249–69.

———. "The United States, the United Nations, and Human Rights." In Margaret P. Karns and Karen A. Mingst, *The United States and Multilateral Institutions: Patterns of Changing Instrumentality and Influence*. Boston: Unwin Hyman, 1990, 261–84.

Gargarin, Michael. "The Torture of Slaves in Athenian Law." *Classical Philology* 91, no. 1 (1996), 1–18.

Gasser, Hans-Peter. "An Appeal for Ratification by the United States." *American Journal of International Law* 81, no. 4 (1987), 912–45.

Genefke, Inge. "Some Steps towards a World with Less Torture." In Rehabilitation and Research Centre for Torture Victims, *Annual Report 1995*. Copenhagen: Rehabilitation and Research Centre for Torture Victims, 1996, 15–16.

Glickman, Stephen E. "Hebb, Donald Olding." In Alan E. Kazdin, ed., *Encyclopedia of Psychology*. New York: Oxford University Press, 2000, 105–6.

Green, Judy, and Jeanna LaDuke. "Mina Spiegel Rees (1902–1997)." *Notices of the AMS* 45, no. 7 (1998), 867.

Grodzynski, Denise. "Tortures mortelles et catégories sociales: Les *Summa suplica* dans le Droit Romain aux IIIᵉ et IVᵉ Siècles." In *Du châtiment dans la Cité: Supplice corporels et peine de mort dans le monde antique*. Rome: L'École Française de Rome, 1984, 361–403.

Gup, Ted. "The Coldest Warrior." *Washington Post Magazine*, December 16, 2001, W-9.

Haggbloom, Steven J. "The 100 Most Eminent Psychologists of the 20th Century." *Review of General Psychology* 6, no. 2 (2002), 139–52.

Hartmann, Lawrence, et al. "Psychopathology of Torture Victims." *Torture* 3, no. 2 (1993), 36–38.

"Harvard Law Professors Urge Congress to Review Interrogation Policy and Hold Executive Branch Accountable." Posted June 14, 2004, http://www.iraq-letter.com.

Hebb, D. O. "Drives and the C.N.S. (Conceptual Nervous System)." *The Psychological Review* 62, no. 4 (1955), 243–54.

Hebb, D. O., et al. "Experimental Deafness." *Canadian Journal of Psychology* 8, no. 3 (1954), 152–56.

Heron, W., W. H. Bexton, and D. O. Hebb. "Cognitive Effects of a Decreased Variation in the Sensory Environment." *The American Psychologist* 8, no. 8 (1953), 366.

Heron, Woodburn. "The Pathology of Boredom." *Scientific American* 196 (January 1957), 52–56.

Heron, Woodburn, and D. O. Hebb. "Cognitive and Physiological Effects of Perceptual Isolation." In Philip Solomon et al., eds., *Sensory Deprivation: A Symposium Held at Harvard Medical School*. Cambridge: Harvard University Press, 1961, 6–33.

Hersh, Seymour M. "The Gray Zone: How a Secret Pentagon Program Came to Abu Ghraib." *The New Yorker*, May 24, 2004, 38–44.

———. "Torture at Abu Ghraib." *The New Yorker*, May 10, 2004, 42–47.

Hinkle, Lawrence E., Jr. "A Consideration of the Circumstances under Which Men May Be Interrogated, and the Effects that These May Have upon the

Function of the Brain," File: Hinkle, Box 7, CIA Behavior Control Experiments Collection, National Security Archive, Washington.

Hinkle, Lawrence E., Jr., and Harold G. Wolff. "Communist Interrogation and Indoctrination of 'Enemies of the States': Analysis of Methods Used by the Communist State Police (A Special Report)." *Archives of Neurology and Psychiatry* 76 (1956), 115–74.

Hirsh, Michael. "A Tortured Debate." *Newsweek,* June 21, 2004, 50–53.

Horowitz, Michael. "Interview: Albert Hofmann." *High Times* 11 (July 1976), 25–28, 31, 81.

Holst, Erik. "International Efforts on the Rehabilitation of Torture Victims." In June C. Pagaduan Lopez and Elizabeth Protacio Marcelino, eds., *Torture Survivors and Caregivers: Proceedings of the International Workshop on Therapy and Research Issues.* Quezon City: University of the Philippines Press, 1995, 8–37.

Ignatieff, Michael. "Lesser Evils." *New York Times Magazine,* May 2, 2004, 46–51, 86, 94.

———. "Mirage in the Desert." *New York Times Magazine,* June 27, 2004, 13–15.

———. "What Did the C.I.A. Do to His Father?" *New York Times Magazine,* April 1, 2001, 56–61.

Irving, Robert. "The Henry X File." http://www.mythologist.co.uk/reading/html.

Johnson, Loch K. "On Drawing a Bright Line for Covert Operations." *American Journal of International Law* 86, no. 2 (April 1992), 284–309.

Jones, R. V. "Tizard's Task in the 'War Years' 1935–1952." *Biographical Memoirs of the Fellows of the Royal Society.* Vol. 7. London: Royal Society, 1961, 331–41.

"Killer Movies." http://www.killermovies.com/p/passion/.

Kordon, Diana, Lucila Edelman, et al. "Torture in Argentina." In Metin Basoglu, ed., *Torture and Its Consequences: Current Treatment Approaches.* Cambridge: Cambridge University Press, 1992, 433–51.

Langbein, John H. "The Legal History of Torture." In Sanford Levinson, ed., *Torture: A Collection.* New York: Oxford University Press, 2004, 93–103.

LeMoyne, James. "Testifying to Torture." *New York Times Magazine,* June 5, 1988, 44–51.

Lilly, John C. "Mental Effects of Reduction of Ordinary Levels of Physical Stimuli on Intact, Healthy Persons." *Psychiatric Research Reports* 5, no. 1 (1956), 1–9.

Mayer, Jane. "The Experiment." *The New Yorker,* July 11 and 18, 2005, 60–71.

———. "Outsourcing Torture: Annals of Justice." *The New Yorker,* February 14, 2005, 106–9.

McConville, Michael, and John Baldwin. "The Role of Interrogation in Crime Discovery and Conviction," *British Journal of Criminology* 22, no. 1 (1982), 165–74.

McCoy, Alfred W. "Cruel Science: CIA Torture and US Foreign Policy." *New England Journal of Public Policy* 19, no. 2 (2005), 209–62.

McWilliams, John C., and Alan A. Block. "On the Origins of American Counterintelligence: Building a Clandestine Network." *Journal of Policy History* 1, no. 4 (1989), 353–72.

Meek, James. "Nobody Is Talking." *The Guardian,* February 18, 2005.

Milgram, Stanley. "Group Pressure and Action against a Person." *Journal of Abnormal and Social Psychology* 9, no. 2 (1964), 137–43.

NewsHour with Jim Lehrer, May 4, 2004. http://www.pbs.org/newshour/bb/military/jan-june 04/abuse1_05_04.html.

Nickson, Elizabeth. "My Mother, the CIA and LSD." *The Observer,* October 16, 1994, 48–52.

Page, H. E. "The Role of Psychology in ONR." *The American Psychologist* 9, no. 10 (1954), 621–28.

Posner, Richard A. "The Best Offense." *The New Republic,* September 2, 2002, 28–31.

———. "Torture, Terrorism, and Interrogation." In Sanford Levinson, ed., *Torture: A Collection.* New York: Oxford University Press, 2004, 291–98.

Press, Eyal. "In Torture We Trust?" *The Nation,* March 31, 2003, 11–16.

Randall, Steve. "Pro-Pain Pundits." *Extra!,* January–February 2002. http://fair.org/extra/0201/pro-pain.html.

Rasmussen, Ole Vedel. "Medical Aspects of Torture." *Danish Medical Bulletin* 37, no. 1 (1990), 1–88.

Rees-Mogg, William. "The Torture Industry." In Rehabilitation and Research Centre for Torture Victims, *Annual Report 1995.* Copenhagen: Rehabilitation and Research Centre for Torture Victims, 1996, 5–6.

Reichbach, Gustin L. "Sartre's Torture and Ours." *New York Law Journal,* June 8, 2005.

Roth, Kenneth. "The Charade of US Ratification of International Human Rights Treaties." *Chicago Journal of International Law* (Fall 2000), 347–53.

Ruff, George E., Edwin Z. Levy, and Victor H. Thaler. "Factors Influencing Reactions to Reduced Sensory Input." In Philip Solomon et al., eds., *Sensory Deprivation: A Symposium Held at Harvard Medical School.* Cambridge: Harvard University Press, 1961, 72–90.

Sanford, Fillmore N. "Summary Report of the 1954 Annual Meeting." *The American Psychologist* 9, no. 11 (1954), 708–18.

Saporta, José A., Jr., and Bessel A. van der Kolk. "Psychobiological Consequences of Severe Trauma." In Metin Basoglu, ed., *Torture and Its Consequences: Current Treatment Approaches.* Cambridge: Cambridge University Press, 1992, 151–57.

Scarry, Elaine. "Five Errors in the Reasoning of Alan Dershowitz." In Sanford Levinson, ed., *Torture: A Collection.* New York: Oxford University Press, 2004, 281–90.

Scheflin, Alan. "Freedom of the Mind as an International Human Rights Issue," *Human Rights Journal* 3, no. 1 (1982), 1–64.

Shatz, Adam. "The Torture of Algiers." *New York Review of Books,* November 21, 2002, 53–57.

Smith, S., and W. Lewty. "Perceptual Isolation in a Silent Room." *Lancet* 2, September 12, 1959, 342–45.

Solomon, Deborah. "Questions for Trent Lott." *New York Times Magazine,* June 20, 2004, 15.

Sontag, Susan. "Regarding the Torture of Others." *New York Times Magazine,* May 23, 2004, 24–29, 42.

Sta. Romana-Cruz, Neni. "Reformists Night Out: In Uniform but into Fun," *Mr. & Ms.,* March 21–27, 1986, 19–20.

Supreme Court of Israel, "Judgment Concerning the Legality of the General Security Service's Interrogation Methods." In Sanford Levinson, ed., *Torture: A
Collection*. New York: Oxford University Press, 2004, 165–81.

"Torturer in US for Training." *Tanod* (Manila) 1, no. 3 (1978), 3.

Vest, Jason. "Pray and Tell." *The American Prospect* 16, no. 7 (July 2005), 47–50.

Victorian, Armen. "Following in Uncle Sam's Dirty Footsteps: Chemical and Biological Warfare Testing in the UK." *Lobster* 36 (Winter 1998–1999), 25–28.

Weisberg, Richard H. "Loose Professionalism, or Why Lawyers Take the Lead on
Torture." In Sanford Levinson, ed., *Torture: A Collection*. New York: Oxford
University Press, 2004, 299–305.

Wexler, Donald, Jack Mendelson, Herbert Leiderman, and Philip Solomon. "Sensory Deprivation: A Technique for Studying Psychiatric Aspects of Stress."
A.M.A. Archives of Neurology and Psychiatry 79, no. 1 (1958), 225–33.

Worden, Leon. "SCV Newsmaker of the Week: Brig. Gen. Janis Karpinski." *Signal Newspaper* (Santa Clarita, California), July 4, 2004.

Zagorin, Adam, and Michael Duffy. "Inside the Interrogation of Detainee 063."
Time 165, no. 25 (June 20, 2005), 26–33.

Zimbardo, Philip G. "On the Ethics of Intervention in Human Psychological Research: With Special Reference to the Stanford Prison Experiment." *Cognition* 2, no. 2 (1973), 243–44.

Zimbardo, Philip G., et al. "A Pirandellian Prison: The Mind Is a Formidable
Jailer," *New York Times Magazine,* April 8, 1973, 38–39, 46–53, 56–60.

Books

Alleg, Henri. *The Question*. New York: Braziller, 1958.

Annas, George J., and Michael A. Grodin, eds. *The Nazi Doctors and the Nuremberg Code: Human Rights in Human Experimentation*. New York: Oxford University Press, 1992.

Aussaresses, Paul. *The Battle of the Casbah: Terrorism and Counter-Terrorism in
Algeria, 1955–1957*. New York: Enigma, 2002.

Baer, Ron. *See No Evil: The True Story of a Ground Soldier in the CIA's War on
Terrorism*. New York: Three Rivers Press, 2002.

Basoglu, Metin, ed. *Torture and Its Consequences: Current Treatment Approaches*.
Cambridge: Cambridge University Press, 1992.

Biderman, Albert D., and Herbert Zimmer, eds. *The Manipulation of Human Behavior*. New York: Wiley, 1961.

Bigel, Alan I. *The Supreme Court on Emergency Powers, Foreign Affairs, and Protection of Civil Liberties, 1935–1975*. Lanham: University Press of America, 1986.

Blass, Thomas. *The Man Who Shocked the World: The Life and Legacy of Stanley
Milgram*. New York: Basic Books, 2004.

Boulesbaa, Ahcene. *The U.N. Convention on Torture and the Prospects for Enforcement*. The Hague: Martinus Nijhoff, 1999.

Bowart, Walter. *Operation Mind Control*. New York: Dell, 1978.

Browning, Christopher R. *Ordinary Men: Reserve Police Battalion 101 and the Final Solution in Poland*. New York: HarperCollins, 1992.

Clark, Ronald W. *Tizard*. London: Methuen, 1965.

Clarke, Richard A. *Against All Enemies: Inside America's War on Terror*. New York: Free Press, 2004.

Cockburn, Alexander, and Jeffrey St. Clair. *Whiteout: The CIA, Drugs and the Press*. New York: Verso, 1998.

Colby, William, and Peter Forbath. *Honorable Men: My Life in the CIA*. New York: Simon & Schuster, 1978.

Conboy, Kenneth J., and Dale Andradé. *Spies and Commandos: How America Lost the Secret War in North Vietnam*. Lawrence: University Press of Kansas, 2000.

Conroy, John. *Unspeakable Acts, Ordinary People: The Dynamics of Torture*. New York: Knopf, 2000.

Cosculluela, Manuel Hevia. *Pasaporte 11333: Ocho Años con la CIA*. Havana: Editorial de Ciencias Sociales, 1978.

Danner, Mark. *Torture and Truth: America, Abu Ghraib, and the War on Terror*. New York: New York Review of Books, 2004.

Dassin, Joan, ed. *Torture in Brazil: a Report*. New York: Vintage Books, 1986.

DeForest, Orrin, and David Chanoff. *Slow Burn: The Rise and Bitter Fall of American Intelligence in Vietnam*. New York: Simon & Schuster, 1990.

Dershowitz, Alan M. *Why Terrorism Works: Understanding the Threat, Responding to the Challenge*. New Haven: Yale University Press, 2002.

Estabrooks, George H. *Hypnotism*. New York: E. P. Dutton, 1957.

Fisher, Seymour. *The Use of Hypnosis in Intelligence and Related Military Situations*. Washington: Study SR 177-D, Contract AF18 [600] 1977, Technical Report No. 4, Bureau of Social Science Research, December 1958.

Garnsey, Peter. *Social Status and Legal Privilege in the Roman Empire*. Oxford: Clarendon Press, 1970.

Gay, Peter. *Voltaire's Politics: The Poet as Realist*. New York: Vintage, 1965.

Greenberg, Karen J., and Joshua L. Dratel, eds. *The Torture Papers: The Road to Abu Ghraib*. New York: Cambridge University Press, 2005.

Gudjonsson, Gisli H. *The Psychology of Interrogations, Confessions, and Testimony*. New York: Wiley, 1996.

Hansen, Eric. *Orchid Fever: A Horticultural Tale of Love, Lust, and Lunacy*. New York: Pantheon, 2000.

Hebb, D. O. *Essay on Mind*. Hillsdale: Lawrence Erlbaum Associates, 1980.

———. *The Organization of Behavior: A Neuropsychological Theory*. New York: Wiley, 1949.

Hersh, Seymour M. *Chain of Command: The Road from 9/11 to Abu Ghraib*. New York: HarperCollins, 2004.

Hodge, James, and Linda Cooper. *Disturbing the Peace: The Story of Father Roy Bourgeois and the Movement to Close the School of the Americas*. Maryknoll: Orbis Books, 2004.

Hoffmann, Peter. *The History of the German Resistance, 1933–1945*. Montreal: McGill–Queen's University Press, 1996.

Horne, Alistair. *A Savage War of Peace: Algeria, 1954–1962*. London: Macmillan, 1977.

Howland, Nina D., ed. *Foreign Relations of the United States, 1964–68: Volume XXII: Iran*. Washington: Government Printing Office, 1999.

Hunter, Edward. *Brain-Washing in Red China: The Calculated Destruction of Men's Minds*. New York: Vanguard Press, 1951.

Janis, Irving L. *Are the Cominform Countries Using Hypnotic Techniques to Elicit Confessions in Public Trials?* Santa Monica: Rand Corporation, Air Force Project Rand Research Memorandum, RM-161, April 25, 1949.

———. "Excerpt from *Victims of Groupthink*," Swans Commentary. http://www.swans.com/library/art9/xxx.099.html.

Johnson, Loch K. *A Season of Inquiry: The Senate Intelligence Investigation*. Lexington: University Press of Kentucky, 1985.

Karns, Margaret P., and Karen A. Mingst. *The United States and Multilateral Institutions: Patterns of Changing Instrumentality and Influence*. Boston: Unwin Hyman, 1990.

Keith, Jim. *Mind Control, World Control*. Kempton: Adventures Unlimited Press, 1998.

Kessler, Richard J. *Rebellion and Repression in the Philippines*. New Haven: Yale University Press, 1989.

Klare, Michael T. *War without End: American Planning for the Next Vietnams*. New York: Knopf, 1972.

Krepinevich, Andrew F., Jr. *The Army and Vietnam*. Baltimore: Johns Hopkins University Press, 1986.

Kritz, Neil J., ed. *Transitional Justice: How Emerging Democracies Reckon with Former Regimes*. Vol. II, *Country Studies*; Vol. III, *Laws, Rulings, and Reports*. Washington: U.S. Institute for Peace, 1995.

Langbein, John H. *Torture and the Law of Proof: Europe and England in the Ancien Regime*. Chicago: University of Chicago Press, 1977.

Langguth, A. J. *Hidden Terrors*. New York: Pantheon, 1978.

Lifton, Robert Jay. *Thought Reform and the Psychology of Totalism: A Study of Brainwashing in China*. London: Victor Gollancz, 1961.

Mackey, Chris, and Greg Miller. *The Interrogators: Inside the Secret War against Al Qaeda*. New York: Little, Brown, 2004.

Maestro, Marcello. *Voltaire and Beccaria as Reformers of Criminal Law*. New York: Columbia University Press, 1942.

Maglipon, Jo-Ann Q. *Primed: Selected Stories 1972–1992*. Manila: Anvil, 1993.

Marchetti, Victor, and John D. Marks. *The CIA and the Cult of Intelligence*. New York: Knopf, 1974.

Marcus, Maeva. *Truman and the Steel Seizure Case: The Limits of Presidential Power*. New York: Columbia University Press, 1977.

Marks, John. *The Search for the "Manchurian Candidate": The CIA and Mind Control*. New York: Times Books, 1979.

McCoy, Alfred W. *Closer Than Brothers: Manhood at the Philippine Military Academy*. New Haven: Yale University Press, 1999.

———. *Priests on Trial*. New York: Penguin Books, 1984.

McGehee, Ralph W. *Deadly Deceits: My 25 Years in the CIA*. New York: Sheridan Square Publications, 1983.

McNeill, Ian. *The Team: Australian Army Advisers in Vietnam 1962–1972*. St. Lucia: University of Queensland Press, 1984.

Mellor, Alec. *La torture: Son histoire, son abolition, sa réapparition au XXᵉ Siècle.* Paris: Horizons Littéraires, 1949.

Merback, Mitchell B. *The Thief, the Cross and the Wheel: Pain and the Spectacle of Punishment in Medieval and Renaissance Europe.* Chicago: University of Chicago Press, 1999.

Mercade, Reverend La Verne D., and Sister Mariani Dimaranan. *Philippines: Testimonies on Human Rights Violations.* Geneva: World Council of Churches, 1986.

Migliorini, Aldo. *Tortura Inquisizione Pena di Morte: Brevi Considerazioni sui Principali Strumenti Commentati in Merito ai Tre Argomenti dal Medioevo all' Epoca Industriale.* Poggibonsi: Lalli Editore, 1997.

Milgram, Stanley. *Obedience to Authority: An Experimental View.* New York: Harper & Row, 1974.

Miller, Arthur G. *The Obedience Experiments: A Case Study of Controversy in Social Science.* New York: Praeger, 1986.

Moyar, Mark. *Phoenix and the Birds of Prey: The CIA's Secret Campaign to Destroy the Viet Cong.* Annapolis: Naval Institute Press, 1997.

The 9/11 Commission Report: Final Report of the National Commission on Terrorist Attacks upon the United States. New York: Norton, 2004.

Olson, James, ed. *Dictionary of the Vietnam War.* New York: Bedrick Books, 1987.

Orlean, Susan. *The Orchid Thief.* New York: Random House, 1998.

Parry, Robert. *Lost History: Contras, Cocaine and Other Crimes.* Arlington: Media Consortium, 1997.

Peters, Edward. *Torture.* Philadelphia: University of Pennsylvania Press, 1996.

Pines, Maya. *The Brain Changers: Scientists and the New Mind Control.* New York: Harcourt Brace Jovanovich, 1973.

de Preaux, Jean. *The Geneva Conventions of 12 August 1949: Commentary. Geneva Convention III Relative to the Treatment of Prisoners of War.* Geneva: International Committee of the Red Cross, 1960.

Promotion of Church People's Rights. *That We May Remember.* Quezon City: PCPR, 1989.

Pyle, Kevin C. *Lab U.S.A.: Illuminated Documents.* Brooklyn: Autonomedia, 2001.

Ranelagh, John. *The Agency: The Rise and Decline of the CIA.* New York: Simon and Schuster, 1986.

Rejali, Darius M. *Torture and Modernity: Self, Society, and State in Modern Iran.* Boulder: Westview Press, 1994.

Roberts, Adam, and Richard Guelff, eds. *Documents on the Laws of War.* New York: Oxford University Press, 2000.

Rochester, Stuart I., and Frederick Kiley. *Honor Bound: American Prisoners of War in Southeast Asia, 1961–1973.* Annapolis: Naval Institute Press, 1999.

Ruthven, Malise. *Torture: The Grand Conspiracy.* London: Weidenfeld and Nicolson, 1978.

Scheflin, Alan W., and Edward M. Opton Jr. *The Mind Manipulators: A Non-Fiction Account.* New York: Paddington Press, 1978.

Schrag, Peter. *Mind Control.* New York: Pantheon Books, 1978.

Silverman, Lisa. *Tortured Subjects: Pain, Truth, and the Body in Early Modern France.* Chicago: University of Chicago Press, 2001.

Simpson, Christopher. *Science of Coercion: Communication Research and Psychological Warfare, 1945–1960.* New York: Oxford University Press, 1994.

Smith, R. Harris. *OSS: The Secret History of America's First Central Intelligence Agency.* Berkeley: University of California Press, 1972.

Snepp, Frank. *Decent Interval: The American Debacle in Vietnam and the Fall of Saigon.* London: Allen Lane, 1980.

Solomon, Philip, et al., eds. *Sensory Deprivation: A Symposium Held at Harvard Medical School.* Cambridge: Harvard University Press, 1961.

Stevens, Jay. *Storming Heaven: LSD and the American Dream.* New York: Grove Press, 1987.

Sundquist, James L. *The Decline and Resurgence of Congress.* Washington: The Brookings Institution, 1981.

Task Force on Detainees. Association of Major Religious Superiors in the Philippines. *Pumipiglas: Political Detention and Military Atrocities in the Philippines.* Manila: TFDP, 1980.

———. *Political Detainees in the Philippines,* Book 2. Manila: Association of Major Orders of Religious Superiors, March 31, 1977.

———. *Political Detainees in the Philippines,* Book 3. Manila: Association of Major Orders of Religious Superiors, March 1978.

Thomas, Gordon. *Journey into Madness: Medical Torture and the Mind Controllers.* London: Bantam Press, 1988.

Uhler, Oscar M., et al. *The Geneva Conventions of 12 August 1949: Commentary. Geneva Convention IV Relative to the Protection of Civilian Persons in Time of War.* Geneva: International Committee of the Red Cross, 1958.

Ulrich, Roger, Thomas Stachnik, and John Mabry, eds. *Control of Human Behavior.* Glenview: Scott, Foresman, 1966.

Valentine, Douglas. *The Phoenix Program.* New York: Morrow, 1990.

Vernon, Jack A. *Inside the Black Room.* New York: Clarkson N. Potter, 1963.

Vitug, Marites Dañguilan, and Glenda M. Gloria. *Under the Crescent Moon: Rebellion in Mindanao.* Quezon City: Ateneo Center for Social Policy and Public Affairs, 2000.

Vizmanos, Danilo P. *Through the Eye of the Storm: Random Notes of Danilo P. Vizmanos.* Quezon City: Ken Inc., 2000.

Vrij, Aldert. *Detecting Lies and Deceit: The Psychology of Lying and the Implications for Professional Practice.* New York: Wiley, 2000.

Watson, Peter. *War on the Mind: The Military Uses and Abuses of Psychology.* New York: Basic Books, 1978.

Weinstein, Harvey M. *Psychiatry and the CIA: Victims of Mind Control.* Washington: American Psychiatric Press, 1990.

Weschler, Lawrence. *A Miracle, a Universe: Settling Accounts with Torturers.* New York: Pantheon, 1990.

Winkler, Ernst. *Four Years of Nazi Torture.* New York: Appleton-Century, 1943.

Wohlstetter, Roberta. *Pearl Harbor: Warning and Decision.* Stanford: Stanford University Press, 1962.

Zimmerman, David. *Top Secret Exchange: The Tizard Mission and the Scientific War.* Montreal: McGill–Queen's University Press, 1996.

Non-Government Organizations

American Psychiatric Association. *The Principles of Medical Ethics: With Annotations Especially Applicable to Psychiatry.* Washington: American Psychiatric Association, 2001.

American Psychological Association. "Ethical Principles of Psychologists and Code of Conduct." http://www.apa.org/ethics/code/2002.pdf.

American Psychological Association. "Program of the Sixty-First Annual Meeting of the American Psychological Association, September 4–9, 1953, Cleveland, Ohio." *The American Psychologist* 8, no. 7 (1953), 269–98.

American Psychological Association. "Program of the Sixty-Second Annual Meeting of the American Psychological Association, September 3–8, 1954, New York, New York." *The American Psychologist* 9, no. 7 (1954), 275–509.

American Psychological Association. "Report of the American Psychological Association Presidential Task Force on Psychological Ethics and National Security" (June 2005). http://www.apa.org/releases/PENSTaskForceReportFinal.pdf.

Amnesty International. *Amnesty International Briefing: Iran.* London: Amnesty International, 1976.

Amnesty International. "Amnesty International Report 2005, Speech by Irene Khan at Foreign Press Association," May 25, 2005. http://www.amnesty.org/library/print/ENGPOL100142005.

Amnesty International. *Report of an Enquiry into Allegations of Ill-Treatment in Northern Ireland.* London: Amnesty International, March 1972.

Amnesty International. *Report on Torture.* London: Duckworth, 1975.

Association of the Bar of the City of New York. Committee on International Human Rights. Committee on Military Affairs and Justice's Report, Human Rights Standards Applicable to the United States' Interrogation of Detainees, April 2004. In Karen J. Greenberg and Joshua L. Dratel, eds., *The Torture Papers: The Road to Abu Ghraib.* New York: Cambridge University Press, 2005, 557–614.

Human Rights Watch. *Getting Away with Torture?: Command Responsibility for the U.S. Abuse of Detainees.* Vol. 17, No. 1 [G], April 2005. http://www.hrw.org/reports/2005/us0405.pdf.

Human Rights Watch. *The Road to Abu Ghraib,* June 2004. http://www.hrw.org/reports/2004/usa0604.pdf.

Physicians for Human Rights. *Break Them Down: Systematic Use of Psychological Torture by US Forces.* Cambridge: Physicians for Human Rights, 2005.

Government Documents

Bowen, Roderic. *Report by Mr. Roderic Bowen, Q.C., on Procedures for the Arrest, Interrogation and Detention of Terrorists in Aden.* London: Stationery Office, Cmnd. 3165, December 1966.

Compton, Sir Edmund. *Report of the Enquiry into Allegations against the Security Forces of Physical Brutality in Northern Ireland Arising out of Events on the 9th August, 1971.* London: Stationery Office, Cmnd. 4823, November 1971.

European Court of Human Rights. *Ireland v. The United Kingdom,* No. 5310/17, January 18, 1978. http://www.worldlii.org/eu/cases/ECHR/1978/1.html.

Parker, Lord of Waddington. *Report of the Committee of Privy Counsellors Appointed to Consider Authorised Procedures for the Interrogation of Persons Suspected of Terrorism.* London: Stationery Office, Cmnd. 4901, 1972.

Republic of the Philippines. *The Final Report of the Fact-Finding Commission (pursuant to R.A. No. 6832).* Manila: Bookmark, 1990.

Supreme Court of Israel. "Judgment Concerning the Legality of the General Security Service's Interrogation Methods." In Sanford Levinson, ed., *Torture: A Collection.* New York: Oxford University Press, 2004, 165–81.

U.S. Government Documents

Bush, George W. "Notice: Detention, Treatment, and Trial of Certain Non-Citizens in the War against Terrorism." White House, November 13, 2001, 66 *Federal Register* (FR), 57833.

Bush, George W. "State of the Union Address of the President to the Joint Session of Congress," January 28, 2003. http://www.c-span.org/executive transcript.asp?cat+current_event&code+bush_admin&year=2003.

Commission on CIA Activities within the United States. *Report to the President.* Washington: Government Printing Office, 1975.

Department of the Army, Headquarters. *FM 34-52: Intelligence Interrogation.* Washington: Department of the Army, September 28, 1992.

Department of Defense. "Army Regulation 15-6: Final Report: Investigation into FBI Allegation of Detainee Abuse at Guantánamo Bay, Cuba Detention Facility" (April 1, 2005; amended June 9, 2005). http://www.defenselink.mil/news/Jul2005/d20050714report.pdf.

Department of Defense. Special Defense Department Briefing, July 7, 2005. http://www.defenselink.mil/transcripts/2005/tr20050707-3301.html.

Department of State. Bureau of Democracy, Human Rights, and Labor. *Country Reports on Human Rights Practices—2004* (February 28, 2005). http://www.state.gov/g/drl/rls/hrrpt/2004/41584.htm.

Foreign Relations Authorization Act, PL 103–236, Title V, Sec. 506, 108 Stat. 463 (1994), 18 USC§ 2340–2340A.

General Accounting Office. *Stopping U.S. Assistance to Foreign Police and Prisons.* Washington: General Accounting Office, 1976.

House of Representatives, 92nd Congress, 1st sess., Subcommittee of the Committee on Government Operations, Hearings on August 2, 1971. *U.S. Assistance Programs in Vietnam.* Washington: Government Printing Office, 1971.

House of Representatives, 104th Congress, 2nd sess. *Congressional Record.* Washington: 142, pt. 14, 1996.

House and Senate Intelligence Committees. "Hearings on Pre-9/11 Intelligence Failures," September 26, 2002.

In Re Estate of Ferdinand E. Marcos Human Rights Litigation, 910 F Supp. 1460, 1462–63, Case No. 94-16739, MDL No. 840, U.S. Ninth Circuit Court of Appeals.

Mrs. David Orlikow, et al. v. United States of America, 682 F. Supp. 77. US District Court, District of Columbia, January 18, 1988.

Office of the President of the United States. *The Commission on the Intelligence Capabilities of the United States Regarding Weapons of Mass Destruction.* Washington, March 31, 2005.

"President Outlines Steps to Help Iraq Achieve Democracy and Freedom," May 24, 2004. http://www.whitehouse.gov/news/release/2004/05/print/20040424-10 .html.

Senate, Armed Services Committee. "Detainee Interrogation," March 10, 2005. LexisNexis Congressional. http://web.lexis-nexis.com/congcomp/printdoc.

Senate, Armed Services Committee. "Hearing on Guantánamo Bay Detainee Treatment," July 13, 2005. http://web.lexis-nexis.com/congcom/printdoc.

Senate, Armed Services Committee. 93d Congress, 1st sess. *Nomination of William E. Colby to Be Head of Central Intelligence.* Washington: Government Printing Office, 1973.

Senate, 93rd Congress, 2d sess. *Congressional Record.* Washington: Government Printing Office, vol. 120, pt. 25, October 2, 1974.

Senate, 109th Congress, 1st sess. *Congressional Record.* Washington: Government Printing Office, vol. 151, no. 102, July 25, 2005.

Senate, Foreign Relations Committee. 93d Congress, 2d sess. *Foreign Assistance Act of 1974: Report of the Committee on Foreign Relations United States Senate on S. 3394 to Amend the Foreign Assistance Act of 1961, and for Other Purposes.* Washington: Government Printing Office, 1974.

Senate, Foreign Relations Committee. 101st Congress, 2d sess. *Convention against Torture: Hearing before the Committee on Foreign Relations.* Washington: Government Printing Office, 1990.

Senate, Foreign Relations Committee, Western Hemisphere Affairs Subcommittee. 92d Congress, 1st sess. *United States Policies and Programs in Brazil.* Washington: Government Printing Office, 1971.

Senate, Judiciary Committee. 102d Congress, 1st sess. Report 102–249, *The Torture Victims Protection Act.* US Senate, Calendar No. 382, November 26, 1991.

Senate, Judiciary Committee. Confirmation Hearing, Transcript, January 6, 2005. http://www.nytimes.com/2005/01/06/politics/06_TEXT-GONZALES .html?ei+5070&3n+5f.

Senate, Judiciary Committee. Panel II of a Hearing of the Senate Judiciary Committee. Subject: Detainees, Chaired by: Senator Arlen Specter (R-PA), June 15, 2005. http://web.lexis-nexis.com/congcomp/printdoc.

Senate, 95th Congress, 1st sess. *Project MKUltra: The CIA's Program of Research in Behavioral Modification. Joint Hearing before the Select Committee on Intelligence and the Subcommittee on Health and Scientific Research of the Committee on Human Resources.* Washington: Government Printing Office, 1977.

Senate, Select Committee on Intelligence. "Transcript of Proceedings before the Select Committee on Intelligence: Honduran Interrogation Manual Hearing," June 16, 1988 (Box 1 CIA Training Manuals, Folder: Interrogation Manual Hearings, National Security Archives).

Senate, Select Committee to Study Government Operations with Respect to

Government Activities. 94th Congress, 2d sess. *Foreign and Military Intelligence, Book I: Final Report*. Washington: Government Printing Office, 1976.

Senate, Subcommittee on Constitutional Rights, Committee on the Judiciary. 93d Congress, 2d sess. *Individual Rights and the Federal Role in Behavioral Modification*. Washington: Government Printing Office, 1974.

Senate, 100th Congress, 2d sess. Treaty Doc. 100–20, *Message from the President of the United States Transmitting the Convention against Torture and Other Cruel, Inhuman or Degrading Treatment or Punishment*. Washington: Government Printing Office, 1988.

Supreme Court of the United States. Oral Arguments, *Donald H. Rumsfeld v. Jose Padilla*, No. 03-1027. http://www.supremecourtus.gov/oral_arguments/argument_transcripts/03-1027.pdf.

Supreme Court of the United States. *Yaser Esam Hamdi, et al. v. Donald Rumsfeld, Secretary of Defense, et al.*, No. 03-6696. http://caselaw.lp.findlaw.com/cgi-bin/getcase.pl?court=US&navby=case&vol=000&invol=03-6696.

Supreme Court of the United States. *Youngstown Sheet & Tube Co. et al. v. Sawyer*, No. 744, June 2, 1952, *United States Reports. Volume 343*. Washington, 1952.

Torture Victims Protection Act. P.L. 102–256, 106 Stat. 73 (1992), 28 USC§ 1350.

United States. *Congressional Record. Proceedings and Debates of the 93rd Congress. Second Session. Volume 120, Part 25*. Washington: Government Printing Office, 1974.

United States. *Congressional Record. Proceedings and Debates of the 102d Congress. First Session. Volume 137, Part 23*. Washington: Government Printing Office, 1991.

United States. *Congressional Record. Proceedings and Debates of the 102d Congress. Second Session. Volume 138, Part 3*. Washington: Government Printing Office, 1992.

United States. *Congressional Record. Proceedings and Debates of the 103d Congress. Second Session. Volume 140, Part 1*. Washington: Government Printing Office, 1994.

United States. *Weekly Compilation of Presidential Documents 32, no. 34*. Washington: Government Printing Office, 1996.

The White House. Presidential Nomination, Jay Scott Bybee. http://www.whitehouse.gov/news/nominations/187.html.

The White House. Press Briefing by Ari Fleischer, February 7, 2002. http://www.whitehouse.gov/news/releases/2002/02print/20020207-6.html.

U.S. Government Memoranda

Army Intelligence Center and School, Fort Huachuca, Arizona, United States Army, Foreign Intelligence Assistance Program, Project X, Annual List of Instructional Material, August 1977, File: Project X, Consortium News, Arlington, Virginia.

Army Intelligence Center and School, Study Manual: Handling of Sources—1989 (Secret. Not Releasable to Foreign Nationals, Declassified by Authority of the

Secretary of the Army, September 19, 1996), Box 2: Intelligence Training Course Manuals, Folder: Handling of Sources, National Security Archive, Washington.

Bush, George. "Memorandum for the Vice President." Subject: Humane Treatment of al Qaeda and Taliban Detainees, February 7, 2002. http://www .washingtonpost.com/wp-srv/nation/documents/0207026bush.pdf.

Bybee, Jay S., Assistant Attorney General, Office of Legal Counsel, Department of Justice. Memorandum for Alberto R. Gonzales, Counsel to the President, and William J. Haynes II, General Counsel of the Department of Defense, January 22, 2002. http://www.washingtonpost.com/wp-srv/nation/documents/ 012202_bybee.pdf.

Bybee, Jay S. Memorandum for Alberto R. Gonzales, August 1, 2002. http:// www.washingtonpost.com/wp-srv/nation/documents/dojinterrogationmemo 20020801.pdf.

Central Intelligence Agency. "Defense against Soviet Mental Interrogation and Espionage Technique," February 10, 1951, File: Drugs-Artichoke (1), Box 6, CIA Behavior Control Experiments Collection, National Security Archive, Washington.

Central Intelligence Agency. *Human Resource Exploitation Training Manual— 1983*, June 8, 1988, Box 1 CIA Training Manuals, Folder: Resources Exploitation Training Manual, National Security Archive, Washington.

Central Intelligence Agency. *Kubark Counterintelligence Interrogation* (July 1963), File: Kubark, Box 1: CIA Training Manuals, National Security Archive, Washington.

Central Intelligence Agency. Memorandum For: Assistant Director, SI, Subject: Progress on BLUEBIRD, July 9, 1951, File: Artichoke Docs. 59–155, Box 5, CIA Behavior Control Experiments Collection, National Security Archive, Washington.

Central Intelligence Agency. Memorandum For: Chief of Naval Research, Subject: Transfer of Funds for Continuation of a Research Project at the Addiction Research Center, U.S. Public Health Service Hospital, Lexington, Kentucky, August 16, 1957, File: Naval Research, Box 8, CIA Behavior Control Experiments Collection, National Security Archive, Washington.

Central Intelligence Agency. Memorandum For: Director of Central Intelligence, Subject: Successful Application of Narco-Hypnotic Interrogation (ARTICHOKE), July 14, 1952, File: Artichoke Docs. 156–199, Box 5, CIA Behavior Control Experiments Collection, National Security Archive, Washington.

Central Intelligence Agency. Memorandum For: The Record, Subject: Discussion with . . . Chief . . . Division, and . . . , Chief of . . . on Utilization of . . . Assets, August 9, 1960, [Sgd.] Sidney Gottlieb, Deputy Chief, TSD/Research Branch, File: Subproject 121 MKUltra, Box 4, CIA Behavior Control Experiments Collection, National Security Archive, Washington.

Central Intelligence Agency. Memorandum for: The Record, Subject: MKUltra, Subproject 107, January 22, 1960, File: APA-Subproject 107, Box 6, CIA Behavioral Control Experiments Collection, National Security Archive, Washington.

Central Intelligence Agency. Memorandum for the Record, SUBJECT: Project AR-TICHOKE, January 31, 1975, John Marks papers, National Security Archive, Washington. http://gwu.edu/~nsarchive/NSAEBB/NSAEBB54/st02.pdf.

Central Intelligence Agency. Minutes of Meeting, June 6, 1951, File: Artichoke Docs. 59–155, Box 5, CIA Behavior Control Experiments Collection, National Security Archive, Washington.

Central Intelligence Agency. n.d., File: APA-Subproject 107, Box 6, CIA Behavioral Control Experiments Collection, National Security Archive, Washington.

Central Intelligence Agency. Office Memorandum, To: Chief, Technical Branch, From: [Blacked-out], Subject: National Meetings of the American Psychological Association, September 30, 1954, File: APA Subproject 107, Box 6, CIA Behavior Control Experiments Collection, National Security Archive, Washington.

Central Intelligence Agency. Project NM 001 056.0, May 1, 1952, File: Naval Research, Box 8, CIA Behavior Control Experiments Collection, National Security Archive, Washington.

Central Intelligence Agency. Special Group (CI). Memorandum for the Record, Subject: Minutes for Meeting of Special Group (CI), 2 p.m., Thursday, August 9, 1962. Collection: Iran Revolution, National Security Archive, Washington.

Central Intelligence Agency. Summary of Remarks by Mr. Allen W. Dulles at the National Alumni Conference of the Graduate Council of Princeton University, Hot Springs, VA, April 10, 1953, File: Artichoke Docs. 362–388, Box 5, CIA Behavior Control Experiments Collection, National Security Archive, Washington.

Congressional Fact Sheet, 8 June 1988, introduction to Central Intelligence Agency. Human Resource Exploitation Training Manual—1983, Box 1, CIA Training Manuals, National Security Archive, Washington, DC.

Department of the Army. Inspector General, Detainee Operations Inspection (July 21, 2004). http://www.washingtonpost.com/wp-srv/world/iraq/abughraib/detaineereport.pdf.

Department of the Army. Office of the Deputy Chief of Staff for Intelligence, Robert W. Singleton, Memorandum Thru the General Counsel, ATTN: PWC, Subject: History of Project X, November 4, 1991, File: Project X, Consortium News, Arlington, Virginia.

Department of the Army. Army Intelligence Center and Fort Huachuca, Memorandum for Deputy Chief of Staff for Intelligence, Subject: History of Project X, [Sgd.] William J. Teeter, September 12, 1991, File: Project X, Consortium News, Arlington, Virginia.

Department of Defense. Assistant to the Secretary of Defense, Memorandum for Secretary of Defense, Subject: Interim Report on Improper Material in US-SOUTHCOM Training Manuals (U)–Information Memorandum, [Sgd.] Werner E. Michel, October 4, 1991, File: Project X, Consortium News, Arlington, Virginia.

Department of Defense. Subject: USSOUTHCOM CI Training–Supplemental Information (U), July 31, 1991, File: Project X, Consortium News, Arlington, Virginia.

Department of Defense. Assistant to the Secretary of Defense, Report of Investigation: Improper Material in Spanish-Language Intelligence Training Manuals, March 10, 1992, File: Project X, Consortium News, Arlington, Virginia.

Department of Defense. Office of the Assistant Secretary of Defense Command, Control, Communications and Intelligence, Memorandum for the Record, Subject: USSOUTHCOM CI Training–Supplemental Information (U), July 31, 1991, File: Project X, Consortium News, Arlington, Virginia.

Department of Defense. Office of the Assistant Secretary of Defense Command, Control, Communications and Intelligence, Point Paper Concerning US-SOUTHCOM Proposed Counterintelligence (CI) Training to Foreign Governments, July 30, 1991, File: Project X, Consortium News, Arlington, Virginia.

Department of Justice, Office of Legal Counsel, Memorandum for William J. Haynes, II, General Counsel, Department of Defense, From: John Yoo, Deputy Assistant Attorney General, and Robert J. Delabunty, Special Counsel, January 9, 2002. In Karen J. Greenberg and Joshua L. Dratel, eds., *The Torture Papers: The Road to Abu Ghraib*. New York: Cambridge University Press, 2005, 38–79.

Department of Justice, Office of Legal Counsel, Memorandum for William J. Haynes, II, General Counsel, Department of Defense, December 28, 2001, From: Patrick F. Philbin, Deputy Assistant Attorney General, and John C. Yoo, Deputy Assistant Attorney General. In Karen J. Greenberg and Joshua L. Dratel, eds., *The Torture Papers: The Road to Abu Ghraib*. New York: Cambridge University Press, 2005, 29–37.

Detainee Interviews (Abusive Interrogation Issues), 5/6/04. http://www.aclu.org/torturefoia/released/FBI_4194.pdf.

Executive Summary (U). http://www.defenselink.mil/news/Mar2005/d20050310 exe.pdf.

Fay, MG George R. "AR 15-6 Investigation of the Abu Ghraib Detention Facility and 205th Military Intelligence Brigade (U)." http://news.bbc.co.uk/nol/shared/bsp/hi/pdfs/26_08_04_fayreport.pdf.

Federal Bureau of Investigation. To: Inspection, From: CIRG, Title: Counterterrorism Division, GTMO, Inspection Special Inquiry, Date: 7/13/2004. http://www.aclu.org/torturefoia/released/FBI_4499–4501.pdf.

From: (INSD) (FBI), To: Harrington, FJ (CTD) (FBI), Sent: August 17, 2004. http://www.aclu.org/torturefoia/released/FBI_4737–4738.pdf.

Gonzales, Alberto R. Memorandum for the President, Subject: Decision Re. Application of the Geneva Convention on Prisoners of War to the Conflict with Al Qaeda and the Taliban, January 25, 2002, DRAFT 1/25/2002—3:30 pm. http://www.msn.com/id/4999148/site/newsweek/.

Gonzales, Alberto R. Responses of Alberto R. Gonzales, Nominee to Be Attorney General of the United States, to Written Questions of Senator Richard J. Durbin. E-mail attachment from Martin Lederman, March 18, 2005.

Harrington, T. J., Deputy Assistant Director, Counterterrorism Division, Federal Bureau of Investigation. Letter to Major General Donald J. Ryder, Criminal Investigation Command, Department of the Army, July 14, 2004. http://www.aclu.org/torturefoia/released/FBI_4622-2624.pdf.

Haynes, William J., II, General Counsel, Department of Defense. For: Secretary of Defense, Subject: Counter-Resistance Techniques, November 27, 2002. http://www.washingtonpost.com/wp-srv/nation/documents/dodmemos.pdf.

Hinkle, Lawrence E., Jr. "A Consideration of the Circumstances under Which Men May Be Interrogated, and the Effects That These May Have upon the Function of the Brain." File: Hinkle, Box 7, CIA Behavior Control Experiments Collection, National Security Archive, Washington.

Hoar, General Joseph (Ret. USMC), et al. Letter to Senator John McCain, July 25, 2005. http://www.humanrightsfirst.org/us_law/etn/pdf/mccain-072205.pdf.

Jernegan, John D. "Memorandum from the Acting Assistant Secretary of State for Near Eastern and South Asian Affairs (Jernegan) to the Special Group (Counterinsurgency), Washington, March 2, 1964." In Nina D. Howland, ed., *Foreign Relations of the United States, 1964–68. Vol. XXII, Iran*. Washington: Government Printing Office, 1999, 15.

Joint Interrogation and Debriefing Center, Abu Ghurayb, Iraq. http://www.publicintegrity.org/docs/AbuGhraib/Tag29.pdf.

Komer, Robert. Memorandum to McGeorge Bundy and General Taylor, "Should Police Programs Be Transferred to the DOD?" Secret (declassified), April 18, 1962.

Levin, Daniel, acting Assistant Attorney General, Office of Legal Counsel, Department of Justice. "Memorandum for James B. Comey, Deputy Attorney General, Re: Legal Standards Applicable under USC§§ 2340–2340A," December 30, 2004.

Lohr, Rear Admiral Michael F. Subj: Working Group Recommendations Relating to Interrogation of Detainees, February 6, 2003, Senate, 109th Congress, 1st sess., *Congressional Record* (Washington: vol. 151, no. 102, July 25, 2005), S8795.

Memo 2: Executive Orders, Federal Register: November 16, 2001, Military Order of November 12, 2001. In Karen J. Greenberg and Joshua L. Dratel, eds. *The Torture Papers: The Road to Abu Ghraib*. New York: Cambridge University Press, 2005, 25–28.

Michel, Werner E., Assistant to the Secretary of Defense (Intelligence Oversight). Subject: Improper Material in Spanish-Language Intelligence Training Manuals, March 10, 1992. Box 2, Intelligence Training Source Manuals, Folder: Untitled, National Security Archives, Washington.

Philbin, Patrick F., Deputy Assistant Attorney General, and John C. Yoo, Deputy Assistant Attorney General, U.S. Department of Justice, Office of Legal Counsel. Memorandum for William J. Haynes, II, General Counsel, Department of Defense, December 28, 2001. In Karen J. Greenberg and Joshua L. Dratel, eds., *The Torture Papers: The Road to Abu Ghraib*. New York: Cambridge University Press, 2005, 29–37.

Powell, Colin L. Memorandum, To: Counsel to the President, Subject: Draft Decision Memorandum for the President on the Applicability of the Geneva Convention to the Conflict in Afghanistan, n.d. http://msnbc.com/modules/newsweek/pdf.powell_memo.pdf.

Report of the International Committee of the Red Cross (ICRC) on the Treatment by the Coalition Forces of Prisoners of War and Other Protected Persons by the Geneva Conventions in Iraq during Arrest, Internment and Interrogation, February 2004. http://www.redress.btinternet.co.uk/icrc_iraq.pdf.

Rives, Major General Jack L. Memorandum for SAF/GC, February 5, 2003, Senate, 109th Congress, 1st sess., *Congressional Record*. Washington: vol. 151, no. 102, July 25, 2005, S8796–97.

Rives, Major General Jack L. Memorandum for SAF/GC, February 6, 2003, Senate, 109th Congress, 1st sess., *Congressional Record*. Washington: vol. 151, no. 102, July 25, 2005, S8794–95.

Romig, Major General Thomas J. Memorandum for General Counsel of the Department of the Air Force, March 3, 2003, Senate, 109th Congress, 1st sess., *Congressional Record* (Washington: vol. 151, no. 102, July 25, 2005), S8794.

Rumsfeld, Donald. Memorandum for the Commander, Southern Command, April 16, 2003. http://www.washingtonpost.com/wp-srv/nation/documents/041603rumsfeld.pdf.

Rumsfeld, Donald. Memorandum for the General Counsel of the Department of Defense, Subject: Detainee Interrogations, January 15, 2003. http://www.washingtonpost.com/wp-srv/nation/documents/011503rumsfeld.pdf.

Sanchez, Ricardo S. Memorandum for: C2, Combined Joint Task Force Seven, Baghdad, Iraq 09335, Subject: CJTF–7 Interrogation and Counter-Resistance Policy, September 14, October 12, 2003. http://www.aclu.org/SafeandFree/SafeandFree.cfm?ID=17851&c=206.

Schlesinger, James R., et al. "Final Report of the Independent Panel to Review DoD Detention Operations," August 24, 2004. http://news.findlaw.com/cnn/docs/dod/abughraibrpt.pdf.

Secretary of Defense. Memorandum for Chairman of the Joint Chiefs of Staff, Subject: Status of Taliban and Al Qaeda, January 19, 2002. In Karen J. Greenberg and Joshua L. Dratel, eds., *The Torture Papers: The Road to Abu Ghraib*. New York: Cambridge University Press, 2005, 80.

Taguba, M. G. Antonio M. Article 15-6 Investigation of the 800th Military Police Brigade, February 26, 2004. http://www.cbsnews.com/htdocs/pdf/tagubareport.pdf.

To: Bald, Gary, Battle, Frankie, Cummings, Arthur, Subject: Impersonating FBI at GTMO, Date: December 5, 2003. http://www.aclu.org/torturefoia/released/FBI_3977.pdf.

To: Caproni, Valene E (OGC) (FBI), Subject: FW GTMO, Sent: July 30, 2004. http://www.aclu.org/torturefoia/released/FBI_4737–4738.pdf.

Working Group Report on Detainee Interrogations in the Global War on Terrorism: Assessment of Legal, Historical, Policy, and Operational Considerations, March 6, 2003. http://www.informationclearinghouse.info/pdf/military-0604.pdf.

Yoo, John, Deputy Assistant Attorney General, and Robert J. Delabunty, Special Counsel, U.S. Department of Justice, Office of Legal Counsel. Memorandum for William J. Haynes II, General Counsel, Department of Defense, January 9, 2002. In Karen J. Greenberg and Joshua L. Dratel, eds., *The Torture Papers: The Road to Abu Ghraib*. New York: Cambridge University Press, 2005, 38–79.

UN Documents

United Nations, Commission on Human Rights. *Advisory Services and Technical Cooperation in the Field of Human Rights: Report of the Independent Expert on the Situation of Human Rights in Afghanistan, M. Cherif Bassiouni.* New York: United Nations Economic and Social Council, ECN 4/2005/122, March 11, 2005.

United Nations, Commission on Human Rights. *Report of the United Nations High Commissioner for Human Rights and Follow Up to the World Conference on Human Rights.* Geneva: Commission on Human Rights, 61st Session, E/CN.4/2005/4, Advance Edited Edition, June 9, 2004.

United Nations, Department of Public Information. *Outlawing an Ancient Evil: Torture. Convention against Torture and Other Cruel, Inhuman or Degrading Treatment or Punishment.* New York: United Nations, Department of Public Information, 1985.

United Nations. *Human Rights: A Compilation of International Instruments of the United Nations.* New York: United Nations, 1973.

Dissertations, Papers, and Manuscripts

Arrigo, Jean Maria. "A Consequentialist Argument against Torture Interrogation of Terrorists" (Joint Service Conference on Professional Ethics, 30-31 January 2003, Springfield, Virginia). http://atlas.usafa, af.mil/jscope/JSCOPE03/Arrigo03.html.

Chairman, Defense Research Board, Canada, May 29, 1951, Sir Henry T. Tizard Papers, Imperial War Museum, London.

Gildner, R. Matthew. "Torture and U.S. Foreign Policy," honor's thesis, Department of History, University of Wisconsin–Madison, 2001.

Gunn, Kenrick. Letter to Sir Henry Tizard, June 7, 1951, Sir Henry T. Tizard Papers, Imperial War Museum, London.

Horton, Scott. "Betr: Strafanzeige gegen den US–Verteidigungsminister Donald Rumsfeld, u.a." An den: Herrn Generalbundesanwalt, Beim Bundesgerichtshof, Karlsruhe, January 29, 2005. http://www.rav.de/StAR_290105_Horton.htm.

Kangleon, Father Edgardo. "A Moment of Uncertainty." (Ms, December 8, 1982), enclosed in letter To: Dear Papa/Mama/Rey, 30 September 1983. Copy furnished by Father Niall O'Brien, St. Columban's Mission Society, Bacolod City.

Lobe, Thomas David. "U.S. Police Assistance for the Third World," doctoral dissertation, University of Michigan, 1975.

Maynard, Harold W. "A Comparison of Military Elite Role Perceptions in Indonesia and the Philippines," doctoral dissertation, American University, 1976.

Tizard Diary. May to June 1951, Sir Henry Tizard Papers, Imperial War Museum, London.

Private Papers and Collections

CIA Behavior Control Experiments Collection, National Security Archive, Washington.
Project X Papers, Consortium News, Arlington, Virginia.
Tizard, Sir Henry T., Personal Papers, Imperial War Museum, London.

Film and Television

ABC News. *Nightline,* "Broken Chain of Command," May 12, 2005.
CBS Broadcasting. *60 Minutes,* January 20, 2002.
Fox News Channel. *Fox News Sunday,* June 5, 2005.
Hendrickson, Kim. *The Battle of Algiers: Remembering History.* Criterion Collection, 2004.
Moore, Michael. *Fahrenheit 9/11.* Lions Gate Films, 2004.
National Public Radio. *Talk of the Nation,* June 6, 2005.

Newspapers and Mass Media

American Forces Information Service News Articles
The Associated Press
The Australian (Sydney)
The Baltimore Sun
The Boston Globe
Bulletin Today (Manila)
The Capital Times (Madison, Wisconsin)
CBS NEWS.com
Chicago Sun-Times
Chicago Tribune
Clarkson Integrator (Potsdam, New York)
The Daily Cardinal (Madison, Wisconsin)
The Denver Post
The Economist
The Guardian
Honolulu Star-Bulletin
Indianapolis Star
International Herald Tribune
Los Angeles Times
Malaya (Manila)
MSNBC.com
National Public Radio
The New York Times
Newsweek
The Observer (London)

Philippine Daily Inquirer
Public Broadcasting System
The Record (Bergen County, New Jersey)
Scotland on Sunday
The Star-Ledger (Newark, New Jersey)
Sunday Telegraph
The Times (London)
Toronto Star
USA Today
The Wall Street Journal
The Washington Post

Interviews

Alleg, Henri. In *The Battle of Algiers: Remembering History,* produced by Kim Hendrickson, Criterion Collection, 2004.
Ang, Maria Elena. Sydney, Australia, May 9, 1989.
Behnke, Stephen. Washington, e-mails exchanged, July 13, 2005.
Coronel, Sheila. Manila, January 5, 1988.
Detainee Interviews (Abusive Interrogation Issues), 5/6/04. http://www.aclu.org/torturefoia/released/FBI_4194.pdf.
Echanis, Randall. University of the Philippines, Interdisciplinary Forum on Political Detainees, n.d.
"Gene." University of the Philippines, Interdisciplinary Forum on Political Detainees, April 16, 1986.
Horne, Sir Alistair. In *The Battle of Algiers: Remembering History,* produced by Kim Hendrickson, Criterion Collection, 2004.
Jazmines, Alan. University of the Philippines, Interdisciplinary Forum on Political Detainees, April 16, 1986.
Ocampo, Satur. Quezon City, August 27, 1996.
Sison, Jose Ma. University of the Philippines, Interdisciplinary Forum on Political Detainees, April 16, 1986.
Sison, Julieta. Quezon City, July 18, 1986.
Stora, Benjamin. In *The Battle of Algiers: Remembering History,* produced by Kim Hendrickson, Criterion Collection, 2004.
Trinquier, Colonel Roger. By Oliver Todd for "La Bataille de Alger," BBC Panorama, 1970, replayed in *The Battle of Algiers: Remembering History,* produced by Kim Hendrickson, Criterion Collection, 2004.
Vizmanos, Captain Danilo P. Makati, November 6, 1998.
Yacef, Saada. FLN military commander for the Casbah in 1956–57. In *The Battle of Algiers: Remembering History,* produced by Kim Hendrickson, Criterion Collection, 2004.

ACRONYMS

ACLU	American Civil Liberties Union
AFP	Armed Forces of the Philippines
AFP	Agence France Presse
AMA	American Medical Association
APA	American Psychological Association
BDE	Brigade
BSCT	Behavioral Science Consultation Teams
BSSR	Bureau of Social Science Research
CI	Special Group-Counter Insurgency
CIA	Central Intelligence Agency
CIO	Central Intelligence Organization (Republic of Vietnam)
CITF	Criminal Investigative Task Force (FBI)
CORDS	Civil Operations and Rural Development Support
CSU	Constabulary Security Unit (Philippines)
FLN	Front de Libération National (Algeria)
GAO	General Accounting Office
GPW	Geneva Convention III on the Treatment of Prisoners of War
ICRC	International Committee of the Red Cross
IPA	International Police Academy (Washington, D.C.)
IRA	Irish Republican Army
ISAFP	Intelligence Service, Armed Forces of the Philippines
JAG	Judge Advocate General
LTG	Lieutenant General
MAP	Military Advisor Program

MG	Major General
MI	Military Intelligence
MIG	Military Intelligence Group
MP	Military Police
NLF	National Liberation Front
NPA	New People's Army (Philippines)
NSA	National Security Agency
NSC	National Security Council
NSF	National Science Foundation
OGA	Other Government Agencies [official euphemism for CIA]
ONR	Office of Naval Research
OPS	Office of Public Safety
OSS	Office of Strategic Services
OVRA	Organizzazione di Vigilanza Repressione dell'Antifascismo
PIC	Provincial Interrogation Center
PMA	Philippine Military Academy
PNP	Philippine National Police
PRU	Provincial Reconnaissance Unit (Republic of Vietnam)
PW	Prisoner of War
PX	Post Exchange (U.S. Army)
RCT	Rehabilitation and Research Centre for Torture Victims
SAP	Special-Access Program
SIHE	Society of the Investigation of Human Ecology
TSD	Technical Services Division (CIA)
UCMJ	Universal Code of Military Justice
UN	United Nations
U.S.	United States
U.S. AID	United States Agency for International Development
USC	United States Code
VCI	Viet Cong Infrastructure (South Vietnam)
WTC	World Trade Center

ACKNOWLEDGMENTS

THROUGHOUT THE FIFTEEN-YEAR journey that led to this book, I have accumulated countless intellectual debts and learned much about torture, from both perpetrators and victims. In the late 1980s, as I explored torture's impact on the Philippine military—the real start of this book—my travel there was eased by the hospitality for which that island nation is so justly famous. In Manila, I had the good fortune to meet a generation of talented journalists—Melinda Quintos de Jesus, Sheila Coronel, and Marites Danguilan Vitug—whose courage and professionalism were as inspiring as their information was invaluable. My host in Manila, Dr. Helen Mendoza, is a tireless civil-society advocate, with contacts high and low throughout Filipino society.

During my early interviews in Manila, I was stunned, then intrigued, to learn that many of the colonels whose abortive coup d'état had sparked Marcos's downfall in 1986 had once worked as interrogators during his dictatorship. Yet even they took time from their busy schedules trying to overthrow the government for interviews filled with inadvertent insights into their formative years as torturers. I am particularly grateful to Navy captain Rex Robles, then the coup group's political theorist, for his extraordinary frankness about the mind-set of his colleagues. On the other side of the generational divide, the aging alumni of the Philippine Military Academy's class of 1940, led by Colonel Deogracias Caballero and Commodore Ramon Alcaraz, were equally generous with their time. And across the country's ideological barricades, activists Satur Ocampo, Julieta Sison, and Maria Elena Ang were sadly expressive describing the effects of torture.

At the University of Wisconsin, conversations with an old friend, Dr. Michael Cullinane, led me to the possibility that the distinctive Filipino torture techniques may have come from some sort of CIA training. An invitation to a conference on the legacies of authoritarianism, at Robben Island, off Capetown, where Nelson Mandela had once been jailed, prompted a paper on the history of CIA torture, thus laying the conceptual cornerstone for this book. Colleagues from Madison helped shape the seminal first draft, including Leigh Payne, who solicited the paper, Steve Stern, who questioned some of my assumptions, and JoEllen Fair, who offered insight into media dimensions. In my travels to both Manila and Capetown, Louis Bickford engaged me in some challenging conversations about the problems of bringing justice to the perpetrators of torture during such delicate democratic transitions.

For four years following the conference, I put the paper aside, thinking that the Cold War and this sordid topic were now, thankfully, relegated to a troubled past. When my former research assistant Matthew Gildner called periodically to prod me toward publication, I always found an excuse, any excuse, to avoid returning to a miserable topic that left me depressed. Then, in the aftermath of the attack on the Twin Towers, I was disturbed to note the growing public support for torture and tracked the debate in the media and on the Internet. Though torture was emerging from the shadows where it had resided since the end of World War II, I was still loath to resume work on a subject so sordid, so demoralized, so utterly dispiriting. But once the Abu Ghraib photos leaked in April 2004, it became undeniably clear that the Cold War past was the prologue to our post-9/11 present. It was, I felt, irresponsible to leave the field open to the pro-pain pundits and professors who seemed determined to make torture America's weapon of choice in the war on terror.

In the summer of 2004, I launched into this work with the support of staff and faculty members at the University of Wisconsin–Madison. My research associate, Ellen Jarosz, proved extraordinarily agile in unearthing information from a wide range of elusive sources. In our work at the university's remarkable Memorial Library, we were assisted by its dedicated staff—notably, Judy Tuohy, chief of Inter-Library Loan, who unfailingly tracked down even the most obscure source, and Larry Ashmun, our resourceful Southeast Asia bibliographer. At the venerable Wisconsin State Historical Society, Nancy Mulhern, the chief of government documents, lent her years of experience to finding key sources through an otherwise impenetrable maze. Colleagues in the History Department, including Jeremi Suri, Andrew Wolpert, and Marc Kleijwegt, were equally generous in helping identify sources.

Elsewhere, the staff of the National Security Archive in Washington graciously flexed their schedules for our flying visit; while Robert Parry of Consortium News generously loaned documents on "Project X," hard-won from the Pentagon under Freedom of Information provisions. The staff of the Canadian National Archives in Ottawa was prompt and polite in explaining why I did not have a prayer of ever seeing the papers of the Canadian Defence Research Board, at least not in this lifetime. In London, by contrast, the staff of the Imperial War Museum, particularly archivist Katherine Martin, moved quickly to facilitate my access to the papers of Sir Henry Tizard. At the War Museum, my researcher, Alexander Baron, was assiduous in his attention to detail even though our only contact was a slender e-mail thread across the Atlantic.

An earlier, much abbreviated version of the manuscript was first published in the *New England Journal of Public Policy,* where editors Padraig O'Malley and Paul Atwood were very supportive. Their production editor, Patricia Peterson, was patient in helping me get this long, demanding essay into print. Others then helped disseminate the article's core findings to a wider audience. At the *Boston Globe,* reporter Tom Palmer and editor Nick King helped me publish a short op-ed in the paper. In New York, Tom Engelhardt, the editor of an exemplary Web site at the Nation Institute, deftly extracted a short essay from my longer paper and posted it on the Internet at Tomdispatch. Through the reach and reputation of his site, my e-essay was posted on over thirty Web sites worldwide and published in hard copy as an op-ed in the *San Francisco Chronicle,* with the help of editor James Finefrock, and in *La Jornada,* in Mexico City, through the efforts there of editor Tania Molina.

The move from academic essay and newspaper article to this book was made possible by some equally generous assistance. When reporter James Meek cited my essay in an article for the *Guardian,* the work came to the attention of Dr. Till Tolkemitt at the Frankfurt publishing house, Zweitausendeins, who offered to publish it as a pamphlet in German translation. As documents and reports tumbled off the Internet, this putative pamphlet quickly grew into a book—one that needed a New York publisher to bring it to an American audience. Again, I turned to Tom Engelhardt, also consulting editor at Metropolitan Books, who agreed to squeeze a quick read into a transcontinental flight. His colleagues at Metropolitan pledged their support, and my editor there, Riva Hocherman, proved a most creative critic of my work.

Working on the book, I was fortunate to find myself in Madison, Wisconsin, one of those rare communities with a lively public intellectual life. Although straining under its recent prosperity and pell-mell growth, Madison still deserves its reputation as the most liberal city in America—indeed, a city with its own foreign policy. As I moved out of the tower into the town, Professor Susanne Wofford of the university's Humanities Center invited me to give a public lecture at my local library, the Sequoya branch of the Madison Public Library, where its head, Anne Michalski, proved an eloquent, gracious host. With over two hundred people spilling out of the room and tough questions continuing for more than two hours, this intense engagement helped me craft a more accessible approach to a troubling topic. This small city is also home to a major national magazine, *The Progressive.* Its editor, Matthew Rothschild, asked provocative questions during an interview for his syndicated radio show, and his associate editor, Amitabh Pal, offered equally probing reflections at a public media conference.

When the manuscript was almost done, a routine lecture became an extraordinary experience. Professor Joseph Elder and his continuing-education students at the University of Wisconsin— retired professors, professionals, and one veteran CIA analyst—

listened courteously to my critique of psychological torture for an hour. Then, freed from academic politesse, one student dared to say, "So what are we going to do, just sit there and ask these terrorists polite questions? Can't we do something, anything, to stop them?" After the rough-and-tumble debate that followed, I pounded out an answer to his questions, which appears as the book's concluding pages. The undergraduates in my own seminar, "History 600: CIA Covert Warfare and the Conduct of U.S. Foreign Policy," were ideal companions for a voyage into this clandestine netherworld. A mix of anti-globalization activists and aspirant intelligence officers, these students were always reflective and unfailingly measured in their discussions, a tribute to the University of Wisconsin's ideal of fearless "sifting and winnowing."

For close, thoughtful readings of the manuscript, I am indebted to Professor Jeremi Suri, a generous colleague at the University of Wisconsin–Madison, and my superb research associate, Ellen Jarosz. Whenever I write, each clause reminds me of a lifelong debt to Dr. Robert Cluett, who taught me this craft, with the skills of clear prose and close-textual analysis, at a small Connecticut boarding school before he moved on to chair the English Department at York University. Closer to home, my mother, Margarita P. McCoy, professor emerita at California Polytechnic University–Pomona, read this text with the same care and precision she usually reserves for urban planning proposals. My wife, Dr. Mary E. McCoy, took time from the hectic final stages of her dissertation at Northwestern University to critique this text with uncommon analytical and moral insight. My initial work on this project with the indefatigable Matthew Gildner was funded by a Hilldale joint faculty-undergraduate research grant from the University of Wisconsin–Madison. A professorial chair from the Graduate School funded the help of Ellen Jarosz. No other funding, public or private, contributed to this work.

For all this help, I am most grateful. But for all the inevitable errors, factual and moral, in this frail process, I alone am responsible.

INDEX

About the Author

ALFRED W. MCCOY is the J. R. W. Smail Professor of History at the University of Wisconsin–Madison. He is the author of numerous books and articles, including *The Politics of Heroin in Southeast Asia* and *Closer Than Brothers*.

THE AMERICAN EMPIRE PROJECT

IN AN ERA of unprecedented military strength, leaders of the United States, the global hyperpower, have increasingly embraced imperial ambitions. How did this significant shift in purpose and policy come about? And what lies down the road?

The American Empire Project is a response to the changes that have occurred in America's strategic thinking as well as in its military and economic posture. Empire, long considered an offense against America's democratic heritage, now threatens to define the relationship between our country and the rest of the world. The American Empire Project publishes books that question this development, examine the origins of U.S. imperial aspirations, analyze their ramifications at home and abroad, and discuss alternatives to this dangerous trend.

The project was conceived by Tom Engelhardt and Steve Fraser, editors who are themselves historians and writers. Published by Metropolitan Books, an imprint of Henry Holt and Company, its titles include *Hegemony or Survival* by Noam Chomsky, *The Sorrows of Empire* by Chalmers Johnson, *Crusade* by James Carroll, *How to Succeed at Globalization* by El Fisgón, *Blood and Oil* by Michael Klare, and *Dilemmas of Domination* by Walden Bello.

For more information about the American Empire Project and for a list of forthcoming titles, please visit www.americanempire project.com.